THE NEW
VICTORY GARDEN

PHOTOGRAPHS BY
GARY MOTTAU

DRAWINGS BY
DANA GAINES

**LITTLE, BROWN
AND COMPANY**

BOSTON TORONTO

THE NEW VICTORY GARDEN

BY BOB THOMSON

WITH JAMES TABOR

FIRST EDITION

Library of Congress Cataloging-in-Publication Data

Thomson, Bob.
  The new victory garden.

  An updated and expanded version of Crockett's victory garden.
  Includes index.
  1. Vegetable gardening.   2. Fruit-culture.   3. Herb
gardening.   I. Tabor, Jim.   II. Crockett, James Underwood.
Crockett's victory garden.   III. Title.
SB321.T615 1987   635   87-3808
ISBN 0-316-84337-7
ISBN 0-316-84336-9 (pbk.)

Published simultaneously in Canada
by Little, Brown & Company (Canada) Limited

PRINTED IN THE UNITED STATES

ACKNOWLEDGMENTS

This book owes a great deal to many whose names do not appear on the cover but without whom it would not have come into being. First, thanks must go to Russell Morash, creator of the "Victory Garden" series on Public Television. He's an acknowledged leader in how-to television, and viewers everywhere must count themselves fortunate for his talents in bringing good gardening to American television. William D. Phillips, my editor at Little, Brown, is the stuff of every author's fondest dreams. Through a seemingly endless project, he never lost his sense of direction — or humor. James Tabor, the book's writer, patiently transformed manuscripts and tapes into finished form. John Pelrine, the "Victory Garden" series producer, contributed endless hours of his time and an inestimable reservoir of gardening knowledge. Former gardener Rudy Perkins added to that vast pool of gardening wisdom, as did Kip Anderson, current overseer of the Victory Garden itself. Gary Mottau, whose photos make this book a true feast for the eye, displayed an uncanny ability to catch the garden over and over at just the right time. Dianne Schaefer's artistry blended all the elements together into a beautiful union, and Dana Gaines's illustrations have added clarity to difficult-to-describe processes. Michael Mattil's tireless scrutiny (and well-timed comic relief) as copy editor assured that the book would come to you without flaw or inconsistency.

Special thanks must go to those who helped with the features that complement the book's gardening chapters. The National Wildlife Federation's Craig Tufts supplied invaluable information about birds and their habitats. Gladys Phillips helped create a lovely section on wreathmaking. The Goodell family of Westminster West, Vermont, whose extraordinary cider has been famous in New England for a good many years now, gave professional depth to my amateur's love for cidermaking.

My literary agent, Donald Cutler, deserves special mention along with Colleen Mohyde, Bill Phillip's able assistant, who kept all the many pieces together.

All of us at the Victory Garden are grateful to those who have made our regional gardens a reality: Lexington Gardens in Lexington, Massachusetts, Callaway Gardens in Pine Mountain, Georgia, and Rogers Garden Center in Newport Beach, California.

A final word of thanks to those who have supported "The Victory Garden" over its very fortunate long life. First, WGBH-TV in Boston, our producing station, and all public television stations across the country for bringing "The Victory Garden" to their viewers. And our corporate underwriters — those businesses who believe gardening is so worthwhile and want to be a part of bringing it to American viewers: Peter's Professional Plant Food, Monrovia Nursery Company, and the Mantis Manufacturing Company.

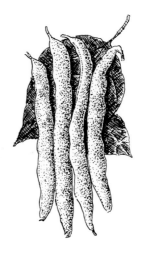

All photos by Gary Mottau with the exception of the following:

Max E. Badgley — pages 189 (left), 190 left column (bottom 3 photos), right column top photo, 191 middle column (both photos), 192 middle column

Lee Jenkins — pages 190 right column (bottom), 191 left column, right column. 192 right column

Robert L. Wick — pages 193 (all), 194 left column, 195 center column

Russell Morash — pages 5, 17, 36 (bottom), 100, 272–3

Rudy Perkins — pages 232, 233, 235

This book is dedicated to my wife, Betty,
my daughter, Kathy,
and to my sons, Scott and David

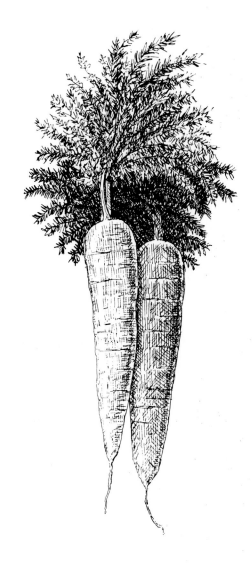

CONTENTS

THE NEW
VICTORY GARDEN

WELCOME TO THE VICTORY GARDEN

WELCOME TO
THE VICTORY GARDEN

In the spring of 1979, I was beginning my twenty-fifth year in the gardening business. My predecessor, Jim Crockett, was getting ready for his fourth season as host of "Crockett's Victory Garden," the acclaimed PBS series. As a fellow "media gardener" (I'd been doing a Boston-based radio show for almost twenty years), I was keenly aware of Jim Crockett's work. I admired it very much and never missed an opportunity to watch Jim as he puttered around the little patch behind the WGBH-TV studios in the shadow of Harvard Stadium.

One day that spring, quite unexpectedly, I received a call from Russell Morash, the show's producer. We chatted a bit, and then Russ came to the point. Jim Crockett was ailing. If the current season was to be completed, the Victory Garden would need a little help. Russ asked if I could lend a hand. I agreed at once, feeling that it would be a privilege to work with Jim, who had helped create a truly unique television series.

We began working together about the middle of May 1979. I quickly discovered that Jim was as straightforward and friendly in real life as he was on camera. We worked well together, and I admired not only his considerable gardening expertise but his sheer courage, as well. Jim Crockett was suffering from cancer then, but he never once complained. His gaze and handshake remained firm throughout those months, and his spirit was bright, though I knew he was hurting. One afternoon, when we had finished taping a segment of the show, Jim drew me aside. "I need to talk to you," he said, and went on to explain that his latest prognosis had not been encouraging. "I'm flying out to a special clinic," he told me. "I want you to keep on doing the program while I'm gone, Bob. Will you do that?"

I assured him that I would, and promised to do my best until he returned. He said that he expected to be gone a month, maybe two. Tragically, four weeks later we received word that he had passed away. I was terribly saddened, as were millions of viewers who had fallen in love with this exceptional man.

"The Victory Garden" needed a new host, and Russ Morash asked me to step in. I thought that carrying on the "Victory Garden" heritage would be a fine way to honor Jim's memory, so I agreed to give television a try. That was seven years ago.

They've been a momentous seven years for vegetable gardening. In that time, I've seen more exciting changes and advances than in my previous three decades in the business. The plant breeders have created wondrous new vegetable varieties, for one thing. Ten years ago, there was no such thing as Sugar Snap peas or supersweet corn. These well-known varieties are

Jim Crockett, who loved a garden of beautiful flowers and fresh vegetables, in the original Victory Garden at WGBH-TV.

only two of a whole host of newcomers that are changing the face — and flavor — of gardening. We've also been blessed with many new hybrid varieties, giving us increased disease resistance, vigor, and plants bred specifically for small-space culture. And it's not only the vegetables themselves that have changed. Cultural practices have kept pace, too, and I've stayed abreast of them in the Victory Garden with raised beds, intercropping and succession planting, and high-yield techniques. There have also been dramatic changes in pest-control methods. Not so long ago, gardeners drenched their soil with strong chemicals. Few do so any longer, and my practice in the Victory Garden reflects this changing consciousness. I use physical barriers, manual removal, and organic pesticides. Nor have I ignored the generation of new gardening aids — black plastic mulch, Wall O' Water, spun polyester row covers, and more.

So much has happened, in fact, that a whole new book for vegetable gardeners really is necessary. I wrote this one both to bring you up to date on the remarkable advances in varieties, tools, techniques, and cultural practices, and to supply as well all the timeless basic information you need to grow vegetables successfully. This book is organized very much like its distinguished companions in the Victory Garden book series, in a month-by-month format, because that's how gardeners garden. When you're thinking about peas in May, you should be able to look them up in the May chapter and find what you need to know about their care and culture at that time of year. Thus the bulk of the book is devoted to eight chapters representing the gardening months of March through October. Each chapter begins with an alphabetized list of crops and the things we do with them in that month. If you want to know when to harvest tomatoes, simply check the front page of each month under the "Harvest" heading, then locate the "Tomatoes" section in the appropriate month. (Believe it or not, it's June!) If you need to know how to start summer squash seeds indoors in March or April, turn to those months, find the "Summer Squash" entries, and start reading. And if you want to learn about the entire cultural cycle of a crop — corn, let's say — simply start reading in the first month that crop appears (April, in this case, when I plant the seeds in peat pots) and follow the entries all the way through the subsequent months.

In addition to these comprehensive monthly chapters, there are two more chapters, "Beginnings" and "Endings," which detail early- and late-season activities. "Beginnings," which precedes the March chapter, describes the things I do to prepare for a long, intensive growing season in the Victory Garden. And in "Endings," which follows the October chapter, I tell you how to put the garden to bed for the winter, and suggest some worthwhile activities for the long, cold hiatus.

For gardeners just getting started, or for those who'd like to update their know-how, I've put all the information on the latest cultural practices up front in the very next chapter, "Steps to Victorious Gardening." This is the chapter to begin with for a thorough immersion in the skills I've been teaching on the "Victory Garden" television series for so long. And even serious veteran gardeners will find this chapter to be "must reading," because it distills the years of Victory Garden experience into essential knowledge and techniques they just won't find anywhere else.

Finally, I've included special features as companions to the gardening months themselves. In some cases, these features provide additional information on certain topics that most gardeners will find especially useful — container gardening, say, or the selection and care of tools. In others, I've focused on topics that have given me great pleasure over the years in the Victory Garden, such as wreathmaking and gardening to attract birds. I've even included a feature profiling several Victory Garden contest winners, drawing valuable cultural lessons from each victorious garden.

Conspicuously absent from this book are the complicated frost maps found in many other gardening tomes. After having squinted over such maps and charts for many years, I've finally

I'm getting ready to share my enthusiasm for oak leaf lettuce as the television camera focuses in.

concluded that they're worse than useless. Because they cannot indicate the frost characteristics for any local microclimate, they invite gardeners to risk their crops on dangerously general information. I think that's a disservice. A valley garden and a mountainside garden in the same-color area on one of those maps have very different frost dates and microclimatic conditions. Instead of including one of those colorful but misleading little maps, I'm going to offer this advice: To learn about the growing conditions in your particular microclimate, consult your local county extension service agent. He or she will know about the frost dates and growing conditions for *your* backyard, and that's what you need to grow the best vegetables.

I've also avoided giving a general planting timetable other than the one I use for my crops in the Victory Garden. It's just not possible for me, a New England gardener, to tell you, a gardener in Spokane or Tallahassee, when to plant, with utter precision. What I *can* do is describe the principles I use to arrive at my gardening schedule for planting, fertilizing, harvesting, and so on. Those principles, applied to your garden, will be as useful there as they are in the Victory Garden itself. My last expected spring frost date, April 20 (determined after consultation with my county extension agent and years of practice), is the pivotal day upon which all the rest of my gardening year is based. Once you've established that date for your own garden, the rest of the schedule and planning falls into place rather easily. I'll tell you exactly how to make the plan and create the schedule — for *your* garden — in the chapter titled "Beginnings."

And there you have it. That's enough introducing. Let's get right to the heart of things. As I've said so many times on the air, welcome to the Victory Garden!

My Victory Garden
techniques assure a boun-
tiful harvest, including a
well-grown spring
cauliflower that I'm especially happy about. I
replant open areas as soon
as a harvest is taken. The
black-plastic-covered
raised beds provide added
warmth for cucumbers on
the A-frame trellis and
some newly set out squash

STEPS TO VICTORIOUS GARDENING

STEPS TO VICTORIOUS GARDENING

Tending a garden is a never-ending learning experience. I experiment constantly with new varieties, schedules, and techniques, carrying on my semiscientific campaigns in the least exact but most exciting laboratory of all: the great outdoors. There, no two springs are ever alike, no single harvest is ever exactly the same as any other, no frost is absolutely predictable. Thus, I set down my steps to victorious gardening with confidence tempered by an awareness that my own education is ongoing. When I say "victorious" gardening, I mean that these steps are lessons that the garden has taught me, and that have worked well. I never feel as though I have made the garden submit to my whims, any more than the adventurous climbers who reach the summits of big mountains feel that they "conquer" peaks. Like them, I view my adventure as a partnership with nature. I consider myself a good steward on this bit of land I call the Victory Garden, but never its master.

In this chapter, you'll find all the lessons I've learned from the years of intensive culture in the Victory Garden and that I've been sharing on the television program. Included are site selection, soil preparation, varietal selection, starting seeds indoors, buying seedlings, planting out, mulching, using season extenders, watering, thinning, weeding, managing pests and diseases, harvesting, making and using compost, and more. All the skills and techniques are laid out in the order in which you'll use them in the garden itself, beginning at the beginning with site selection and ending with harvesting.

Site Selection

A good vegetable garden demands sun — the more the better. Six hours is really minimum. Those hours should be full, not filtered, for sturdy growth. Step one, then, is to give the garden all the sun a piece of property allows. Everything else will be severely compromised if the garden does not receive those essential hours of sunlight.

Ideally, the garden should be located away from the shade cast by buildings and trees. That should also keep the garden well away from the root systems of trees, which will steal essential nutrients and water. Tree roots will reach out at least as far as the trees' outermost branches — the so-called drip line. Keep the garden's borders beyond that line, and the vegetables will be safe from thirsty tree roots.

Slope is important, too. If the garden is located on too steep a slope, soil will erode and nutrients will be washed away. Terracing is advisable on hillsides much steeper than 15 degrees. A

gentle slope to the south is actually ideal, as it promotes drainage and exposes the garden to more sunlight.

Size is another consideration. The Victory Garden has expanded over the years, from the small Boston garden to several other locations. Each of the new gardens is larger than the original. From that experience comes one of my cardinal rules: Start small and build on success, rather than retreating from large failure. I've found that I can always push back fence lines when time, confidence, and energy allow. For beginning gardens and gardeners, I think that a 15x15-foot plot is perfectly adequate.

Soil Preparation

Along with lots of sunlight, a successful vegetable garden requires well-prepared soil. Bad soil is a handicap, but *any* soil (as so many Victory Garden contest winners have demonstrated) can be improved tremendously. The Victory Garden itself is a case in point. When the first Victory Garden was born in the parking lot behind the WGBH-TV studios in Boston, the land was rubble, and what little soil there was served only to separate the debris. That first season, Jim Crockett added dozens of bales of peat moss to improve the structure of that junkyard soil. In my years, I've continued to add peat moss, homemade compost for tilth and fertility, and coarse builder's sand for drainage. There's premium soil in that garden now, soil that holds moisture, retains nutrients, provides good aeration, and crumbles like chocolate cake in my hand. It took a lot of work, year after year, to create that superb soil, and from that genesis comes another cardinal gardening rule: Great soil is not built overnight, but it *can* be built. Never be discouraged by bad soil. With patience and work, virtually any soil can be improved enough to produce excellent vegetables.

Soil quality is determined by three characteristics: composition, pH, and fertility. These three are like the legs of a stool. All must be present; if any one is missing or impaired, vegetables will grow poorly or not at all. If soil is too loose and sandy, or too heavy and clayish, aeration, drainage, and nutrient retention will suffer. Similarly, because vegetables require a pH range of 6.0–7.0 for optimum growth, soil that is too acid or alkaline will impair their development. And soil that is deficient in nutrients (especially in any of the "big three" — nitrogen, phosphorus, or potassium) cannot support healthy crops.

Composition   The first step in preparing soil for vegetable gardening is understanding soil composition. Basically, there are three types of soil: clay, sand, and loam. Clay soils are composed of densely packed clay particles. They do not drain well, nor do they provide good aeration. Clay soil is hard to work, and, because of its density, is slow to warm and dry in the spring. Sandy soil is made up of large, irregular granules that neither adhere to each other nor retain moisture well. Water flows through unimpeded, washing out nutrients. Loam, the third basic soil type, is a combination of sand, silt (particles that are between clay and sand on the soil spectrum), and clay, with varying amounts of organic matter.

Each soil type has a different feel. Clay soil, when squeezed, will form a dense, sticky ball. When wet, clay soil feels slick and greasy. Sandy soil feels gritty, and is so loosely structured that it may not hold its shape even when squeezed hard into a ball. Loam molds readily into a ball when squeezed, but crumbles easily, too.

All gardeners long for loam. The ideal gardening soil would be a deep loam, a bit on the sandy side, with a crumbly, chocolate-cake feel. This dream soil would have a high *humus* content — at least 5 percent and preferably more. (Humus is decayed plant and animal material, a dark, crumbly substance that is essential

Spring soil preparation and pea seedlings in peat strips, ready to be set out.

for good vegetable gardening.) As much as 50 percent of its total volume would be given over to pore space, which in turn might contain water or air. This loose, crumbly structure is open enough to allow penetration by roots, and firm enough to support the plants above those root systems. Equally important, the high proportion of organic matter allows the soil to retain enough moisture, nutrients, and air.

Not many of us are lucky enough to find that kind of soil ready and waiting for our vegetables, so improving the soil structure is a basic part of any vegetable gardener's activity. The foundation of soil improvement is organic matter. *Any* soil — heavy clay or dusty sand — benefits from the addition of organic matter. Fortunately, there are lots of sources for this prime ingredient of good soil. Peat moss, which I mentioned above, is one. It's available in bales from garden supply houses and, while relatively expensive, is an excellent way to improve soil structure quickly. Sawdust is fine, too, if you have access to a sawmill or woodworker's shop. Animal manure is another amendment that improves soil structure. Manure contains some nutrients, and contributes to soil fertility as well. Green manures are grassy or leguminous crops that can be planted any time and later dug into the soil. Winter rye and buckwheat are two green manure crops that have become Victory Garden standards. And of course there is compost, perhaps the best all-around soil improver. Compost is a potpourri of organic materials (plant residues, grass clippings, kitchen wastes, and so forth), soil, lime, and fertilizer that decomposition has blended into a dark, crumbly, humus-rich mass. Later in this chapter, I'll give detailed instructions for creating large amounts of rich compost with a minimum of effort. For now, it's enough to know that compost is an unbeatable addition to any garden.

There are good reasons for all this stress on organic matter. It's full of large, spongy particles that "open up" the soil, making it easier for water to percolate in and then helping retain that water once it has entered. Organic matter is also a repository for soil nutrients. It holds minerals absorbed from the soil, provides a medium in which beneficial bacteria thrive, and fuels soil microorganisms that help produce nutrient-rich humus. Finally, organic matter increases soil's porosity, and it is in the porous spaces between particles that air — which the plants need for growth — resides.

I like to add most soil amendments to the Victory Garden in the fall. The beds are ready for replenishment after producing successive crops all season long, and the winter months provide time for manure and partially decomposed organic matter to break down fully. When the beds have produced their last, I add 2 inches of well-rotted manure or compost. (If I can find only fresh manure, I'll use that now, because it will have a chance to break down over the months.) I also add ground limestone to adjust the pH, and fertilizer to boost nutrient content. Fertilizer

My summer-sown buckwheat cover crop is turned under just at flowering. Green manure crops like this add invaluable organic material at a very low cost.

goes down at the rate of 2 pounds of 10-10-10 for every 100 square feet of bed area. I'll explain how much limestone to add in the next part of this chapter. I turn all this — manure or compost, limestone, fertilizer — into the soil. Then I rake the beds into shape and sow a cover crop of winter rye, using 1 pound of rye seed for every 100 square feet of area sowed. I rake the seed in lightly, water it well, and keep the beds moist until germination occurs. Come spring, that rye will be turned under 4 to 6 weeks before planting time, adding still more organic matter to the soil.

Fall is not the only time I can add organic matter to the soil, of course. Finished compost and well-rotted manure can be turned into the soil at any time, as can peat moss and other organic materials. Similarly, coarse builder's sand (the remedy of choice for gluey clay soils) can be worked in any time.

Gardeners just getting started will have to strip sod from the ground before they can add any amendments to the soil. For this bit of work there is nothing more valuable than a *very* sharp spade. First, I cut down through the grass, making parallel cuts 12 inches apart to form strips of sod. Then I lever up the foot-wide strip as I go, working the spade along underneath, cutting off the top inch or so, and rolling the sod back on itself until the mass becomes too heavy to move easily. When that happens, I

REMOVE SOD SECTIONS WITH MINIMUM OF TOPSOIL

cut the roll loose and lay it to one side. After the whole garden area is cleared, I use my spading fork to turn up the topsoil to a depth of 12 inches, forking in organic material (compost or manure) as I go, and adding enough lime to bring the pH into the 6.5 range. The stripped sod goes into the compost pile, where it will decompose into more rich, organic matter.

pH Level The second important indicator of soil quality is pH, which is nothing more than the degree of soil acidity or alkalinity as described by a number from 0 to 14. Zero is completely acid, 14 completely alkaline. The midpoint, 7, indicates neutrality. The pH level is important in vegetable gardening because soil for most vegetables must be between 6.0 and 7.0 on the pH scale for best plant growth. In acid soils with a pH below 5, phosphorus is not released readily, and other nutrients (notably magnesium, potassium, and calcium) tend to wash out. High acidity deters the breakdown of humus, invites diseases like clubroot, and discourages earthworms. Very alkaline soils (with pH above 7.5) have their own problems. High alkalinity keeps trace elements locked up in the soil, deters the production of humus, and can contribute to a toxic buildup of chemical salts.

I've heard stories about gardeners who assess their garden's pH by tasting the soil, but I've never actually *met* anyone who does it that way. I've experimented with some of the do-it-yourself testing kits available at hardware stores and garden supply centers, but I don't much like them. The color-coded reagent has always seemed difficult for me to match with the little charts they provide. I much prefer the more accurate and dependable alternative of having my sample tested by the county extension service. For a very reasonable fee, the service gives me a computerized printout on my soil, including the current pH, levels of nitrogen, phosphorus, and potash, and levels of important trace elements like iron and boron. The test report also includes helpful recommendations for amending the garden soil, tailored to my particular needs. When I take a soil sample, I make sure to take soil from at least four different locations throughout the garden, to give the chemists a true cross-section. I also make sure to use a clean trowel to dig the soil, and clean double plastic bags to hold it. I avoid touching the soil with my hands, because body oils can contaminate the sample. Finally, I avoid any area that's recently been enriched by fertilizer, compost, or manure, because all of those will affect the test results.

I like to test for pH in the fall and again in the spring. The fall test, performed after the long, intensive growing season, tells me how much lime I must add to bring the pH back to the 6.5 level that's optimum for most vegetables. Lime works slowly in the soil, which is why I add it in the fall — by spring, it will have done its job. The tests usually reveal that our season-end pH has dropped to around 6.0, and I add lime accordingly. My rule of thumb is that 70 pounds of ground limestone will raise

When collecting soil samples for testing, be sure the trowel is clean and use double plastic bags. To provide a good cross-section for analysis, I take samples from at least four different locations in the garden.

the pH of 1000 square feet of garden soil one full point — that is, from 5.5 to 6.5. There's nothing esoteric about liming. When I add organic matter in the fall, I work limestone in at the same time, incorporating enough to bring the pH back into that desirable 6.5 range.

I test the soil pH again in the spring, before planting time, so that I can make any last-minute adjustments that may be needed — usually only a light dusting of ground limestone before I turn under the cover crop of winter rye, adding well-rotted manure or finished compost if I have any available.

The methods described above will work for most gardeners east of the Mississippi River, where centuries of heavy rainfall have leached away alkaline elements and left the soil generally acidic. Western gardeners may find themselves with the opposite problem. On the other side of the Mississippi, where rainfall is somewhat lighter, alkalinity has remained higher. Soil tests there may indicate the need for agricultural sulfur, which will lower the pH. Twenty pounds of sulfur will lower the pH of 1000 square feet of garden soil one full point, from 7.5 to 6.5. Sulfur can be incorporated just like limestone, by broadcasting or mechanically spreading over the soil and then forking or rototilling in.

Fertility Fertility is the third component of healthy soil. For successful vegetable gardening, soil must contain adequate amounts of the "big three" macronutrients — nitrogen, phosphorus, and potash. Nitrogen is important to plant protein formation and to the creation of chlorophyll, the pigment that fuels photosynthesis. Nitrogen is also essential for strong foliar growth. Yellowing leaves are one sure sign of nitrogen deficiency. Phosphorus is required for strong root development, disease resistance, and fruit formation. Phosphorus-poor plants will look stunted, and may have reddened stems or leaves. Potash is necessary for vigorous growth, and plays a key role in disease resistance. Browning leaves and retarded growth are telltale signs of potash deficiency.

Plants also need substantial amounts of three secondary nutrients — calcium, magnesium, and sulfur. These are usually found in adequate supply in most soils. Also generally present in sufficient amounts are the important micronutrients, also called trace elements: iron, manganese, boron, chlorine, zinc, copper, and molybdenum.

As I've already mentioned, I use a lot of organic matter in the Victory Garden, and this has some nutritive value. Manure is relatively high in nitrogen, for instance, and compost will introduce adequate amounts of micronutrients. I also use chemical fertilizers, though, and I think it's silly to avoid one or the other as a matter of rigid principle. Both organic matter and chemical fertilizers have their place in any soil management program. It's my feeling that a balance of organic matter and chemical fertilizers is best for the garden and the gardener. I advocate the use of chemical fertilizers mostly because they're efficient. Organic materials, whatever their virtues, are not as efficient suppliers of plant nutrients, for example. It takes twenty pounds of cow manure to provide the same amounts of nitrogen, phosphorus, and potash found in *one* pound of 5-10-5 fertilizer. It's also true that organic materials do not contain balanced proportions of essential plant nutrients. They must be combined in various ratios to give growing vegetables an adequate diet, and it can become downright confusing juggling recipes of bonemeal, blood meal, greensand, wood ashes, tankage, and the like.

My preference, then, is to rely heavily on organic matter (animal manure, compost, green manure crops) to improve soil *structure*, and more on chemical fertilizers to produce balanced fertility. I've found that this combination is both good for the soil and very efficient in terms of time and labor. As I'll say over and over again in this book (and on the air!), I believe strongly in achieving maximum yield from every hour I spend in the garden.

All chemical fertilizers carry a three-number designation. Among the most common are 5-10-5, 10-10-10, and 5-10-10. These numbers refer to the percentages of nitrogen, phosphorus, and potash (in that order) contained in the bag of fertilizer. The remaining material in any bag is simply inert matter used for binding and forming. Different formulations of the "big three" are useful for different crops. A 5-10-5 fertilizer is best for fruiting crops like squash and tomatoes, which benefit from

Side-dressing corn: Here I've opened up a narrow, shallow trench to apply the fertilizer, which I'll cover up with soil.

extra phosphorus; 10-10-10 is better for leafy vegetables like lettuce, spinach, and cabbage, as the extra nitrogen promotes vegetative growth. And certain crops, most notably peppers, benefit from 5-10-10 because they need extra potash.

Fertilizers like those described above release their constituents into the soil quickly. Their breakdown begins as soon as they're dug into the soil and come into contact with water contained in it. They continue to release their nutrients for a period of time that varies depending on rainfall, temperature, and soil disturbance. No standard chemical fertilizer will provide nutrients steadily over an entire Victory Garden growing season of five to six months, though. To provide certain crops with additional nutrition during the season — especially long-term crops like winter squash or melons, which can take from 100 to 120 days to mature — I rely on slow-release fertilizer. Chemically the same as other commercial fertilizers, the granules of slow-release types are coated with a water-permeable material that releases the nutrients more gradually than do standard fertilizers.

I also use a balanced liquid fertilizer for foliar feeding, initial watering-in of seedling transplants, and as a quick-fix boost for any plants that show a nutrient deficiency during the season. Water-soluble fertilizers, as their name implies, are meant to be mixed with water. They come in crystalline and liquid forms, and my favorite is a balanced 20-20-20 formula.

Fertilizing in the Victory Garden is really an ongoing process. In the spring, when I turn under our cover crops of winter rye, I like to add 5 pounds of 5-10-5 fertilizer for every 100 square feet of bed area for most of the crops. I'll use the same amount of 10-10-10 for leafy vegetables (lettuce and Swiss chard, for example), and 5-10-10 for the peppers, with their big appetite for potash. During the season, when I'm preparing the raised beds of long-term crops like squash and melons, I add 5 pounds of slow-release 14-14-14 per 100 square feet of bed area before laying down the beds' black plastic mulch.

Side-dressing is another way to make sure that each crop receives all the nutrients it needs throughout the growing season. Peppers, for instance, benefit from additional fertilizer after their first fruits set. It's good to side-dress broccoli, after harvesting the primary head, with half a handful of 10-10-10 per plant. In the calendar-month chapters that follow, I give specific, month-by-month instructions for side-dressing, but the thing to understand here is that there's nothing at all complicated about the process. It's nothing more than using my cultivator to scratch half a handful of fertilizer per plant into the soil around the plant's base.

I use balanced water-soluble fertilizer liberally. When seedlings are transplanted from 4-inch pots to individual cell-packs after having been started indoors, I water them in with a starter solution of 20-20-20 liquid fertilizer diluted to half strength. Later, when these transplants are set out into the garden, they receive another watering-in with half-strength solution. I keep my eye on all the crops during the growing season, too, and whenever I spot yellowing leaves, unusually slow growth, or other signs of nutrient deficiency, I give the needy plants a drink of 20-20-20 at full strength.

Finally, when fall arrives and the Victory Garden beds are coming empty, I fertilize the soil with 2 pounds of 10-10-10 for each 100 square feet of area before sowing the cover crop of winter rye.

There are a few fertilizer cautions worth mentioning. One is to keep chemical fertilizer 3 or 4 inches away from plant roots and stems. Direct contact with either will cause burning, resulting in checked growth or a dead plant. Be careful, also, to avoid overfertilizing, which can be more harmful than underfertilizing. Finally, don't use fertilizer during very dry weather, unless you can water adequately. Roots can't take up the nutrients unless there is enough moisture in the soil. In the Victory Garden it's not a problem, because I can water the crops pretty much at will, and I make sure they receive at least 1 inch of water per week during the growing season. Gardeners who live in very dry areas, or who are subject to water-use restrictions during the summer, will need to be more careful with the chemical applications.

Compost

As I indicated in the previous section on soil preparation, compost is probably the best all-around soil improver available to the vegetable gardener. I've used compost in the Victory Garden from the beginning, but my method for producing compost has improved a bit. At first, I used a conventional three-bin compost system. One bin was for ready-to-use, fully reduced compost. Another contained partly decayed, intermediate material. The third was for new matter. This three-bin system, in optimal conditions and with lots of turning, could produce finished compost in three months. Note well that phrase, "lots of turning," and then understand when I say that all the turning was the rock upon which my three-bin system finally came to grief. As I got busier in the Victory Garden, the turning just wasn't getting done. More pressing activities always seemed to demand my attention and, though I am as devout a lover of compost as any gardener on earth, my compost production dwindled.

Now I've hit upon a different and better way to make compost. The new system eliminates one bin altogether. Instead, I fill two larger bins with the same ingredients that went into the three-bin system. But here's the big difference: no turning. The larger bins generate enough heat to speed decomposition without requiring all that turning, and I like that. Physicists talk about elegant formulas, by which they mean formulas that work with utmost efficiency. I like to garden by that same principle: maximum output from minimum input. It's not that I don't en-

Adding ground limestone will hasten the breakdown in our compost.

FERTILIZER
LIME
2" SOIL
6" ORGANIC MATERIAL

joy spending time in the garden — I've been at it for more than thirty years and loved every minute. But as I've said on the air, gardeners in this day and age just can't afford to waste time or energy.

In the next chapter's feature, "Victory Garden Structures," I give detailed instructions for building a sturdy two-bin composter like the one I use. Here, I'll explain how I make the rich compost that goes into the Victory Garden beds. To start my first pile, I lay down a 6-inch layer of organic material or manure, or a mixture of both. The organic material might include leaves, garden refuse, tomato vines, and lawn clippings. The latter should not be used alone, because they will mat together and prevent air circulation. It's also important to use clippings from lawns that have not been treated with weed killers or insecticides, because these can remain active and damage crops later on. Similarly, diseased garden refuse of any kind is denied entry into the Victory Garden composter. I also stay away from bones or meat, which decay too slowly, cause bad smells, and attract digging animals. I do include household waste whenever possible: vegetables, fruits, eggshells, and coffee grounds. On top of this first 6-inch layer I add 1 to 2 inches of soil, then 2 handfuls of lime, and 2 more of any garden fertilizer. The lime ensures a correct pH, and the fertilizer maintains a proper balance of essential nutrients. After the first layer's sequence is complete, I repeat it several times until the bin is filled. Then I go to work on bin number two.

As I build the layers, I'm careful to leave a depression in each pile's center. This collects water and channels it down into the pile, where it's needed — along with oxygen — for decomposition to occur. Moisture control is important, too. Each layer should be about as wet as a damp sponge, but not soaking. Too much water drives out air, which causes anaerobic decomposition to occur. From anaerobic piles come bad smells that will not endear you to your neighbors, so avoid overwatering.

If I complete a pile in early summer, that will give me ready compost for fall. My second bin, completed at season's end, will be ready during the following spring. Decomposition takes place more quickly during the heat of summer, so the March-started compost is often finished faster than my fall batch. I know that the compost is finished when there is no longer any heat in the pile, and — more important — when the compost is dark brown and crumbly.

Raised Beds

The practice of raised-bed culture was probably originated by the Chinese thousands of years ago. French market gardeners near Paris improved some of the techniques in the late 1800s, and in the last ten years, raised-bed culture has undergone a real renaissance.

In the Victory Garden, I now grow almost everything (corn and a few vining crops are about the only exceptions) in raised beds. The advantages are many. Raised beds provide a greater depth of rich topsoil, which is the primary growing medium for all vegetables. This extra helping of premium soil allows for a greater concentration of nutrients, and a more economical use of fertilizer and amendments. In traditional flat-plane culture, all the garden areas — walkways as well as growing areas — receive fertilizer and organic matter, though they do no good in noncultivated areas. With raised beds, the amendments go only to those areas where crops will grow, cutting down on wasted material — and time. It's also true that because feet and machines travel on the footpaths and not over the beds, soil compaction is kept to an absolute minimum. This means that the soil remains loose and friable, providing excellent drainage and aeration and allowing growing roots to penetrate without difficulty. The high fertility of the beds allows for very intensive gardening practices: intercropping, succession planting, and extended seasons. The soil warms up earlier in spring, and stays 6 to 10 degrees warmer throughout the growing season. Raised beds also lend themselves nicely to the most efficient way to keep the garden watered — drip or trickle watering. And when heavy rains drench other gardens, washing away seeds or seedlings and submerging young plants in early spring, the raised beds float snugly above the deluge. The only extra attention raised beds require is a bit more watering during the hottest days of summer, when their greater exposed surface area causes them to lose more moisture than flat beds.

I've heard people say that the big drawback to raised beds is the work required to create them, but I think that's a myth.

Opening up a trench to bury the corners of the black plastic. ▲ I've stretched the plastic taut before burying the edges all around. ▶

Any garden requires a certain amount of working-up in the spring: tilling, forking, raking, and so on. Raised-bed gardens require about the same work. When I make my raised beds, instead of raking the soil smooth and flat, I rake it into the raised formations that will be our beds. It's not really any more work than that required for flat culture.

Here's how I go about making raised beds in the Victory Garden. The best time to do this is in the spring, following a thorough fall program of soil amendment like that described earlier. As soon as the soil can be worked, I add any last-minute amendments (compost or manure, lime, fertilizer) and till or fork them under, along with the green manure cover crop that's been growing all winter. Next, I excavate the pathways that will separate the beds. I like to have fairly wide pathways, about 24 inches, and I string two lines to help me keep my digging straight. I take about 3 or 4 inches of soil from the pathway and deposit it on top of the adjacent soil, working the length of the bed. All my Victory Garden raised beds are 48 inches wide, and most are 8 feet long. I string lines 48 inches apart to help me form the beds, too, so that they're just as neat and eye-pleasing as the pathways. To make the beds themselves, I use my rake to form the soil between the paths into a flat-topped mound about 8 inches high, with a base width of 48 inches and sides that taper up at about a 45-degree angle to a top that's 36 inches wide. (See accompanying illustrations.) I have to work a bit with the flat side of my rake to shape the top and sides of the bed and to smooth the pathways in between beds, but when I'm finished I have raised beds that will last the whole growing season. Once created, these raised beds need only minor reshaping with the rake at the beginning of each season.

Planting in raised beds is easier than flat-plane planting because the beds are higher, requiring less bending and stooping. The 48-inch width is not only convenient for the gardener — the bed can be worked from both sides — but good for the vegetables, too, since I never have to stand on the growing surface. My actual planting practice is the same as it would be for conventional gardens, whether I'm setting in seedlings or seeds. I can sow in single rows, wide rows, or simply broadcast the seed, depending on the crop I'm growing.

Varietal Selection

In my thirty-plus years of gardening, I've stayed with a few varieties for a long time. I still grow Butter and Sugar corn, for instance, and I've grown Buttercrunch lettuce for over a decade. Most of the Victory Garden crops, though, are of more recent vintage. I spend a lot of time reviewing seed catalogs and trying out the new varieties. I'm always on the lookout for varieties that combine disease and insect resistance and good eating quality. I'll hazard an observation here, too, that a good many growers still use the same varieties they were seeding twenty years ago. I think that's a shame. Though I'm pretty conservative in most matters, I'll try any new, promising varieties as soon as I can get my hands on them. Many problems that plague the garden can be overcome only when breeders discover a wild strain of disease-resistant plants and work that desirable quality into a new variety for home gardening. Other kinds of advances, as well, make new varieties attractive. Dr. Clint Peterson's new A+ carrot is one example. The A+ is sweet and delicious, and packs *twice* the vitamin A content of previous varieties. I want vegetables like that in my garden — and on my table.

The best way to stay abreast of such developments is to read as many seed catalogs as possible. I'm on the mailing lists of dozens of companies, and I spend many enjoyable winter hours poring over the catalogs. Though the catalog descriptions occasionally run to extremes, many have excellent cultural information. I also read as many articles as I can in the leading garden magazines, and I talk to lots of other gardeners, all of whom have something to tell me. They're just like me: Whenever I produce a masterful new crop, bragging rights come with it.

Another excellent source of information on new varieties is an organization called the All-America Selections Committee. This

A recent All-America favorite of mine — Jersey Golden Acorn — yields a good harvest of superb-tasting squash on compact vines. Good yield with great taste in less space is a real improvement.

group of seed industry professionals conducts annual field trials of promising vegetables and flowers in regional gardens across the country. Qualified judges give awards to varieties that display superior performance when grown alongside the best existing varieties. Before long, these varieties show up in the catalogs and on seeds racks. While All-America Selections may not show spectacular results in all gardens, using them increases the chances of producing healthy, vigorous crops. For more information on garden planning and crop choice, see the chapter entitled "Beginnings," which immediately follows this one.

Starting Seeds Indoors

I start the vast majority of crops grown in the Victory Garden indoors, rather than planting out directly in the soil, even when warm summer weather would allow me to direct-seed if I wished. I emphasize indoor starts for my crops because of the greater control this gives me over growing conditions during the critical early stages of the plants' lives. Indoors, the plants are assured freedom from wind, cold, and drought. They are started from seed in a sterile growing medium, so diseases can't attack them, nor are they subject to assaults from insects or other pests. I can control the amount of light they receive, and keep them free from competition with larger, more established garden crops. All in all, starting seeds indoors lets me produce the hardiest, healthiest seedlings possible.

I start a few tomatoes (my super-early crop) and some onions and leeks indoors in February, but the bulk of my indoor seeding takes place in March and April. I use a soilless growing medium called "Redi-Earth," which is a commercial variety developed at Cornell University. The mix is a blend of peat moss, vermiculite, and nutrients, and is available at garden centers and from some seed catalogs. The mixture is free of weeds and disease organisms. In addition, it's porous enough to keep the seeds moist without inviting rot, while providing good aeration and drainage. I add this mix to plastic 4-inch pots that have been sterilized by washing in a solution of 1 part chlorine bleach and 7 parts hot water. New pots need not be sterilized.

Before I fill the pots, I moisten the growing medium in its bag, which not only prevents my being smothered by billowing clouds of fine peat moss but saves time, as well. Next, I fill my 4-inch pots to the brim, and firm the surface by pressing down with the bottom of another 4-inch pot, leaving a ½-inch space to allow for watering. To compensate for the various kinds of attrition that can keep new seed from coming up or attack it once it does, I sow twice as many seeds as I plan to transplant into the garden. Thus the eventual growth of 10 cabbages, say, requires my sowing 20 seeds at this early stage.

To sow, I crimp the seed packet into a V and then tap the seed out with my index finger. After they are sown, I cover the seeds with this same soilless mix to a depth equal to about three times their diameter. Planting too deeply retards emergence, while shallower planting increases the risk of drying out.

I set the pots in a tray of warm water and let them remain there until capillary action has drawn water up and moistened the surface of the growing medium. When I can see the moisture from this bottom-watering, I remove the pots from their tray. Thereafter, I keep a close eye on them. The medium must never be allowed to dry out, or to become soggy. Either will spell the demise of germinating seeds. This bottom-watering is the technique I use for all my indoor-started seeds. It's much neater than top-watering, but — more important — it prevents seeds from being washed out of the growing medium.

To germinate, seeds need constant moisture and bottom heat, but not fertilizer. Like camels, seeds carry a long-distance supply of nutrients with them, and at first the sprouting seeds will

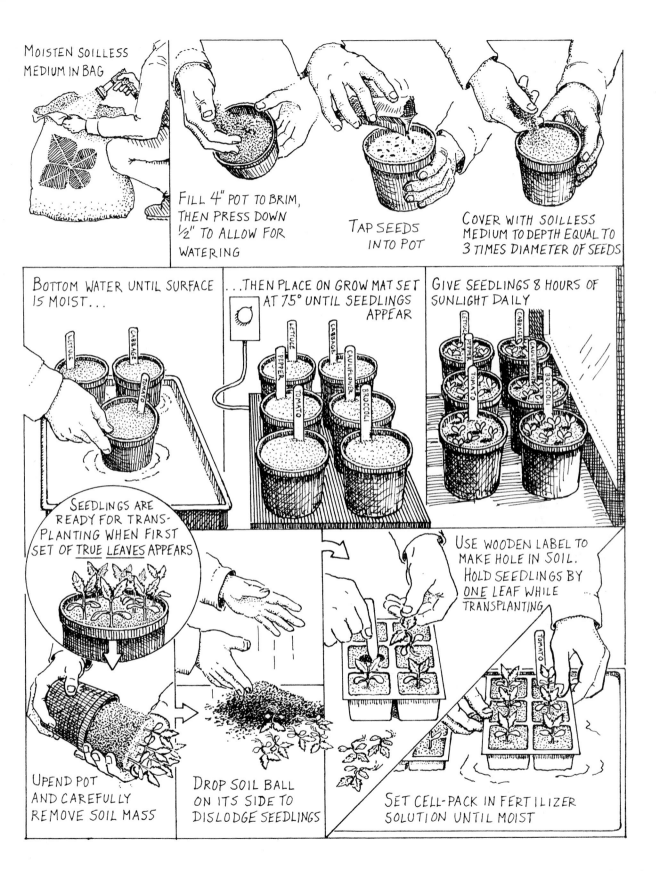

MOISTEN SOILLESS MEDIUM IN BAG

FILL 4" POT TO BRIM, THEN PRESS DOWN ½" TO ALLOW FOR WATERING

TAP SEEDS INTO POT

COVER WITH SOILLESS MEDIUM TO DEPTH EQUAL TO 3 TIMES DIAMETER OF SEEDS

BOTTOM WATER UNTIL SURFACE IS MOIST...

...THEN PLACE ON GROW MAT SET AT 75° UNTIL SEEDLINGS APPEAR

GIVE SEEDLINGS 8 HOURS OF SUNLIGHT DAILY

SEEDLINGS ARE READY FOR TRANS- PLANTING WHEN FIRST SET OF TRUE LEAVES APPEARS

USE WOODEN LABEL TO MAKE HOLE IN SOIL. HOLD SEEDLINGS BY ONE LEAF WHILE TRANSPLANTING

UPEND POT AND CAREFULLY REMOVE SOIL MASS

DROP SOIL BALL ON ITS SIDE TO DISLODGE SEEDLINGS

SET CELL-PACK IN FERTILIZER SOLUTION UNTIL MOIST

feed on these quite satisfactorily. While the professional growers adjust temperatures precisely to the needs of different crops, the home gardener need only provide a soil temperature of about 75 degrees to insure optimum germination of vegetable seeds. At the Victory Garden, I set the pots directly on a grow mat to give them this steady bottom heat. Made especially for propagating, a grow mat is a 2-foot square of rubber in which electrical cables are embedded. Setting the mat's thermostat at 75 degrees provides ideal soil temperature and foolproof germination.

As soon as the seedlings poke through the surface, I move the pots off the heat and into bright light, then water them conscientiously, for they must not be allowed to dry out. Full, strong sun, coupled with nighttime temperatures of 55 to 60 degrees, will produce the sturdiest seedlings that will survive later transplanting outdoors. At this stage, at least half a day of full sunlight is important. Without that much, I would be reluctant to grow seeds indoors unless I supplemented natural light with fluorescent grow-lights.

Standard blue-white fluorescent tube lights are adequate for growing seedlings indoors. These can be used to supply all the light seedlings receive, as in a basement, or they can be used to augment sunlight from windows. It's possible to buy special

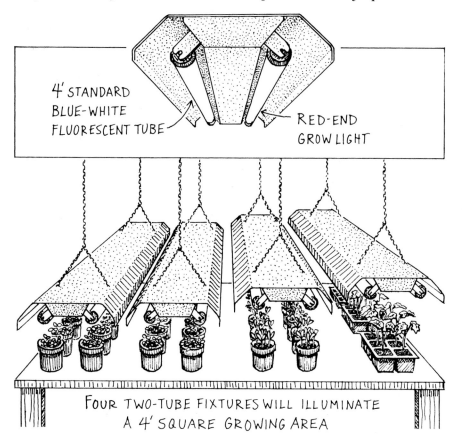

4' STANDARD BLUE-WHITE FLUORESCENT TUBE

RED-END GROW LIGHT

FOUR TWO-TUBE FIXTURES WILL ILLUMINATE A 4' SQUARE GROWING AREA grow-lights, at hardware stores and garden centers, that emit more light from the red end of the spectrum and that have been designed especially for indoor plant growing. Probably the best arrangement is to combine a standard blue-white tube with one of these special red-end grow-lights, thus providing the plants with a wide range of red and blue light wavelengths. Two 4-foot fluorescent tubes provide enough light for a growing area 4 feet long and 1 foot wide. By aligning 4 two-tube fluorescent fixtures, a 4-foot-square growing area can be lit. Fluorescent lights do not heat up, so plants can be placed very close to them — 3 inches or so. Most growers don't know this, but more light comes from the center of the tubes than from the ends, so it's a good idea to move the seedlings around every few days to make sure they all receive equal amounts of light. And don't make the mistake of leaving the lights on twenty-four hours a day. Plants need some darkness to develop properly. Eight hours of darkness is enough, and an automatic timer never forgets.

Germinating seeds will stay in their 4-inch pots for 2 to 4 weeks, until they produce their first set of true leaves. These aren't the first leaves that appear. Those are seed leaves (also called cotyledons), and they will dry up and shrivel as the seedling grows. The true leaves are the *next* to appear, and they look like smaller versions of the plant's real leaves. When the true leaves are evident, it's time to move the seedlings on to cell-packs. These are light plastic containers that vaguely resemble egg cartons and may have 4, 6, 8, or more individual cells for growing seedlings.

To separate the seedlings, I gently upend the 4-inch pot, so that the soil mass drops into my hand, and here I am very careful not to damage any of the delicate seedlings. Then I drop the soil ball, from a height of about 6 inches, onto its side on the potting bench. This breaks up the soil, loosens the seedlings, and makes it much easier for me to isolate individuals without undue damage to roots and stems. My cell-packs are filled with the same soilless growing medium, pre-moistened, and each cell is firmed. A 4-inch wooden label is the perfect tool for making a hole in the growing medium. Into this I insert my seedlings, holding them by the leaves, never by the stem, and burying them up to their seed leaves, one seedling per cell. Setting them in too deeply could check growth or kill weak ones; not deeply enough gives spindly, weak seedlings. I firm the medium gently. Once transplanted, the seedlings are given a watering-in with a solution of balanced water-soluble fertilizer (I like 20-20-20) diluted to half strength. I use the same bottom-watering technique with the cell-packs that I used earlier when the seeds were first planted in the 4-inch pots. The planting medium takes up the liquid until fully saturated, and the delicate seedlings are not disturbed by a heavy shower of water. This bottom-watering settles the medium, and also eliminates the inadvertent washing away of soilless mix.

The object of all these steps — planting seed indoors, watching for true leaves, transplanting to cell-packs — is to provide unchecked growth for the plants. Any number of mishaps (temperature fluctuations, insufficient or excessive watering, inadequate light, overly aggressive fertilization, to name a few) can check plant growth, but one of the surest ways to accomplish it is to leave a plant growing too long in one container. Progress halts when root mass exceeds soil volume, and while the plant may survive thereafter, it will never be as healthy or productive as it would have been without overcrowded roots. To prevent this, I periodically pop my plants from their containers to check the roots. If I see that the roots have filled up the soil mass, I move them to larger containers. But if I have my planting times figured correctly, I should not have to do this, and, in fact, I prefer not to. All this potting-up takes time from a busy gardener's spring schedule.

I transplant most of my seedlings only this one time, from 4-inch pots to cell-packs. Then, after they've hardened off (spent 5 days in the cold frame adjusting to outdoor temperature and moisture conditions), I set the individual seedlings into the garden soil as soon as temperature and soil conditions allow. This produces plants more vigorous than those that have been pampered and nursed along under limiting indoor conditions for too long. On the rare occasions when I want a few larger seedlings (broccoli, perhaps, or tomatoes), I'll move them from their cell-packs into individual 4-inch pots. This will give me very sturdy seedlings that could be set out in the cold frame or (in the case of tomatoes) in plastic-wrapped cages that will give me a 3- to 4-week jump on the season.

The only variation in the procedures described above occurs when I'm seeding crops that are extremely sensitive to transplant shock: melons, for instance, or cucumbers. To minimize this shock, I sow seeds for crops like these in peat pots or peat strips filled with soilless growing medium. Peat pots can be set directly into the garden soil, where they disintegrate, allowing young roots to expand unimpeded. The one drawback to peat pots is that they tend to dry out. I pay them special attention after the seeds have germinated, keeping them moist at all times. When they're set into the garden, I peel the tops from the peat pots, because those tops, if left exposed to air, would wick away moisture and dry out the root mass below.

Buying Seedlings

Though I like to start my own crops from seed whenever possible, I realize that I'm fortunate to have a greenhouse and the good conditions necessary to grow strong seedlings. Without the light and temperature needed for strong seedling development, it makes sense to buy them at a good nursery or garden center. I like to shop early for best selection and to get the seedlings before they've grown too long in their containers. I look for

These peat strips for starting peas, beans, and sweet corn have meant weeks-earlier harvest for all three.

healthy foliage and I check the undersides of leaves to make sure they're free of insects. I like young, stocky seedlings, and avoid, weak, leggy, long-stemmed plants. And I'm never afraid to slip the plant out of its cell-pack to check its root system. If all I see is a mass of roots and no soil, it goes back on the shelf. Plants like that have sat too long in the container and won't perform well in the garden. Finally, I shop at garden centers that enjoy good reputations. They're never the cheapest, but customer satisfaction and repeat business are important to them. They'll have the best plants, and the really good ones will replace any seedlings that die off quickly — an indication that something was amiss in the greenhouse — or show signs of disease that could have been incurred early in their development.

Planting

There are two primary ways to plant vegetables in the garden: sowing seeds directly in the soil, and transplanting seedlings that have been started indoors. Sowing seeds directly involves no magic. It does require knowledge of the soil temperature each crop needs to germinate and of the crop's sensitivity to frost (if I'm planting in the spring). In the monthly chapters that follow, I give specific, crop-by-crop requirements for direct seeding, so that's the place to look for individual instructions for beans, say, or pumpkins. There's a good bit of variation between crops' germination temperature requirements and frost sensitivity, so it's hard to generalize. Once the timing is established, though, the planting procedures are similar for all the crops. I head for the garden with my seed packets, rake, trowel, and planting board. When I plant single or wide rows, I cover the seeds with soilless growing medium three times as deep as their diameter. I use the growing medium rather than soil because it's free of weed seeds, disease organisms, and insects, and because it offers less resistance to the germinating seedlings than more solid soil does. I gently firm the growing medium with my hand, then water the seeds in well with a very fine spray from the watering can or hose. As is the case when starting seeds indoors, seeds sown in the garden must be kept moist to germinate.

A straight line and careful seeding make for a neat look to the garden and less thinning later on. The watering can at the end of the row won't let me forget to water in.

The other way to get plants into the garden is to transplant established seedlings. Before *that* happens, though, they must be "hardened off" in the cold frame for 5 days. The Victory Garden cold frame is nothing more than a portable wooden box, about 4 feet square, with a hinged top covered with clear plastic. Full instructions for building a cold frame just like the one I use appear in next chapter's feature. Seedlings rushed directly from the indoors to the open garden can suffer shock from the sudden temperature fluctuations, wind, and reduced water supply, and this shock can impair their growth forever after. In the cold frame, they become accustomed more gradually to wider temperature variations, reduced water, blowing wind, and longer hours of direct sunlight.

I like to set the cell-packs of seedlings or individual pots into the cold frame on an overcast day to ease them into the harsher outdoor conditions. I try to keep the frame cover closed that first day, and here I'll admit that managing a cold frame takes some getting used to. It must be vented on warm, sunny days so that the seedlings don't overheat, but it must be closed early enough on cool days to build up heat for the evening. Though I don't use one, it's possible to buy cold frames with automatic venting devices, which can be set to open and close the cover at a certain time each day, or when the internal temperature reaches a certain point. There's nothing wrong with automatic venters like this, but I've come to prefer the intimacy with my crops that I gain from making the adjustments myself.

When the seedlings have been hardened off, they go into the garden. I dig their planting holes one by one, pop a plant from its cell-pack, and set it into the hole. Planting depth varies from

A warm spring day means my cold frame is opened wide to keep cool seedlings of lettuce, broccoli, leeks, and Chinese cabbage.

These broccoli seedlings are set in deeper than they grew in their cell-packs because they will root along their stems. To fill in the space until the broccoli needs it, I've interplanted quick-growing leaf lettuce.

crop to crop. Those that root all along their stems, like tomatoes, go in deeper than they were growing in the cell-packs or pots, so that strong root systems will develop. Others (like lettuce) that will not root along the stem are planted the same depth they were growing in their seedling containers. I add soil to fill the hole around the seed ball, then firm the soil on top, leaving a slight depression around the stem to collect water. When all the seedlings have been planted this way, I give them a thorough watering with a solution of balanced water-soluble fertilizer diluted to half strength.

Mulches

Mulches are one of the gardener's best friends. Where they're used, they reduce or eliminate weed growth and, therefore, weeding. Mulches help the soil retain moisture by slowing evaporation. They stabilize soil temperature, and lessen the likelihood of rot for crops like squash and melons. One type of mulch, black plastic, even discourages a few types of insects from attacking plants. A welcome by-product of all this is that mulches reduce the gardener's work load. You'll never hear me complain about that.

Mulches may be organic or inorganic. Organic types include salt marsh hay, grass clippings, compost, sawdust, newspapers, and more. Inorganic mulches include aluminum foil and clear and black polyethylene plastic. Organic mulches must be at least several inches thick to quell weeds effectively and conserve moisture, and they must be replenished throughout the growing season as they become compacted and decompose. Not so the inorganic plastic mulches, which is one main reason why I favor them, in the Victory Garden, over the organic types. Black plastic mulch — the kind I use most widely — can be forgotten, once it's in place.

I use black plastic mulch throughout the Victory Garden, and will confess right here to an unabashed fondness for the homely stuff. It makes weeding a thing of the past, greatly reduces the need for watering, and helps warm spring soil for those early crops. Plentiful moisture, the absence of weed competition, and warm soil produce great crops. Every one I've grown under black plastic has outperformed those left unmulched.

Plastic mulch is available at garden centers in rolls of varying length, width, and thickness. For the Victory Garden's raised 48-inch-wide beds, I use black plastic that is 6 feet wide and 3 mils (or .003 inch) thick. It's possible to buy mulch plastic in thinner, .002-inch versions, but I like the thicker type, which resists ripping and is sure to last a whole season.

Which crops do I single out for black plastic treatment? Heat-lovers like peppers, eggplants, and cucumbers benefit especially from the soil-warming effect of the plastic. Weed control with rambling, long-vining crops like melons and winter squash is much easier with black plastic, so they're covered, as well. I don't use it for crops that come quickly — radishes, spinach, beets — because all the laying down and taking up would be too much work. Nor do I use it for crops that are spaced very closely in the rows, like carrots or lettuce. Finally, it's not helpful to crops that like to grow cool: the brassicas, spinach, and kale, to name three. (I'll give specific mulching instructions for each crop later, in the monthly chapters.)

Here's how I use the plastic mulch. Bed preparation comes first. I make sure that all soil prep — adding manure or compost, lime, turning under cover crops — is complete. Then, before the plastic goes down, I add 5 pounds of slow-release 14-14-14 fertilizer per 100 square feet of bed space. Next, while the crop in question is hardening-off, I lay the black plastic over the bed and bury its edges all the way around the bed's borders. The extra foot on each side of my 6-foot-wide strips gives me plenty of plastic to work with. In addition to giving the garden a nicely tailored appearance, this anchors the plastic securely, even in the wildest New England gales. Come planting time,

The soil under the black plastic mulch will be many degrees warmer than ground uncovered, which means quick, unchecked growth for these tomato seedlings.

whether for seeds or seedlings, I cut 4-inch squares in the plastic and plant my seeds or seedlings through the openings. At one time I just cut crosses in the plastic, but stopped that practice after discovering that wind whipped the little flaps back and forth, administering quite a beating to delicate seedlings.

Now that I've expressed this fondness for black plastic, let me admit that I also use organic mulches for certain crops. Asparagus, for instance, is mulched with salt marsh hay or grass clippings when newly planted shoots appear above the soil. Leeks, late in the season, will receive a thick mulch of salt marsh hay or grass clippings to keep them from freezing in the rapidly chilling soil. (Neither of these trench-grown crops lends itself to black plastic mulching.) Organic mulches, when used in the spring, are not laid down until the soil has had a chance to warm up because, unlike the heat-absorbing black plastic, they'll keep the heat *out*. That makes them valuable during the hot summer months, though, and they're laid down at that time to protect certain crops from too much heat, and to help conserve moisture as well. Let me give this general warning for grass clippings, one of my favorite organic mulches: They must not be laid down too thickly (about 2 inches deep is maximum) in hot weather, or they will mat and generate too much heat for the safety of the plants beneath.

Broccoli appreciates an organic mulch like salt marsh hay to keep its root zone cool. It will cut down on weeds, also. ▲

The Wall O' Water tower fits over young plants to protect them from the cool nights and gusty winds of spring. ▼

Season Extenders

People mark their garden victories in different ways, but one of my goals is to harvest something from the garden every day from mid-April through Thanksgiving. In our New England climate, that takes some doing. I've come to rely heavily on my season extenders for that 8-month harvest season. I use the cold frame, Wall O' Water towers, and a spun polyester fabric. I'm especially enthusiastic about this fabric, which helps the crops in many ways. It offers several degrees of frost protection, for one thing. For another, it keeps insects at bay. I don't have to disturb it for watering, because water passes right through. Finally, it affords excellent light penetration. It's possible to lay the spun polyester right on top of the emerging seedlings of some crops, and it's so light that the growing plants will lift it right up. I prefer to support it with hoops of PVC tubing or #12 wire, though, so that the plants are spared even the minimal resistance that the very light fabric offers.

The Victory Garden cold frame is used primarily for hardening off, but it does extend the growing season of a few crops — especially lettuce — several weeks in the spring and fall. As I've said elsewhere, the cold frame is essentially a 4-foot-square box with a hinged lid that is covered with plastic. Heat is trapped inside the covered box, and the inside temperature can be adjusted by opening the lid to vent off excess warmth.

To protect tomatoes, peppers, and eggplants against frost, I use Wall O' Water towers. These are flexible plastic tubes, large

This beautiful crop of spring brassicas was protected from early cold and troublesome insects by spun polyester fabric, which is supported by hoops of bent PVC tubing.

enough to fit over the young plants. Once in place, channels in the Wall O' Water are filled with water, which retains warmth from the sun through cool nights. They also protect seedlings from wind and, to some extent, from insects.

Basic Care Techniques

Watering Plants obviously need water for good growth. They need it consistently, and I make sure the garden gets 1 inch of water per week throughout the growing season. That amount is easily measured by putting a can in the path of my sprinkler with a mark 1 inch from the bottom. I water in late afternoon, so that little is lost to evaporation from a hot midday sun, but early enough so that the plants dry off before evening. Early in the season, when the plants are delicate, I prefer hand-watering with a hose-end sprayer that has a fine rose attachment to break the force of the spray. After the seedlings have developed, my watering device of choice is an oscillating sprinkler that provides a fine spray and even distribution.

The most economical way to water a garden where water is precious is a drip or trickle system. Either of these delivers water very slowly, and the water is absorbed completely and deeply, avoiding runoff, because the rate of flow is so gradual. The Israelis have used this principle to make the desert bloom — literally — and drip and trickle systems can also be used to deliver fertilizer and insecticides in liquid form. A drip or trickle system, which uses a tube or hose with many small holes in it, may be above ground or dug in permanently below the surface. These systems can be quite complex, with different zones, timers, and programs for different crops. Such systems are quite expensive, though, and these days you can spend a

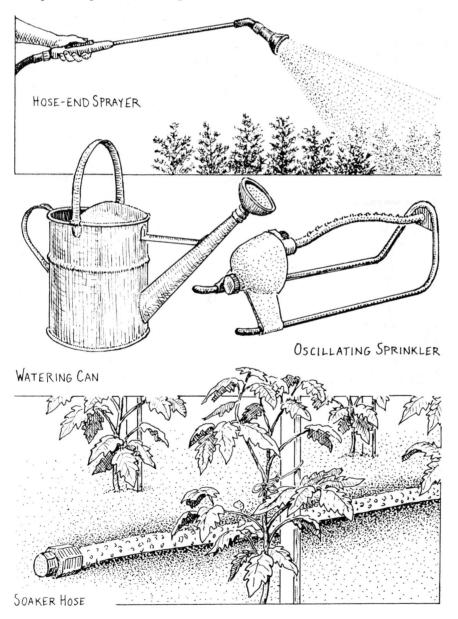

HOSE-END SPRAYER

WATERING CAN

OSCILLATING SPRINKLER

SOAKER HOSE

Another good choice in sprinklers is the impact type. Here it's raised on a basket to get good even distribution over tall plants.

fortune on watering technology — as on many areas of gardening equipment — if you choose. I've had excellent luck with my tried-and-true oscillating sprinkler and rose-equipped watering can, however, and recommend those for all but the biggest, most elaborate gardens.

Thinning Plants must be thinned to their appropriate spacing, or they will never develop fully. I thin early, always after a rain or watering, when the plants can be pulled most easily from the moist soil. This first thinning is done when the seedlings are 1 to 2 inches tall. I cull out weaker seedlings and leave the sturdiest

40 **Steps to Victorious Gardening**

The bag of Victory Garden tricks for beating the season and the bugs includes raised beds, black-plastic-covered beds, plastic-wrapped tomato cages, cold frame, spun polyester over PVC hoops, and cheesecloth to protect delicate carrot seeds.

behind — or at least that's the rule by which I *try* to do my thinning. In many cases, *all* the seedlings will look equally strong, but I still have to thin to the correct spacing, hard-hearted though it may seem. Not all thinnings are discarded, by the way. Some are transplanted to fill gaps left by poor germination, and others (spinach, say) are eaten in salads. When I'm thinning in the garden beds, I use one hand to protect the strong seedlings in place while I pull the culls with my other hand. Individual spacings vary from crop to crop, and I describe each detail in the monthly entries.

Weeding   In any good growing environment, weeds thrive, too. They compete with vegetables for moisture and nutrients, and they can harbor insect pests. Where I've used thick organic or black plastic mulch, my weeding is eliminated or reduced. Where weeding is necessary, I do it every week, after a rain or thorough watering, but not while the foliage is still soaking wet, because disease can be spread through the wet leaves. When possible, I work the soil over with my scuffle hoe (see the "Victory Garden Tools" feature in March for a detailed description of this largely undiscovered marvel), which is the easiest way I've found to accomplish this task. The three-pronged cultivator is handy for in-close weeding like that required for onions, beets, and some brassicas.

Pests

One of the biggest differences between the way things used to be done in the Victory Garden and the way they are done now is my handling of insect pests. Over the years, I've developed a philosophical attitude toward them. Yes, it's possible to wage all-out chemical warfare and produce a relatively insect-free garden. But I, for one, am exceedingly wary of chemical pesticides. As I will say throughout this book, I don't think it makes sense to treat crops with exotic compounds that may do worse things to me than to the bugs. As a result, I've developed a pest management program in the Victory Garden that relies heavily on nonchemical deterrents. Experience has proven that I can produce beautiful, healthy crops without toxic chemicals.

My first line of defense is varietal selection. Whenever possible, I choose varieties that I know are resistant to attack from insects, or that have demonstrated an ability to take a few licks and keep on producing. Timing is my next weapon. My overwintered spinach will be ready to eat before the leaf miners become troublesome. A second sowing of summer squash, in midsummer, is usually spared from vine borer infestation. Whenever possible, I time plantings to minimize contact with insects. This requires an intimate knowledge of their rhythms and cycles in my garden, of course, but taking the time to keep records and plan my plantings is, to my mind, a better way than soaking the soil with insecticides. We're really talking about vigilance here, and I *am* vigilant when it comes to insects. I visit the garden often, so that I spot problems early on. It's often easy to deal with insects when they've just begun their invasion. Aphids, for instance, can be hosed off. Colorado potato beetles can be picked off by hand. Vine borers can be surgically removed from plant stems. It doesn't really take all that much more time or effort than spraying or soil drenching, and the end result leaves me feeling more secure. In the feature titled "Pests and Plagues" in June, I give descriptions, accompanied by color photographs, of insects most troublesome to the home gardener. Refer to that section for a thorough grounding in insect identification.

I'm very enthusiastic about the spun, bonded polyester fabric (one brand name is Reemay) that I now use in the Victory Garden. As I mentioned in the "Season Extenders" section of this chapter, this fabric provides some frost protection, and is also effective against insects that chew, lay eggs, bore, or otherwise attack the plants. The fabric can be laid directly onto the soil, after which it is lifted by the growing seedlings, but I prefer to support it with hoops of PVC tubing or #12 wire. Mosquito netting, which I've used in the past on beet crops, also works well, but the spun, bonded polyester seems to be more effective.

My use of crop selection, timing, black plastic, and polyester fabric has greatly reduced insect problems in the Victory Garden. Usually, the few bugs that do manage to infiltrate my barriers can be removed manually or sprayed off. Once in a great while, however, I'll still need to apply an organic pesticide. Three of these form my Victory Garden organic arsenal. *Bacillus thuringiensis*, sold under the trade names Attack, Dipel, and Thuricide, is effective against caterpillars like cabbage

loopers, cabbage worms, corn earworms, European corn borers, and gypsy moths. Despite its scary name, *Bt* is a bacteria that is harmless to humans. It can be dusted or sprayed on the plants, but I prefer to spray a solution because it gives more complete coverage, especially on the undersides of leaves. Rotenone is another organic insecticide, which means in this case that it is derived from plants. It is effective against asparagus beetles, cucumber beetles, flea beetles, aphids, and caterpillars. Though potent, its toxicity is short-lived. I apply it as a 1-percent-solution spray. Pyrethrum, derived from the flower heads of some chrysanthemum varieties, is a good choice for white fly control. Red Devil is a particularly handy commercial mixture of rotenone and pyrethrum.

Even with organic pesticides, I practice careful handling techniques. I wear gloves when mixing the solutions, and gloves and a mask when spraying or dusting. I never store unused solution, but dispose of it when I'm finished.

My last line of defense against insects is really no defense at all, but tolerance. I know that no matter how religiously I observe the garden, and no matter how carefully I erect my barriers and apply organic insecticides, I'm going to lose a few plants here and there to bugs. That's okay. Bugs, bothersome as they may be, are a part of nature's scheme, too. I figure they're entitled to a leaf or two, as long as they don't get out of control.

Harvesting

In the Victory Garden, I plan to stagger my harvests, so that I don't suddenly find myself with 50 crookneck squash in their prime, or 100 lettuce plants ready for pulling. Lettuce is a good example of how I do this, because I harvest lettuce from May through October. I've always got a cell-pack or two of lettuce seedlings coming along. I use the cold frame to get lettuce seedlings off to an early start, and then use it again later to keep them going into the fall. Staggering techniques also apply to cabbage, tomatoes, corn, and many of my other crops. By planting successive generations, I receive successive, smaller harvests that just keep on coming. This requires a sense of timing, but that's where my garden plan (see the chapter titled "Beginnings") comes in handy.

I believe in harvesting early and often. I give specific harvesting instructions for each crop in the monthly chapters that follow, but that early-and-often principle is my guiding light throughout the season. Vegetables that are harvested young are the tenderest and most flavorful. There's no sense in leaving vegetables on the vine or in the ground beyond their prime. And after harvesting, I use them as soon as possible. If there's a surplus, it goes to friends and neighbors. I never made an enemy by handing over a bagful of fresh-picked ears of corn.

The payoff!

BEGINNINGS

A sunny late winter day is a great time to prune fruit trees and berry bushes.

BEGINNINGS

My gardening year begins quietly in January, pleasantly antic-
ipated as I shovel snow or cut firewood, taking shape by the
fireplace as I mull over the many seed catalogs that have
arrived in the mail, and culminating in a day of serious planning,
when I sit down with graph paper, pencil, and seed packets to
plot out my garden beds. It's certainly possible to throw a garden together in May on a wing and a prayer, but I much prefer
not to. I do think of gardening more as an artistic creation than
a scientific project, but I also like to create my garden in an organized, systematic way. Planning minimizes labor and mistakes
and maximizes output. Planning is also an instrumental part of
the Victory Garden philosophy of constant, three-season productivity. With all the intercropping and succession planting and
crop rotating I do, I'd be lost without a coherent plan to make
sure everything's in the proper place at the proper time.

The first step, really, in planning the garden is varietal selection, making a list of all the vegetables I'll be growing in the
coming season. The majority of these will be modern varieties
that have performed well, but I always have my eye out for
new vegetables that promise improved taste, better disease
resistance, greater insect tolerance — or a combination thereof.
I'm especially amenable to All-America Selections. These vegetables have been test-grown by specialists at twenty-eight sites
across the country. Each year, new candidates are grown next
to the best similar varieties. Thus the newest grows next to the
best, and must show clear improvement under widely varying
growing conditions to be judged a winner. I've rarely been dis-
appointed by All-America Selections, which include such
triumphs as Sugar Snap peas, Gypsy peppers, and Savoy Ace
cabbage.

Next, I use pencil and graph paper to draw a diagram of the
garden, showing every bed. I use a ½ inch to 1 foot scale, but
that's less important than making the diagram accurate enough
to show each raised bed and vegetable-planting area. That may
sound overly meticulous, but it's not. It's the only way to judge
accurately how much seed I need to buy, and to provide an adequate supply of vegetables for the number of people I want to
feed.

When I assign crops to beds, I consider several things. Long-
term crops like parsnips go on the perimeter of the garden,
where they won't be disturbed by the comings and goings related to other beds. Corn I locate on the north or west side of
the garden, so that the tall mature plants won't shade lower
crops. I plant brassicas (broccoli, cabbage, Chinese cabbage,
cauliflower, and Brussels sprouts) in beds where they have *not*

Start indoors
Celery
Leeks
Onions
Tomatoes (super-early)

**A sure sign of the season
to come — seed catalogs
and seed orders.** ▶

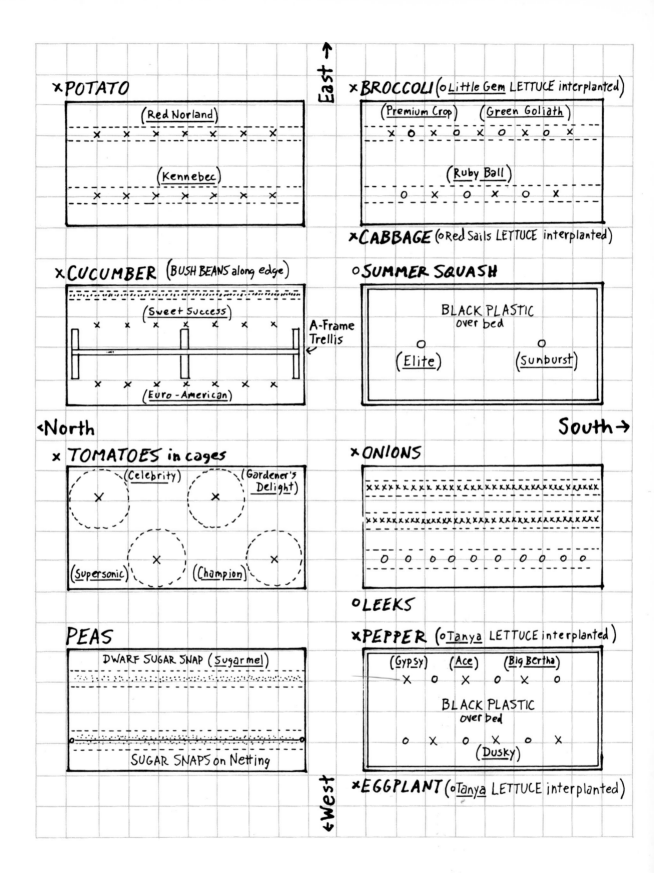

x POTATO

(Red Norland)

× × × × × × × ×

(Kennebec)

× × × × × × ×

East →

x BROCCOLI (o Little Gem LETTUCE interplanted)

(Premium Crop)   (Green Goliath)

× o × o × o × o ×

(Ruby Ball)

o × o × o ×

x CABBAGE (o Red Sails LETTUCE interplanted)

x CUCUMBER (BUSH BEANS along edge)

(Sweet Success)

× × × × × ×

(Euro - American)

× × × × × ×

A-Frame
Trellis ←

o SUMMER SQUASH

BLACK PLASTIC
over bed

o
(Elite)

o
(Sunburst)

‹ North

South →

x TOMATOES in cages

(Celebrity)   (Gardener's
Delight)
×   ×

×   ×
(Supersonic)   (Champion)

x ONIONS

xxxxxxxxx xxxxxxxxxx xxxxxxx

xxxxxxxxx xxxxxxx xxxxxxx

o o o o o o o o o o

o LEEKS

PEAS

DWARF SUGAR SNAP (Sugarmel)

SUGAR SNAPS on Netting

x PEPPER (o Tanya LETTUCE interplanted)

(Gypsy)   (Ace)   (Big Bertha)
×   o   ×   o   ×   o

BLACK PLASTIC
over bed

o   ×   o   ×   o   ×
(Dusky)

‹ West

x EGGPLANT (o Tanya LETTUCE interplanted)

grown for a year or more, to stave off clubroot. And where legumes have grown, fertilizing the soil with their nitrogen-fixing roots, I plan to plant heavy feeding crops like squash.

With seed lists and diagrams in hand, it's time for scheduling. I write down *lots* of projected dates. For each crop, I record the date it will be started indoors, the date it will be moved to the cold frame for hardening-off, the date of planting in the soil, and the projected date of harvest. Planting dates for direct-seeded crops are also faithfully recorded. April 20 — my last expected spring frost date — is the linchpin for all this scheduling, and I give specific dates for all the above steps, for each crop, in the monthly calendar entries. Here, though, I'll say that experience has taught me to be flexible, and to consider my carefully recorded schedules as educated guesstimates. I'm never offended by having to juggle the schedule a bit to accommodate late blizzards or early warm periods. That's all part of the game, and it's great fun later to compare actual harvest dates with those I projected back in January. Whenever a bed will be used for succession planting, I record the pertinent dates for the crop and bed, too. Finally, I double-check estimates of indoor growing time, amount of seed required, and harvest dates.

My growing season is really divided into three periods: spring, summer, and fall. Each subseason has a plan of its own, and a schedule. And all my plans go into the Victory Garden journal, where they're kept year after year. I make notes on them during the season, recording thoughts on timing, weather, soil conditions, and each variety's performance. A final word about plans and schedules: I'm not rigid about either of them. No gardener can afford to be, if he values his sanity. I make adjustments to the garden plan every year, and each season rearranges some of my best-laid schedules. Even with these necessary and inevitable changes, though, the Victory Garden is vastly more efficient — and enjoyable — for having been created according to plan.

As January draws to a close, I set aside my completed garden plan and schedule and make sure that I have everything I'll need for the next growing season. I prepared my tools back in November and December, so I don't have to worry about them. I make sure that I have a good supply of pots, cell-packs, peat pots, and peat strips for seed starting and transplanting. I check my supply of sterile potting medium and 4-inch wooden labels. (A label in each pot gives a quick chart of seed-starting and transplanting times, as well as the correct variety that's growing there.) I check the heating pad, and make sure that I have enough lime, fertilizer, black plastic, and spun, bonded fabric to get through the spring. As seeds come in, I sort them and file them alphabetically in a shoe box or plastic file cabinet.

And then, at last, February arrives, bringing with it the very first planting of the new Victory Garden year. It all starts with celery . . .

Celery   While the television crew was traveling through Utah one year, I met an ingenious "Victory Garden" contest finalist named Delbert Thompson. A lanky, booted Westerner, Delbert was also a bishop in the Mormon Church. Since growing food was one way Delbert had found to practice the Mormon philosophy of self-sufficiency, he took his gardening very seriously. All of Delbert's crops were impressive, but his long, creamy stalks of celery really caught my eye. I asked him how he grew such beautiful celery, and he showed me his secret weapon: 10-inch sections of PVC pipe that he collected, free, from the discard piles of nearby construction projects. Delbert simply slipped these over the growing celery plants when they were young.

In order to produce the most nutritious celery possible, I've given up blanching in the Victory Garden, but that story about Delbert and his PVC pipe does point up the fact that celery is a crop which needs a bit of extra attention. It's a *very* long-term crop, which can take the whole growing season to mature, and that means some extra care. My variety of choice has been Improved Utah-52-70R.

I'll be transplanting celery seedlings to individual cell-packs in mid-March, so I start them from seed indoors in mid-February. I plant the seeds ½ inch deep in 4-inch pots filled with soilless medium, bottom-water thoroughly, and set them on the heat pad at 75 degrees. I'll have seedlings up in 5 to 7 days, and as soon as they're evident I move the pots to full sunlight — a windowsill or shelf in the greenhouse. There they will remain until mid-March, when they've moved into individual cell-packs.

Leeks   Leeks are relatively disease resistant and insect free, and few things are more rewarding than pulling a trophy leek from the ground in September. Garden-grown leeks will make grocery-store specimens (if you can find them) seem puny and bland by comparison. I'm quite a fan of leeks now, but must confess that it was not always so. I guess I thought that the gourmets just made too much fuss over this crop, which does require a lot of care and a very long growing season. A cold day in late November changed all that, however. I was working in the garden, covering strawberries with a deep mulch of hay. The ground was frozen iron-hard, and it looked as if snow would begin to fall at any moment. I came inside frozen to the bone, and discovered my television colleague, Marian Morash (chef-in-residence for the "Victory Garden" TV series), rehearsing a segment we'd be shooting soon. "Hey Bob, want some soup?" she asked, and I quickly agreed. *Anything* hot would have been welcome at that point! After a few spoonfuls from the bowl she handed me, though, I realized that her creation was not only hot — it was the best soup I'd ever tasted. "What *is* this stuff?" I asked her. "Why, leek and potato soup," she exclaimed. "What *else* would you eat on a day like this?" Thus occurred my conversion to leek-lover. Leeks take a *long* time to grow, so I start

A good variety of leek seedlings ready for Victory Garden evaluation. Modest beginnings for our fall-harvested giant leeks.

my leek crop indoors in late February. In 4-inch pots filled with soilless medium I sow the seeds and cover them with ¼ inch of the medium, then bottom-water until the pots are moist all the way from top to bottom. The pots are set onto my heat pad at 75 degrees, which will produce seedlings in about 7 days.

Giant Musselburgh and Titan are my favorite varieties. As their names imply, they produce *big* vegetables — 1½ inches in diameter and up to 18 inches long. Giant Musselburgh has been around for more than seventy-five years, so I know that it's stood the test of time and emerged as one very dependable performer.

Onions   I want to be able to plant onion seedlings in the garden in late April, and that means starting them indoors in mid-February. I've started onions in plastic trays and Speedling flats, but I've returned to my standard 4-inch pot. It's plenty deep, easy to handle, and easy to buy in quantity. I fill the pots with soilless medium, sow the onion seeds ¼ inch deep, bottom-water well, and set the pots on my 75-degree heat pad. I'll have seedlings up in a week, and I move them into full sun. After a couple of weeks, I thin the seedlings so that there's about ½ inch of space between them in the 4-inch pots. I don't bother transplanting these onions to cell-packs (there are too many of them), but let them grow along in the 4-inch pots until it's time to transplant them into the garden in April.

Tomatoes   One of my goals with tomatoes is to be the first kid on my block with red, ripe fruit. By breaking all the rules, I'm now able to do that. I actually grow two crops of tomatoes in the Victory Garden these days — my steady, dependable main crop, which I begin to harvest in July, and my super-early, labor-intensive crop, which I begin to harvest — are you ready? — by June 1. To do that, I have to alter my planting schedule radically. Tomatoes cannot produce ripe fruit until they have matured. A variety that must grow 65 days to maturity, in other words, can't produce fruit in 55 days, no matter how ideal the growing conditions. To allow for this rather elementary fact, I seed my super-early tomatoes, indoors, in February.

For this crop, I like Jet Star and Early Girl. Both are prolific producers with relatively compact vines. In mid-February, while the winter winds are still howling outside, I start one 6-cell-pack of each variety, sowing 2 seeds per cell ½ inch deep in the soilless medium. I bottom-water the packs until the growing medium is thoroughly moist, then set them on my 75-degree heat pad to germinate. The seedlings will be up in a week. I move them to full sun in a warm location (70 degrees or more is good) and, after another week, thin to the strongest seedling in each cell.

In mid-March, I transplant each seedling to an individual 4-inch pot filled with soilless medium, setting the seedlings deeper now than they were growing in their cells — right up to their true leaves, in fact, because tomatoes will root all along the stems. I bottom-water them at this transplanting with a solution of balanced, water-soluble fertilizer diluted to half strength, give them a day out of full sun to recover from the trauma of transplanting, and then set them back in the sunniest, warmest location I have.

In mid-April, each seedling is transplanted once more, this time to individual 1-gallon plastic containers filled with soilless medium. Again they're set in deeper than they were growing in their previous pots, to allow for more root formation. By now the seedlings will be 6 to 8 inches tall and growing very vigorously. I feed them again with a drink of water-soluble fertilizer (again diluted to half strength), give them another day's respite from full sun, and then put them back on my sunny windowsill or in the greenhouse. During the next 3 weeks, I keep a close eye on the weather. Whenever there is a warm, sunny day without high wind, I carry the tomatoes outside to take advantage of those prime conditions. (I'm also ready to hurry them back

Tomatoes are worth that special effort.

inside at the first hint of dropping temperatures, rising winds, or heavy precipitation.) These outdoor visits serve to harden the seedlings off, and to give them as much of a head start as possible before I set them out — permanently — on May 5. A week before, I work in 5 pounds of 5–10–5 for every 100 square feet of bed. Then I plant them in the open garden, setting them in deeper than they were growing in their gallon pots, spacing them 36 inches apart in the raised beds. The plants will be up to 3 feet tall by this time, which makes them too big for Wall O' Water protection. Instead, I surround them with cages made

Turning in soil-improving winter rye *in small batches* makes this task much easier.

from concrete reinforcing wire. For detailed instructions on building these cages see this chapter's feature, titled "Victory Garden Structures."

When the tomatoes have been transplanted, I water them in with full-strength water-soluble fertilizer and then cross my fingers. Actually, the mini-greenhouses, coupled with the very early start in February and successive transplantings, have just about eliminated tomato fatalities. I can almost always count on harvesting red, ripe tomatoes now by June 1. And when I bite into that first sweet, juicy Early Girl, I know all the work was worth it.

Winter Rye   My cover crop of winter rye has been green all through the cold, blustery months of New England winter, keeping the raised beds in shape, protecting against wind deformation and runoff damage. The cover crop has also been storing nutrients that will be released when it's turned into the soil. Winter rye's contribution to soil structure is even more important. When it's turned in, and decomposes, the organic material helps produce a loose, friable soil that is ideal for vegetable growing.

I've found that winter rye in the Victory Garden takes from 2 to 4 weeks to break down completely, so during our inevitable January thaw I turn under the beds that I'll be using for early spring plantings — crops like the brassicas, for example. (I give specific planting schedules for each crop in the monthly chapters that follow.) Then I follow along with a turning-under schedule that anticipates sowing times by 3 or 4 weeks. I turn the rye under with my spading fork, working from one end of a raised bed backward, taking 4-inch sections with each lift. I turn the mass over to bury as much green matter as possible, then break up the turned soil by smacking it sharply with my fork.

VICTORY GARDEN STRUCTURES

During the long winter months, I ease the burden of indoor captivity by spending time in the workshop, repairing some of the Victory Garden's structures or making new ones. Over the years, through trial and error, I've come up with designs for five important gardening aids that I think are worth passing on.

Composter You'll hear me say over and over that good gardens are built on a solid soil improvement program, and the heart of soil improvement is composting. A compost bin is simply essential. My new, two-bin composter is a real improvement over former designs.

Here, step-by-step, is how I built the new composter. See the accompanying illustration for construction details.

Materials

11 8-foot pieces of pressure-treated 2x4

6 ⅜x3-inch lag bolts (bottom)

6 ⅜x6-inch carriage bolts (sides to back)

4 ⅜x4-inch carriage bolts (top rails)

20x4-foot piece of galvanized dog wire (2x4-inch mesh)

¾-inch galvanized staples

The durable, indispensable Victory Garden cold frame. ◄

1. Make three 4x4-foot panels, using 2x4 lumber cut into 48-inch lengths and then nailed together.

2. Make one 4x8-foot panel, also using 2x4 lumber.

3. Attach galvanized "dog wire," using galvanized staples, to all four frames.

4. Attach the panels to each other, as shown, using 5-inch carriage bolts inserted through drilled holes.

5. Nail 2x4x8-foot bars of 2x4 onto the bottom and top of the bin's front. These make the bins more rigid and keep them from deforming under the pressure of all that compost they'll eventually contain. (You'll find my detailed instructions for making compost in the chapter entitled "Steps to Victorious Gardening.")

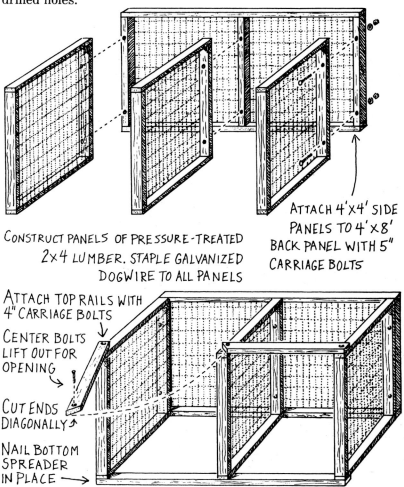

CONSTRUCT PANELS OF PRESSURE-TREATED 2x4 LUMBER. STAPLE GALVANIZED DOGWIRE TO ALL PANELS

ATTACH 4'x4' SIDE PANELS TO 4'x8' BACK PANEL WITH 5" CARRIAGE BOLTS

ATTACH TOP RAILS WITH 4" CARRIAGE BOLTS

CENTER BOLTS LIFT OUT FOR OPENING

CUT ENDS DIAGONALLY

NAIL BOTTOM SPREADER IN PLACE

Cold Frame A second essential piece of garden hardware is the cold frame, which gives me at least 2 months of extra growing time. It also provides a place to harden-off seedlings and hold over plants that might need help through the winter. I've designed a Victory Garden cold frame that's built to last. Here's the step-by-step construction method. Refer to the accompanying illustration for details.

1. Cut a 48½-inch 2x8 diagonally, as shown. This cut can be made with a table saw, or by using a circular saw with a cutting guide tacked in place. These diagonals will eventually become the slanting top pieces of the cold frame.

2. Next, cut the cold frame sides, front, and back from 2x8 lumber. For the sides, cut two pieces 45½ inches long. For the front, cut one piece 48½ inches long. For the back, cut two pieces 48½ inches long.

3. Now assemble the sides by nailing 1x3 cleats in place, as shown. Assemble the two back pieces the same way.

4. Insert eye screws near the ends of the sides, front, and back. Connect the four sections together by threading ½-inch wooden dowels through the aligned eye screws.

5. Cut 2x4 lumber for the cold frame top. The two side pieces should be 45½ inches long. The front and back pieces should be 48½ inches long.

Materials

32 feet of pressure-treated 1x1

3 8-foot pieces of pressure-treated 2x8

2 8-foot pieces of pressure-treated 2x4

1 8-foot piece of pressure-treated 1x4

4 3-inch galvanized corner brackets

2 galvanized or brass loose-pin hinges (heavy duty)

1 4-foot piece of ½-inch dowel

2 8-foot wooden battens, ¼x1½ inches

4x4-foot piece of plastic sheeting (4 mil)

4x4-foot piece of galvanized dog wire (2x4-inch mesh)

36 1½-inch galvanized screws (#8)

1¼-inch galvanized box nails

¾-inch galvanized staples (#14)

1 4x⅜-inch carriage bolt

10 galvanized screw eyes

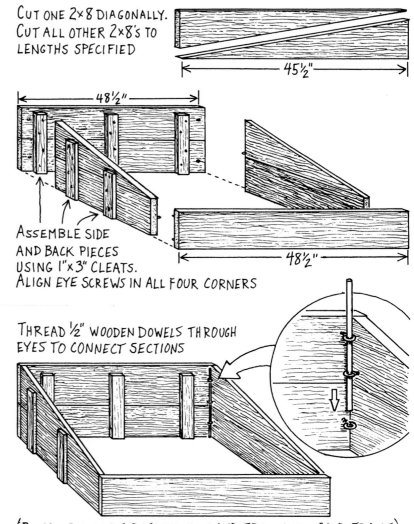

CUT ONE 2×8 DIAGONALLY. CUT ALL OTHER 2×8's TO LENGTHS SPECIFIED

45½"

48½"

48½"

ASSEMBLE SIDE AND BACK PIECES USING 1"x3" CLEATS. ALIGN EYE SCREWS IN ALL FOUR CORNERS

THREAD ½" WOODEN DOWELS THROUGH EYES TO CONNECT SECTIONS

(REMOVE DOWELS TO DISASSEMBLE AND TRANSPORT COLD FRAME)

6. Nail or screw the four top pieces together.

7. Now cover the top of the frame with galvanized wire fencing (with 4-inch holes) and staple the fencing to the 2x4s with galvanized staples.

8. Lay clear plastic (polyethylene sheeting) over the fencing, cut so that there is a 3-inch overlap of plastic all around.

9. Fix the plastic in place by nailing furring strips along the outside of the 2x4 frame.

10. Attach the top to the cold frame box with loose-pin hinges.

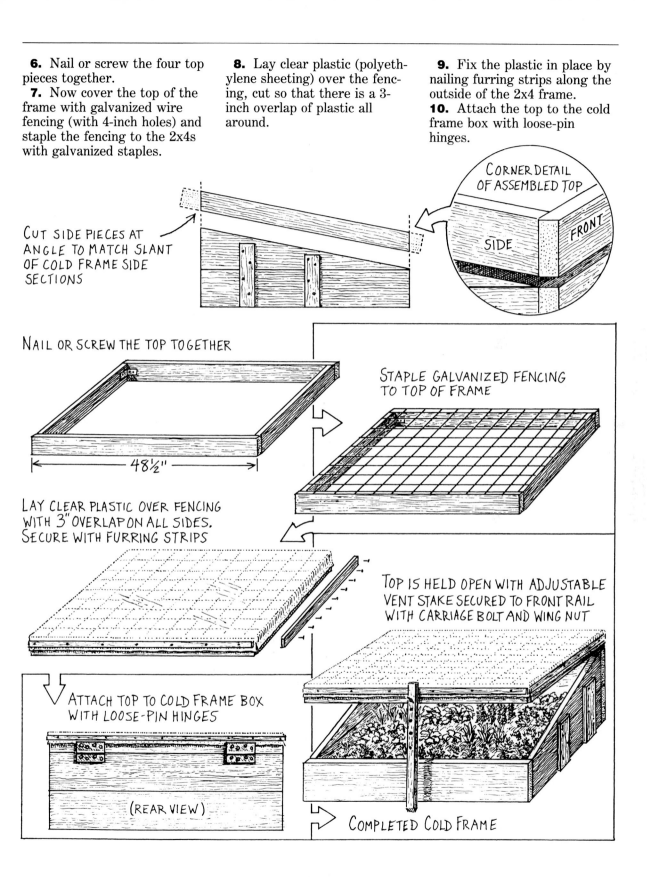

CORNER DETAIL OF ASSEMBLED TOP

FRONT

SIDE

CUT SIDE PIECES AT ANGLE TO MATCH SLANT OF COLD FRAME SIDE SECTIONS

NAIL OR SCREW THE TOP TOGETHER

48½"

STAPLE GALVANIZED FENCING TO TOP OF FRAME

LAY CLEAR PLASTIC OVER FENCING WITH 3" OVERLAP ON ALL SIDES. SECURE WITH FURRING STRIPS

TOP IS HELD OPEN WITH ADJUSTABLE VENT STAKE SECURED TO FRONT RAIL WITH CARRIAGE BOLT AND WING NUT

ATTACH TOP TO COLD FRAME BOX WITH LOOSE-PIN HINGES

(REAR VIEW)

COMPLETED COLD FRAME

Planting Board   In addition to the composter and cold frame, I've had fun making planting boards in the Victory Garden workshop. Planting boards are unbeatable for creating furrows and easily spacing transplants. I use redwood, spruce, or pine. Redwood is more expensive, but it stands up to weather better than pine, which requires a coat or two of preservative stain. Here's how to make the Victory Garden planting board:

1. Start with a 48-inch piece of 1x6 redwood, spruce, or pine.
2. Bevel both sides of one of the plank's long edges to 45 degrees. A table saw or a circular saw can be used to do this cutting.
3. Cut notches at 6-inch intervals in the other edge. Large notches are 3 inches deep. Small notches are 1½ inches deep. The planting board, as the illustration shows, will have four small notches and three large notches when finished.
4. Drill a ⅜-inch hole near one end for convenient hanging.

Tomato Cages   Another project I like to tackle over the winter is making tomato cages. These are the lazy man's choice for controlling the growth of tomato plants, and I recommend them. I buy raw materials from a masonry supply house: one roll of the reinforcing wire used to strengthen poured concrete. The wire has 4-inch openings, and is quite stiff. I buy wire that's 5 feet high, to make sure that my vigorous tomato plants don't cascade over the top, which happens often with 48-inch cages. Making these cages is easy. I use stout wire cutters to cut through the wire, allowing 80 inches per section, which, when rolled into a cylinder, will make a cage 24 inches in diameter. I secure the cages into their cylindrical shape with several twists of tie-wire, then trim the bottom cross pieces off, leaving a ring of sharp little probes that will stick into the ground and hold the cages upright.

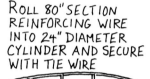

ROLL 80" SECTION REINFORCING WIRE INTO 24" DIAMETER CYLINDER AND SECURE WITH TIE WIRE

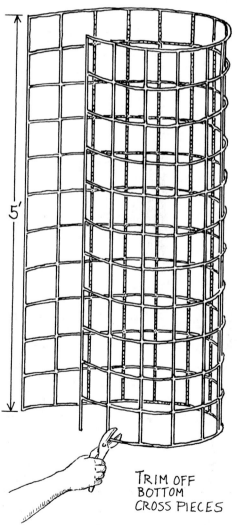

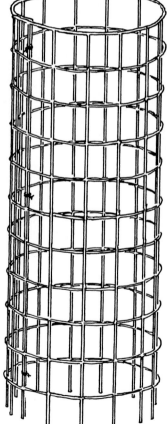

5'

TRIM OFF BOTTOM CROSS PIECES

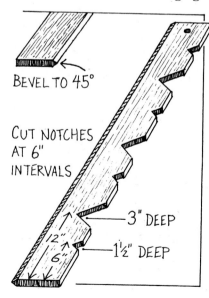

BEVEL TO 45°

CUT NOTCHES AT 6" INTERVALS

3" DEEP

1½" DEEP

12"

6"

Trellis Last but not least, I take time to make the Victory Garden A-frame trellises that I use for cucumbers and some other sprawling crops.

Materials

10 8-foot pieces of 2x3 redwood or weather-treated lumber

16x6-foot piece of galvanized dog wire (4x6-inch mesh)

2 3-inch brass-plated hinges

4 18-inch reinforcing rods

1¼-inch galvanized screws

1. Cut three 6-foot pieces of 2x3 redwood or stained pine.

2. Cut four 4-foot pieces of the same wood.

3. Trim the ends of all the pieces, as shown, to make half-lap joints.

4. Secure the pieces together, as shown, with 3-inch round-head wood screws.

5. Nail or screw braces in place at all four corners.

6. Attach reinforcing wire to the frame with galvanized staples. It's possible to substitute string, or wide-mesh nylon netting, for the metal wire, if you prefer.

7. Repeat steps 1 through 6 to make the second half of the frame, and attach the two sections with brass loose-pin hinges.

The completed A-frame is 6x8 feet, a two-sided trellis that will support 96 square feet of growing space while occupying less than 20 square feet of ground. That's almost a five-to-one return!

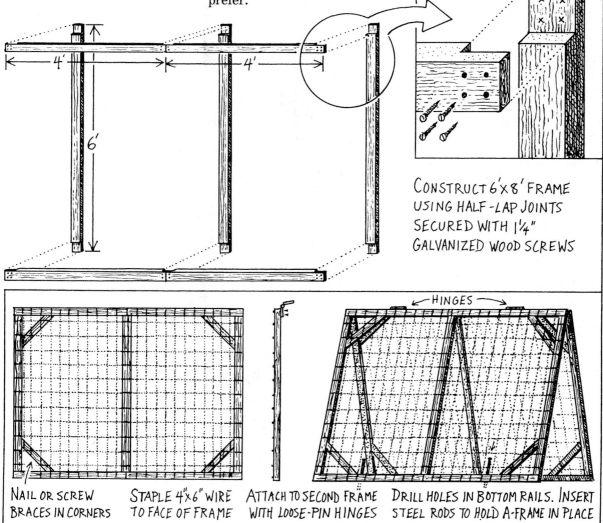

HALF-LAP JOINT

CONSTRUCT 6'x8' FRAME USING HALF-LAP JOINTS SECURED WITH 1¼" GALVANIZED WOOD SCREWS

HINGES

NAIL OR SCREW BRACES IN CORNERS

STAPLE 4"x6" WIRE TO FACE OF FRAME

ATTACH TO SECOND FRAME WITH LOOSE-PIN HINGES

DRILL HOLES IN BOTTOM RAILS. INSERT STEEL RODS TO HOLD A-FRAME IN PLACE

MARCH

MARCH

March is mostly a winter month, and carries the threat of a late-season blizzard, at least in my region, despite those tantalizing, lengthening hours of daylight and occasional balmy days. Thus I have learned the hard way that disappointment awaits if I move too quickly; this is a month of promise, but also one of caution.

Since March provides plenty of sunlight for indoor seed sowing, I do quite a bit of that. I'll also be caring for the celery, leeks, onions, and tomatoes that I started indoors back in February. It's important to keep the seedlings well fed and watered without overdoing it. Plants can use fertilizer only if they are growing vigorously, with all the light and warmth they might require. Reduce the light or turn down the heat, and one must let up on the fertilizer. Otherwise the seedlings will develop as poor, spindly plants. The same advice follows for water. Seedlings kept too wet will suffocate. They must dry out between waterings or precious oxygen will not get to the roots.

Seed sorting occupies some time, as well. I sort all my packets alphabetically. At the same time, I like to double-check all the seed packet instructions to make sure the producers haven't sprung any new techniques on me.

Not all my March activities take place indoors. There's quite a bit to do outside, and planting is the part I always look foward to most. I'll be planting peas and onion sets outside, and spinach, too. Beyond that, I'll be turning under some of the winter rye, pruning raspberries and blueberries, and moving mulch off the strawberry plants. I'll dust off my cold frames and set them up in the garden's sunniest spot. And March is a good time, too, for me to catch up on those little odds and ends that never quite seem to get done when I'm too busy planting and harvesting. Fencing and trellises, for instance, can always use a sharp eye. It's a lot easier to mend the fence now before weeds disguise the weaknesses and before the woodchuck gets hungry. I'll check my hoses, too, repairing the broken sections because I know I won't have the time later. I'll give the compost bins a once-over, replacing any staples that have loosened and making sure the corners are still secure.

Finally, I'll be taking some of my seed from storage, and since I've protected the seed, it should germinate well enough. To reduce identification problems, I store seeds right in their packets, but I put the packets into tightly capped coffee tins or jars sealed with tape. It's important to keep the seeds cool and dry during storage. Humidity should remain below 65 percent, temperature between 32 and 40 degrees. A refrigerator is a good place to store the seeds. Adding rice, silica gel, or cornstarch to the jars will absorb moisture and reduce the chance of unwanted germination.

Start Indoors
Broccoli
Cabbage
Cauliflower
Chinese cabbage
Lettuce
Peas

Transplant
Broccoli
Cabbage
Cauliflower
Celery
Lettuce

Plant in Garden
Onion sets
Peas
Shallot sets
Spinach

Victory Garden broccoli,
ready for harvest: heads
tightly budded, no yellowing or flowering.

Broccoli I am joined by many these days in my fondness for broccoli, which is gaining popularity faster than any other home garden vegetable and giving the traditional front-runners — tomatoes and lettuce — a serious run for their money. Of course I relish the taste of fresh-from-the-garden broccoli, but I like it equally because it is not dauntingly difficult to grow. Nor is broccoli a stingy crop. If I harvest the central heads from my plants when they are tightly budded, before any yellowing or flowering has occurred, the plants will continue to grow tasty side shoots for several more weeks.

I have grown some very fine broccoli in the Victory Garden, but the best stand I ever saw grew happily in a community garden complex in Plymouth, New Hampshire. I'd traveled there to visit one of our contest finalists — a young couple attending a nearby college — and while their whole garden was outstanding, the broccoli was really special. I had never seen bigger, healthier plants, even in the carefully tended show gardens of professionals, and I asked the young people to tell me their secret. Smiling, they pointed to a stream flowing over nearby rocks. They explained that every spring, the stream, swollen with snow melt, overflowed its banks and flooded the surrounding land. When those waters receded, they left a superrich soil in which the broccoli, in particular, thrived.

Though I have no overflowing stream, I do grow very good broccoli each year, thanks in large part to the Victory Garden program of soil improvement and fertilization. I start the broccoli plants indoors in mid-March, following my usual indoor seed-sowing practices, sowing twice as many seeds ¼ inch deep in the 4-inch pots (which are filled with soilless medium) as I will eventually want plants in the garden. The pots are bottom-watered until the medium is thoroughly moist, then set onto the 75-degree heat pad. Seedlings are up in 5 to 7 days. When the first true leaves show, the seedlings are transplanted into cell-packs and then given a one-day respite from full sunlight. Bright, indirect light is fine while they adjust to their new quarters. They are then bottom-watered again, this time with a solution of a balanced liquid fertilizer (20-20-20 is the formula I use, but there are other variations that will work as well) diluted to half strength, then returned to full sun. Three or four weeks later the cold frame receives them for hardening-off. A word here about transplanting depth for broccoli seedlings: Like certain other vegetables (tomatoes, for instance), broccoli will grow roots all along its stem. Thus the plant is set into the cell-pack more deeply than it grew in the 4-inch pot, right up to its seed leaves. This will allow the development of a strong, vigorous root system, and it's a process that I'll repeat with every crop that has this growth pattern.

I have several favorite broccoli varieties. Goliath has consistently performed well in the spring garden, as has Grand Duke. Premium Crop is a recent development, an All-America Selection that has also grown nicely in the Victory Garden. And Green Valiant produced absolutely huge heads in my fall garden.

Cabbage   While most members of the brassica family (which includes broccoli, cauliflower, Brussels sprouts, Chinese cabbage, kale, kohlrabi, and rutabagas) prefer cool weather and do not grow well in hot, cabbage is the exception. *This* brassica will grow well throughout the season, unaffected by warm weather. Despite this advantage, though, I have to admit that I grow less cabbage now than I used to. Time has tempered my tendency to fill up the early spring garden with cabbage plants. Why so? Simply, I don't really need more than half a dozen heads, even though I do love cole slaw.

There are many varieties of cabbage, but only two general types, and I grow them both: the smooth, ball-headed cabbages and the crinkly-leaved Savoys. I'm very fond of Ruby Ball, an early red cabbage, for its good harvest and manageable,

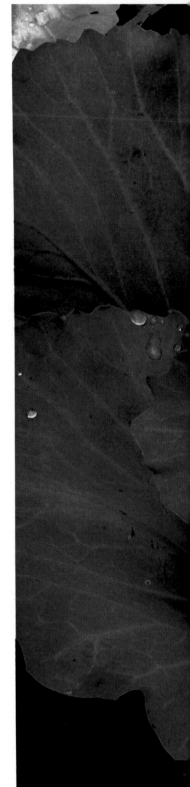

Ruby Ball, one of my favorite early cabbage varieties, produces an abundant harvest of cantaloupe-sized heads that leave room for intercropping lettuce seedlings.

cantaloupe-sized heads. These are somewhat small as cabbages go, but they leave room for the intercropping of lettuce, which maximizes yield from available space. Stonehead is another fine early variety that produces handy, 4-pound heads a week or so earlier than Ruby Ball. And of the Savoys, Savoy Ace is my favorite, an outstanding recent All-America Selections gold medal winner.

In early March, I seed cabbage the same way I seed broccoli, planting twice as many seeds as I will eventually want plants in the garden, in 4-inch pots filled with soilless growing medium. I cover the seeds with ¼ inch of the medium, then bottom-water until it is thoroughly moist. They go onto the heat pad at 75 degrees, which will produce seedlings in about a week. As soon as they're up, they're moved to a sunny windowsill and there they'll remain until they produce their true leaves, at which time I transplant them to individual cell-packs and bottom-water with half-strength water-soluble fertilizer.

Cauliflower   Cauliflower has given me (and I imagine I am not alone) more than a fair share of trouble. Clubroot, a disease caused by soil-borne organisms, is one problem. More serious is cauliflower's sensitivity to temperature. Cauliflower cannot stand heavy frost and bolts in hot weather. It grows best in average temperatures of 60 to 65 degrees. If the plants are subjected to 5 days of temperatures in the 40- to 45-degree range, they will be overstressed and that will initiate premature flowering, a survival mechanism that is wonderful for continuance of the species but that severely limits the harvest.

It is essential, then, to wait until all danger of frost has passed before moving cauliflower seedlings into the garden. It is just as essential for the crop to mature before the hot summer weather begins. In the Victory Garden, April 20 is my last expected spring frost date. Working backward to allow 8 weeks for germination and indoor growth, I start seed indoors in the first week of March. The seeds are planted in 4-inch pots filled with soilless medium, covered with ¼ inch of the medium, and bottom-watered thoroughly. I keep the pots at 75 degrees on the heat pad, and will have seedlings in 5 to 7 days. When they're up, I move them to a sunny windowsill until the first true leaves show. Then I prick out individuals and plant them up to their seed leaves in cell-packs filled with soilless medium. They're bottom-watered with water-soluble fertilizer diluted to half strength, given a day out of full sun, and then set onto the sunniest spot I can find. They will remain there until late April, when I will move them to the cold frame.

Early Snowball and Snow Crown are two early varieties that produce firm 8-inch heads, reaching maturity in about 50 days from setting out into the garden. White Sails has produced gigantic heads for me in the spring garden, and Burgundy Queen has proved to be a good, reliable purple-headed hybrid.

Celery It's time to transplant the celery seedlings from their 4-inch pots to individual cell-packs filled with soilless medium. When the true leaves are visible, I move them to the cell-packs, planting them the same depth they were growing in their 4-inch pots, then feed them with a solution of half-strength water-soluble fertilizer by bottom-watering. A one-day break from full sunlight eases the shock of transplanting, and then they're ready for full sunlight once again.

Chinese Cabbage Chinese cabbage is a very broad category, with many different types that vary in their heading quality. In general, it's a more tender (some would say more refined!) form of the cabbage we Occidentals know as great round heads in the garden. Chinese cabbage is very temperature sensitive, though more recent breeding efforts have produced some relatively weather-tolerant varieties. That aside, timing is still the most important factor in growing this delicious vegetable. Chinese cabbage grows best in cool weather, but can't tolerate more than a light touch of frost. I'll want to move young seedlings into the cold frame in mid-April, so I plant the seeds indoors in mid-March. Chinese cabbage does not tolerate transplant shock well, so I plant 2 seeds in each 3-inch peat pot filled with soilless medium. The seeds are covered with ¼ inch of soilless medium, and the pots are bottom-watered until uniformly moist. Then they go onto the heat pad at 75 degrees, which will produce seedlings in a week or less. When they're up, I move them into full sunlight.

Leeks The leeks I started in 4-inch pots in February will grow along happily in those same pots through the month of March. I feed with liquid fertilizer at half strength every other week until May set-out. I keep them in full sun, water regularly, and just watch them grow. I used to rush the leeks into the spring garden as soon as possible, but I no longer do that. One year, in a scheduling mix-up, I let the leeks remain indoors until early May, about 3 weeks after the last frost date in this area. When I finally got them into the garden, I didn't have much hope for a good crop. Surprise: They turned out to be the best leeks I'd produced in the Victory Garden. Now my practice is to keep those seedlings growing indoors well into May, to give them the longest head start possible. My new rule is that bigger transplants grow the best leeks. The February start indoors, coupled with 3 months of indoor growing time, gives me those big, healthy transplants.

Leeks always look frail in March, but 2½ months of controlled indoor growing conditions will produce super-sturdy seedlings for May transplanting. ▲

My first lettuce harvest, compliments of the cold frame. I keep several generations of lettuce growing at all times; as soon as mature plants are harvested, new seedlings take their place. ▶

Lettuce One of the greatest dividends of my work in the Victory Garden has been the opportunity to share the wisdom of gardeners around the world. That kind of communication is invaluable, and keeps opening my eyes to new wonders. I never really gave lettuce its due, for instance, until I visited Wisley, the Royal Horticultural Society's 250-acre garden not far from London. There I met head gardener Bertie Doe, a small man in his sixties. Bertie managed with absolutely no difficulty whatever to infect me with his passion for lettuce, and my own attitude toward the crop has never been the same.

Bertie showed me more than a dozen different varieties of lettuce developed by English breeders, extolling the virtues of each with unbridled zeal. I followed him dutifully, discovering how much there really was to learn about lettuce, but after more than an hour of crouching and touching and tasting and listening I had to call a halt.

"Bertie," I said, "these are all terrific, but I have to pin you down. Tell me two favorites that will be perfect for the home gardens back in the States."

"Tell them to grow Tania and Little Gem," Bertie said without hesitation. "And don't sell your own Buttercrunch short." He walked me to the end of the garden, and, as we were shaking hands, said, "By the way, the French have a great heading lettuce. It's crisp, tipped with red, and slow to bolt. Called Marvel of the Four Seasons." He hesitated, as though about to say more, and then laughed. "And now you'd better move right

along before I think of six more really good ones!" I have no doubt that he could easily have done so.

I came home and tried Little Gem, perhaps Bertie's true favorite, and found that its soft, buttery leaves really did justify that overused "melt in your mouth" superlative. Marvel of the Four Seasons was just as good. Since then, I've discovered Red Sails and Webb's Wonderful, and both have also become favorites. These days, thanks largely to Bertie Doe, one of my great joys is an early April cold frame filled with six different kinds of lettuce, all resplendent in various shades of red and bronze and green, as rich in textures as they are in colors. These varieties are not only eye-catchers, of course. Their taste makes grocery-store stuff seem like nothing but roughage — which is not far from the truth. Iceberg lettuce, though the least nutritious and blandest tasting, dominates shelves because it is tough enough to store well and to endure the rigors of long-distance travel. That's fine for the merchants, but not so good for us salad lovers.

All three main types of lettuce — headed, looseleaf, and butterheaded — are best grown fast and cool, so I start seeds indoors in the first week of March. I sow the seeds in 4-inch pots filled with soilless medium, cover them with ¼ inch of the medium, and bottom-water. A heat pad temperature of 75 degrees gives me seedlings in 3 days. Then they go to my sunny windowsill. When the true leaves are evident, I transplant the seedlings to individual cell-packs filled with soilless medium, setting them in at the same depth as they were growing in their original pots. They're bottom-watered with half-strength water-soluble fertilizer and given a day out of full sun, then moved to a location where they'll get full sun but cool temperatures in the 60- to 65-degree range. They'll remain there until early April, when I move them to the cold frame for hardening-off.

Starting two dozen lettuce plants in March will produce 24 beautiful, mature heads all ready for harvesting over a 2-week period in May. After that, the lettuce will pass its prime. To avoid overload and to ensure the longest possible harvest, I stagger plantings of lettuce in the Victory Garden. There are always several generations of lettuce seedlings growing, and whenever a space opens up, these youngsters are ready to fill it. My goal is to have 12 to 24 lettuce seedlings every 2 weeks. This guarantees a continued harvest throughout the season, giving fresh greens from April to Thanksgiving.

Onions While onions can be grown throughout the world in soils ranging from muck to loam, certain regions produce superb onions, thanks to a fortuitous coincidence of climate and soil composition. One year, for instance, I visited Ron Andring, a Victory Garden contest finalist living in Walla Walla, Washington. Ron's home sat on a small, in-town corner lot, and in his unusual garden much space was devoted to protein crops like

I plant onion sets in March as soon as the soil is dry enough to work. Stringing a line keeps my garden orderly, and that's important. I believe it should please the eye as well as the palate.

soybeans and peanuts. But his Walla Walla onions, creamy white and big as softballs, were the garden's crown jewels. I admit to a serious case of envy, because I knew that those onions, even with the most meticulous care, would not produce for me back in Boston as they had for Ron there in Walla Walla, where soil and weather were absolutely perfect.

Similar "miracle" onions also grow around Vidalia, Georgia, and on Maui, in the Hawaiian Islands. Naturally, each region claims that its onions are the sweetest on earth. The "Victory Garden" TV show's director, Russ Morash, is relentless in his search for the truths of gardening, and each time we visited one of these famous onion regions, he would ask me to verify the sweetness factor of that region's star performer.

"Come on, Bob, they say they're sweet enough to eat like apples," he would urge. "Tell us if that's true."

Well, I came, I saw, and I tasted. And I can affirm that these are all wonderful onions, excellent cooked, super when sautéed. But I would *not* recommend eating them like apples, and I have dripped a trail of tears from Vidalia, Georgia, to beautiful Maui to bring you that bit of invaluable advice.

In the Victory Garden, I plant onions from seed and from sets. Sets are young onion plants whose growth was interrupted just as they were forming bulbs. In this area, a bag of 100 costs about $1.29, and I mention the price because I know that some gardeners feel that sets are much more expensive than seeds. I disagree. By the time I add up costs for pots, soilless medium, and my own time (the most valuable commodity in any garden), all of which seeds require and sets do not, sets turn out to be cost-efficient indeed. For any garden where time and labor are supershort, they're unbeatable. Sets are also a terrific way to introduce kids to gardening. Little fingers have great fun pushing those onion bulbs down into the soft, cool soil. In fact, the only drawback to sets that I can think of is the fact that fewer varieties are available than is the case with seeds.

Onions I'm growing from seed were started indoors in February, but in March I plant onion sets outside, when the soil is dry enough to work. I buy sets that are no bigger than a dime (½ inch in diameter, maximum, is a good rule) because larger bulbs are more likely to go to seed, and anything smaller may not grow with the vigor I'd prefer. Onions are voracious feeders, so I fortify their raised beds with 5 pounds of 5-10-5 fertilizer for every 100 square feet of bed space. Then I rake the bed smooth and string lines to keep my planting straight.

Planting the bulbs is simple. I push them in with my fingers until their tops are just barely exposed, making sure to leave their stem ends pointing up. The bulbs are spaced 3 inches apart in the rows, with 12 inches between the rows themselves. I water them in well and forget about them for a while. My favorite onion variety from sets has been Stuttgarter Riesen, which has performed well here.

Peas Though winter confinement leaves me itching to get a spade in my hands again, most crops just aren't ready for the great outdoors in March, at least in the Victory Garden area. Peas, happily, are an exception. Not only can they be sown directly in March, the *best* peas are sown and grown in cool, 60- to 65-degree daytime air temperatures. In anticipation of this early planting, I prepare the soil well back in the fall ("Steps to Victorious Gardening" discusses my fall soil amendments), so that when spring arrives and the soil has warmed to the 40- to 50-degree range, all systems are go.

Planting peas, by the way, almost ended my gardening career before it got started. My father was a professional engineer, a precise man who insisted on planting his peas by March 17 — Saint Patrick's Day. This was an admirable enough goal, but in Massachusetts the ground was cold and wet, and the sharp east wind would chill a little guy like me right to the bone. Nothing daunted, Dad and I would bundle up and head for the garden. We'd string a line and make the furrow 2 inches deep and wide as a hoe. Dad wanted a double row of seeds, and he insisted that each seed in each row be 2 inches apart. Not 1½ inches or 2½ inches, but 2 inches — exactly. There *was* a purpose to his precision. He had seen me sow with a heavy hand on occasion, and I think he wanted to add discipline to my gardening skills. Those were Depression times, after all, and there was nothing to waste. His message was clear: Use what you need, but waste not a bit in the process — even if winter winds *are* turning your fingers blue.

My sowing these days is more carefree, but before I head outside with my seeds, I do two things to make the job easier. First, I soak the seeds overnight in room-temperature water to soften the skin and hasten germination. Then I treat the seeds with powdered legume inoculant. Peas belong to that marvelous family of plants called legumes, which feed themselves as well as the garden by pulling nitrogen from the air and storing it on their roots. They can do so probably because they evolved in Spartan growing conditions, which forced them to seek from the atmosphere nourishment they could not derive from poor soils. A bacteria called *Rhizobia* clusters in thick nodules on their roots, and these nodules are the nitrogen factories. *Rhizobia* is contained in the legume inoculant (a black powder, perfectly safe to use) that is available from garden centers and through seed catalogs. One dollar's worth will inoculate 10 pounds of seed. I dust my pre-soaked seeds with the powder immediately before planting, because prolonged exposure to air will reduce the bacteria's potency.

While I'm enthusiastic about legume inoculants, I'm much less so about the fungicide that some growers use to stave off the rot that can attack seeds in cool, damp soils. Commercial growers, who can ill afford to lose crops, counter the problem with a potent fungicide, but it has been under suspicion for some time as

By starting pea seeds in-
doors in March, I produce a
very early June harvest,
and eliminate the need to
treat seeds with chemical
fungicides.

a carcinogen. I stay away from it altogether. Instead, I have
taken to starting some pea plants indoors in March. The benefits
of this indoor start are several. Most obvious, I don't have to
treat the seeds with fungicide. But I also enjoy a much earlier
pea harvest — as early as June 1, in fact. That's a record in my
area, and means I can expect a *doubling* of the pea harvest before the truly hot weather arrives. Indoor starting seems to
work well with English peas, sugar types, and snow peas. I
plant 2 seeds per cell in 2-inch peat cells, which come 12 to a
strip. The cells are filled with soilless growing medium, and the
seeds are covered with ¼ inch of that mix. I bottom-water the
peat strips in a flat plastic tray, and set them on the 75-degree
heat pad to germinate. At that temperature, I have seedlings up
in about 7 days. I move them off the heat pad, let them grow
for another week, and then thin to the stronger seedling in each

cell. They go into the greenhouse to grow on until mid-April, when they'll move to the cold frame for 5 days of hardening-off.

While I'm heartily in favor of started pea plants these days, I also still direct-seed peas, though I start a little later than I used to. At one time, I'd be out digging the pea trench as soon as the soil was dry enough to work in March — old habits die hard, especially those forged by a pea-loving father. Now, though, I wait for the soil temperature to pass 45 degrees, which minimizes loss. To sow my peas, I first excavate a trench 2 inches deep and as wide as the bottom of my square-edged spade: about 8 inches. Then I add 2 pounds of 5-10-5 fertilizer, scratching it in to the bottom of the trench. I just broadcast the seeds into the trench, looking for a casual spacing of about 1 inch between seeds. This thick sowing is closer than many seed catalogs recommend, but I like it because it increases yield and because the closely spaced plants help support each other in bad weather. As soon as the peas are covered with an inch of soil, I erect the trellis that will support them when they grow to their full 6- to 8-foot height. (This is not true of the shorter varieties like Sugar Rae and Sugar Anne, which grow 24 to 26 inches tall.) I make my trellises from snow-fence poles and nylon net-

Four steps to superb peas. When the soil has warmed to 45 degrees, I dig the pea trench 2 inches deep and 8 inches wide, and broadcast the seeds casually. Then I sprinkle the seeds with legume inoculant and cover them with a full inch of soil.

ting with 4-inch-square openings. The metal poles are pushed about 18 inches into the ground at either end of the rows, and the netting is strung between them.

There are many varieties of peas out there — shelling peas, English peas, snow peas — but I will say here and now that I'm devoted to peas of the Sugar Snap family. These remarkable peas were developed first by Dr. Calvin Lamborn of the Gallatin Valley Seed Company in Twin Falls, Idaho. Lamborn was seeking to increase yields and to breed out the distorted pod found on edible-podded peas in the 1960s and before. Ten years of crossing thick-fleshed shell peas with edible-podded varieties finally produced a true breakthrough. This standout had large, sweet peas and a crisp, sweet pod, both of which actually became tastier as the pea grew to full maturity. Lamborn called his creation Sugar Snap, and introduced it in 1979. It was immediately voted an All-America Selection, won a gold medal shortly thereafter, and not long ago was voted the top all-time All-America winner by gardeners across the country.

The Sugar Snap pea is so desirable because it makes for one-stop shopping for the gardener. In their early stage, Sugar

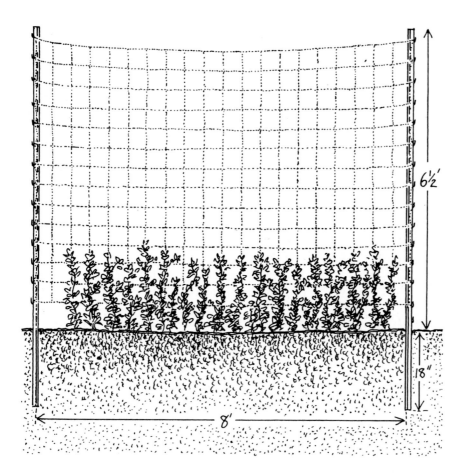

Snaps can be eaten like snow peas. Later, when the pods are developed, they can still be eaten in the pod — no shelling required. And they are exquisite simply munched raw, right off the vine. Because they are so tasty, and because they require no work beyond the growing, I myself see no need now to grow peas that do require shelling. Not everyone will agree with me, of course, but I admit my prejudice right here so·that my frequent references to Sugar Snap varieties later on will be less of a surprise.

Shallots   Just as I will never rival Vidalia's onion, I will never grow exhibition shallots in the Victory Garden. New England is not prime shallot territory. Still, they are delicious enough that they are worth growing.

Shallots are planted from sets — small bulbs — as are some of the other onion members in Victory Garden beds, but my eyebrows raise every time I see the shallot-set prices in seed catalogs. A half-pound of these little delicacies will cost five dollars or more. They're not really as expensive an investment as that price would make them seem, though, because each little bulb will later produce 6 to 10 shallots.

Shallots, planted as sets in March, grow rapidly in the Victory Garden's super-fertile soil. Shallot sets are good investments — each bulb produces 6 to 10 shallots.

To make sure that they receive all the nutrients they need, I work in 1 cup of 5-10-5 fertilizer for every 10 feet of row before planting. Then I space the shallot sets 6 inches apart in the rows, and push each set about two-thirds of its length into the soil, leaving the pointed end up. When green shoots appear, I give the sets a drink of water-soluble fertilizer. I'll also put back into place any sets that have popped up out of the soil or have been disturbed by birds.

Spinach Growing spinach in the Victory Garden has taught me about microclimates. Despite virtually identical cultural practices and soil amendment programs in both the Boston and suburban Victory Gardens, I have never been able to coax a truly fine spinach crop from the Boston garden. In the suburbs, though, the spinach flourishes, and I'd match it against spinach grown anywhere. For a long time I wondered why these two gardens, separated by only ten miles and blessed with the best soils modern care could provide, produced such different spinach crops. After years of observation, I think the reason may be heat. It's possible that the urban garden's March and April weather may be just a few degrees too warm on just a few too many days — enough to make the difference. Despite being one of the most cold-tolerant crops, spinach is very sensitive to warm weather.

Because of that touchiness about heat, I sow the spring crop outdoors in late March. My cultural practice here is unusual, but it's worked very well for me in the Victory Garden, so I can recommend it wholeheartedly. The first step is to work the soil well and add 5 pounds of 10-10-10 fertilizer for every 100 square feet of bed.

Most garden instructions call for planting spinach in single rows, giving adequate spacing between plants in the row. Instead, I make a shallow trench with the back of an iron rake, about 12 inches wide and 1 inch deep. Then I sow seed directly into the depression, leaving about 1 inch between seeds. Happily, spinach seeds are white and not tiny, so they are easy to plant this way. Once covered with ½ inch of soil in this wide row, they will germinate even in cold, wet soils in about 10 days. As the plants become large enough to touch one another, I harvest every other seedling for a fine-tasting spinach salad. Soon the leaves will be big enough for cooking. By then the spacing is 6 inches, just what those seedsmen recommend.

This March planting of spinach helps prevent confrontations with hot weather, and as extra insurance against trouble I choose quick-growing early varieties like Melody and America, which will mature in 40 to 50 days. America is an especially good choice if I'm late sowing seeds, because it's more heat tolerant than some other early varieties and will resist bolting for up to 2 weeks in hot weather.

VICTORY GARDEN TOOLS

In the garden, a few good tools can make an amazing difference between hard times and good times. Visit the shed of any experienced gardener and you will find a set of well-made tools, freshly oiled, their keen edges gleaming. I learned long ago that there are no bargains in tool buying. The only sensible purchase is a tool that is well designed, expertly crafted, and sturdy enough to last season after season. There may be more frustrating things than seeing the spading fork's head part company with its handle right in the middle of spring soil preparation, but I can't think of any just now. Good tools promote both peace of mind and pleasant gardening, and that, after all, is what we're after. Good tools are not cheap, but then neither is it cheap to replace shoddy junk season after season. When you've just laid out money for the third "inexpensive" spade, the wisdom of a strong initial purchase becomes clearer.

This doesn't mean, however, that I spend as much for a garden shovel as for my firstborn's college education. Any number of wily businessmen, capitalizing on gardening's ever-increasing popularity, would have you believe that you simply *must* have aerospace-quality stainless-steel tools, with handles of exotic woods from the dark

forests of distant lands. Nonsense. My philosophy is to buy well, but not to overbuy. Leave zirconium/titanium alloys in the nose cones, where they belong.

When I said earlier that a *few* good tools make gardening easier, I wasn't kidding. Most gardeners — myself included — do perfectly well with the Big Five: *spading fork, rake, hoe, spade,* and *trowel.* There are certainly other tools that I use in the Victory Garden. Some save time, some save labor. But one can do without them and still produce beautiful crops. One can't do without the Big Five, and I'll say honestly here that I think most gardeners would do well to spend more time selecting the basic tools they do use. Consider how much care goes into the choice of a set of golf clubs, for instance, or into the purchase of skis or a tennis racquet. Garden tools, like this other equipment, will be used often in their season, year after year, and a great deal of energy will be directed through them.

Spading fork   This is arguably the most-used tool in the garden. For many years I have had a four-tined steel model. Steel gives, rather than snaps, when it hits large rocks and roots. If the tines are bent, I can re-form them. I have a couple of cast-iron forks, but they are heavier and more brittle, and I'm always afraid they will break when the going gets tough. My favorite spading fork has square tines with a

6-inch spread. You can find models with a much wider bite, but I like a spread of 6 to 8 inches. This lets me get into tight places, but also turns up a respectable swath of earth when I'm digging in earnest. My fork measures 40 inches from tine tips to handle, which is just about right for my six-foot height. Good forks come in shorter and longer lengths, however, so be sure to shop around for the one that fits your body best.

Rake   My preference is a 16-inch model with a straight top. Bow-top rakes may be stronger, but they're heavier, too, and I don't try to move any boulders with my rake. It's a light-duty tool, used for smoothing tilled ground, clearing out small stones, breaking soil clods, and covering seeds. I like the flat top, too, because I can simply flip it over and give my beds a final smoothing. I prefer a long handle — 60 inches or more — to give me a long reach, but I have long arms and a back conditioned by thirty years in the trenches. As with forks, you'll have to choose a weight and length suited to your own comfort.

Cultivating hoe   The number three tool in my arsenal is a cultivating hoe. I use an "action" hoe (called, by some, a "scuffle" hoe), and in my travels I'm continually amazed at how many people *don't* use this marvelous little device. An action hoe allows me to cultivate

The scuffle hoe in action. Though twice as efficient as a conventional hoe, this handy tool is overlooked by most gardeners.

while walking backward *or* forward. The two-edged blade is also twice as efficient as the single-bladed conventional hoe. Whenever I use my action hoe, I think of those animated TV commercials in which safety razors slide along, lopping giant whiskers off below the skin line. That's just how the action hoe decapitates weeds, loosening the soil at the same time. Whenever I hear people complain about how much work it takes to keep their gardens well groomed, I know they haven't discovered the action hoe yet. As with my other tools, I make sure the handle is of good, close-grained wood, and that the head is of sturdy steel — carbon, not stainless. Carbon steel can be sharpened easily, and that's why I choose it for all my edged garden tools.

Spade   I use my flat-bladed spade to excavate trenches, cut pathways, and plant large, container-grown stock. That's heavy construction by garden standards, and my spade will take more punishment and stress than any other garden tool. For that reason, I pay special attention to its selection. The wooden handle must be smooth, tight-grained, and completely free of knots, flaws, or interruptions in the grain. I like a handle that's all one piece of wood, right up to the forked end, and reinforced with a wedge where the handle opens into its Y shape. The uhion between handle and metal spade gets extra attention. Cheap models have a short neck of light-gauge metal with a seam running the neck's length. The wooden handle is inserted into this flimsy tube and then secured, usually with a single rivet. This arrangement can be counted on to split like a scallion the first time any real leverage is applied. I look instead for a one-piece steel throat 10 to 12 inches high — long enough, in other words, to continue a full third of the way up the wooden shaft. The spade's blade is equally important. Stainless-steel spades can be had at considerable cost, but again I prefer a blade of high-quality carbon steel for the same reason that professional chefs use carbon-steel knives: They are easier to sharpen. A sharp spade is one of the greatest labor-savers in the garden, and I sharpen my own with a file frequently. The spade rewards me by slicing easily through turf, roots, and compacted soil.

Trowel   The humble trowel completes my list of must-have garden tools. I use a one-piece cast-aluminum trowel, with a thick, curved handle. The handle fits me so comfortably that I feel as if I'm shaking hands with a friend each time I pick it up. The scoop is 6 inches long, and the handle is encased in red plastic. I've learned the hard way that my trowel is the easiest garden tool to lose, and that red handle makes it the easiest to find, as well.

Additional tools   I can hear gardeners everywhere exclaiming, "What about the rototiller!" To tell the truth, with my raised beds I don't use a heavy one anymore. When the Victory Garden was in its early days, and flat-plane culture was being used, the big rototiller was an important part of the arsenal. I've moved on to 4-foot raised beds, though, keeping pace with gardening advances, and I put a lot of work into preparing and shaping those superfertile raised beds. Once I've done so, I don't want to ruin them by running a heavy tiller down their length. However, the new hand-held lightweight tillers are ideally suited for raised-bed maintenance.

Other hardware does come in very handy. A *pocketknife* is one such item. I use mine so often that I'm almost inclined to make the Big Five a Big Six. Opening a ripe melon, for instance, demands instant access to a keen blade. Squash and eggplants should have their stems trimmed cleanly from their vines, as should pumpkins. I also need to snip lengths of twine to tie up cauliflower leaves. I carry a "Swiss army"–type knife with several blades and tools.

I also find handy a *metal watering can*, big enough to hold 2 or 3 gallons. Mine produces agentle, rainlike flow from its "rose" end, which can be removed for cleaning. Plastic cans are lighter and cheaper than the galvanized steel variety I use, but they won't last as long. Either the handles will give way after a season or two, or the flimsy, screw-on rose will strip its threads.

I use a *garden cart* and a wheelbarrow in the Victory Garden. The cart is the largest I could find, with a 14-cubic-foot capacity and big, bicycle-style wheels. I've used it to haul everything from cordwood to sand, and I'm always amazed at how easily the thing rolls along, no matter how badly I've overstuffed it. A good wheelbarrow with an inflatable tire is useful, too, in the Victory Garden's raised beds and narrow aisles. Here, the maneuverability of the wheelbarrow is hard to beat.

A *gas-powered string trimmer*, for a garden the size of the Victory Garden, is something of an indulgence — but a justifiable one. The trimmer saves me a lot of time cleaning up around the beds, and time is my most valuable commodity. By keeping down tall grass, I minimize insect hideaways and keep the garden looking picture-perfect. With a string trimmer, I'm spared the toil of scuttling along on hands and knees, snapping away at grass with clippers. There are very powerful models available, but for my garden purposes, a light, 2-horsepower trimmer, weighing about 12 pounds, is adequate. I use a shoulder strap to support the trimmer's

My planting board, with cutouts at 6- and 12-inch intervals, eliminates time-consuming measuring.

weight, which makes the going considerably easier.

My homemade *planting board* is very convenient in spring, when I'm laying out the garden. Easy-to-read markers take the guesswork out of spacing plants and save time by eliminating repeated measurements. The board's beveled edge creates a precise seed furrow, too. (See the feature in the chapter titled "Beginnings" for my detailed instructions on how to make the Victory Garden planting board.)

Garden lines on bailers help me mark out straight edges for my beds, and keep planting rows straight, too. I use cast-aluminum bailers wrapped with 50 feet of mason's line, which is sturdier and less likely to tangle than standard twine.

There are several other tools I'm glad to have in the shed, too. A short-handled, *three-prong cultivator* is dandy for weeding close to plants and for scratching in side-dressings of

fertilizer. A standard *garden hoe* is the tool of choice for hilling-up leeks and potatoes. I use a *soil thermometer* to tell me when some very frost-sensitive crops can be planted in spring. (I like thermometers with sturdy metal probes that can be plunged into the soil, and with easy-to-read circular dial scales in sturdy steel casings.) Finally, I've found that a *compression sprayer* with a plastic body is very helpful. The hose-end sprayers work well, but there are times when the portability and superfine spray of the pressure sprayer is unbeatable. A 2- or 3-gallon capacity is adequate without being too heavy for comfortable carrying with a shoulder strap. I make sure that the sprayers I buy have brass components at the spraying end, because steel is sure to rust or corrode after a season or two.

That's about it. My tool philosophy, in a nutshell, is to buy the best without falling for advertisers' gimmicks. And when it comes to tools that I use infrequently — post-hole diggers, say — I rent rather than buy. It just doesn't pay to spend the money and then have the tool sit idle for years and years.

Finally, I take good care of the tools I do buy. After every use I wipe them clean with a brush or coarse cloth like burlap, and then anoint them with a rustproofing coat of oil. I sharpen the edged tools often with a file, and I hang *every* tool in the same place in the shed after each use so that I'll find it, gleaming and ready, the next time I need it. The only thing more frustrating than a broken tool is one that's disappeared entirely.

April showers bring many
splendors to the Victory
Garden, in this case
healthy lettuce seedlings.

APRIL

APRIL

If March is the month of promise, it is in April that the dreams that have sustained me throughout the long winter begin to come true. Plenty of rain will fall early in the month, and days will be, on average, 10 degrees warmer by month's end. April weather is more uniform than was the case with March, and I see the passing of my last expected frost date in the Victory Garden region: April 20. It's still too early for most bugs, a blessing for garden and gardener alike, and all of these fortuitous developments can breed a heady excitement.

These days, I temper that excitement with reserve. It's tempting to rush out every single transplantable item from the greenhouse or windowsill, of course. In fact, at one time I did just that. But over the years, I found that setting plants out too early brought later problems. Even crops that like the cool 40- to 60-degree April temperatures — cabbage, broccoli, and beets, for instance — will suffer quality and bolting problems if jolted by *too* great a fluctuation between day and night temperatures. So with these and other sensitive crops I have learned to be patient rather than pressing. The reward for my April patience is trouble-free crops through the rest of the season.

April may still be, however, the busiest month in the Victory Garden. More than a dozen crops are planted outdoors, and almost that many are started from seed inside. In addition to those important tasks, I'll be turning under more beds of winter rye, laying down black plastic over some of the raised beds to warm them up, and tending to the compost bin. This is the month to start a new asparagus bed, a major project in and of itself. And I'll be getting the trellises and netting ready for use with crops that need them — beans, peas, melons, and cucumbers.

Start Indoors
Beans
Corn
Cucumbers
Eggplant
Melons
Okra
Peppers
Summer squash
Swiss chard
Tomatoes

Transplant
Broccoli
Cabbage
Eggplant
Lettuce
Peppers
Tomatoes

Plant in Garden
Asparagus
Beets
Carrots
Chinese cabbage
Kohlrabi
Lettuce
Onions
Parsnips
Peas
Potatoes
Radishes
Turnips

Screen
Broccoli
Cabbage
Chinese cabbage
Radishes
Spinach

Asparagus   April is the month to create an asparagus bed, and asparagus crowns are the prime ingredient. Crowns are young asparagus plants, one to two years old. It's possible to grow asparagus from seed, but doing so means a minimum three-year wait before first harvest. That's why most gardeners start new beds with crowns, which will shorten the waiting period by a full year.

When I was a youngster, Dad and I would travel to a nearby farmer's spread to buy our asparagus crowns. We paid two cents apiece for them, and they looked like small octopuses or squid. Nowadays I don't have to track down willing farmers for my crowns because they're widely available at garden centers. I pay a bit more for them now, but the varieties on today's market, like Jersey Centennial, are hardier and much more disease resistant.

The secret to producing award-winning asparagus is soil preparation and more soil preparation. Asparagus will come from these beds for decades (some well-preserved beds have produced for more than one hundred years), so it makes sense to prep the soil with extraordinary care. There's only one chance to do so! Step one is to lay out the beds as soon as the soil is workable and dry in the spring. In the Victory Garden, I laid out two beds in an area 30 feet long and 8 feet wide, which gives room for 30 crowns. (Ten plants per person will produce enough stalks to satisfy most asparagus-lovers.) In each 30-foot bed, I dug out

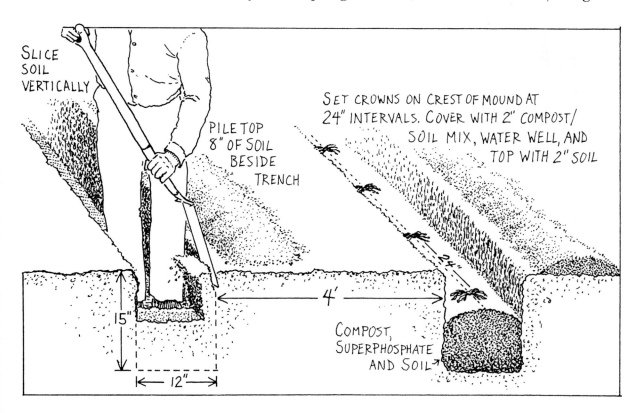

SLICE SOIL VERTICALLY

PILE TOP 8" OF SOIL BESIDE TRENCH

SET CROWNS ON CREST OF MOUND AT 24" INTERVALS. COVER WITH 2" COMPOST/ SOIL MIX, WATER WELL, AND TOP WITH 2" SOIL

15"

12"

4'

24"

COMPOST, SUPERPHOSPHATE AND SOIL

two trenches 12 inches wide and 15 inches deep. The trenches were 4 feet apart. I strung lines to keep my digging straight, and cut the sides of the trench dead vertical. An excavating trick I learned from my father made the earth moving considerably easier. I dug right down to the 15-inch depth, then cleared a space large enough to stand in — about 3 feet long and 1 foot wide. I stood in that hole and just sliced away soil with my spade. The loose slices fell toward me like slices of cake. It was easy to scoop them up and lay them to one side. Here's something else I've learned: I put the top 8 inches of soil (the very best stuff) to one side, and deposited the remaining subsoil in my compost bin.

After digging the trench, I shoveled in about 4 inches of well-rotted manure or compost. Next came a secret weapon: superphosphate, a fast-acting, commercial fertilizer especially effective for root development because of its potent phosphorus content (the analysis is 0-20-0; it's made by treating raw rock phosphate with sulfuric acid, which makes the phosphorus much faster-acting). I scattered 5 pounds per 100 square feet of bed into the trench.

Before planting asparagus crowns, I trim off any broken or torn roots. After soaking the crowns for 10 minutes, I set them atop the mound at 24-inch intervals.

When the compost or manure and superphosphate had been added to the trench, I blended in half of the soil I'd set aside earlier, using a hoe to draw the whole mix together into a mound that ran the length of the trench.

Then, at last, it was time to plant the crowns. I bought mine at a garden center where they were kept refrigerated prior to sale, and I made sure that they didn't dry out before I had a chance to plant them. (Damp peat moss works well to hold them in the interim.) I checked each one carefully for root damage, because the crowns are often pulled roughly from their home beds. Broken or torn roots were trimmed back to healthy tissue, and then I gave the crowns a bath in tepid water for 10 minutes. Properly moistened, they were set out at 24-inch intervals atop the long mound I'd created earlier. The crowns should be centered right over the mound's crest, with their roots flowing downward over the mound's flanks. When all were in place, I gently spaded in a mixture of compost or manure and some of the remaining topsoil I'd laid to one side, covering first one side of each crown and then the other with 2 inches of this mixture. I gently firmed the loose soil, and watered it well to firm and settle it further. Finally, I covered the crowns with 2 more inches of soil. By this time the trench was about half-full, and I was almost finished. As a last step, I blended the remaining loose soil with compost or well-rotted manure, using 1 part compost or manure to 3 parts soil, and piled this mix on the ground back from the edges of my trench. As the new shoots emerged over the next weeks, I added this enriched soil a little at a time, spreading it carefully around them until the trench was filled and level with the surrounding soil. I also side-dressed the rows with 10-10-10 fertilizer in June and October . . . but now I'm getting ahead of myself. I'll remind you about that when the time comes in later monthly chapters.

Cultivation is important to young asparagus plants. Until I saw shoots appear from the planted crowns, I weeded the beds by hand. Once they're up, I use the three-pronged cultivator. It was time well spent, because weeds or grass would have competed for nutrients, moisture, and light.

Beans Beans, like peas, are a most rewarding crop to grow because they feed the garden as well as the gardener. I needn't go into the contribution they make to our own nourishment; the fact that over 500 varieties are cultivated attests to our love affair with the bean. And beans, like all legumes, do their part for garden fertility. A benign bacteria called *Rhizobia* colonizes on the roots of beans and other legumes. *Rhizobia* takes nitrogen from the air and converts it into forms usable by plants — the process we call nitrogen fixation.

In the Victory Garden I grow both bush and pole beans. Bush beans are prolific producers, mature quickly (50 to 60 days), make good use of available space, and require no support sys-

I've broken with tradition and now sow bean seeds indoors in early April. The indoor start gives me an earlier harvest, healthier plants, and a guaranteed full stand of beans.

tems. The only real drawback to bush beans is their relatively short bearing time. Two weeks is usually the extent of my bush bean harvest from any one sowing, though succession plantings every 2 to 3 weeks let me beat that problem. One sowing of pole beans, on the other hand, produces an extended harvest of 6 to 8 weeks. Pole beans do take longer to mature (60 to 75 days) and, though their yield at any one time is smaller, the overall harvest is about the same. Toward the end of their life cycle, they are more susceptible to disease than bush beans. Finally, pole beans, as their name implies, require support of some kind — poles, trellises, or screens.

Several years ago I laughed when I discovered young bean plants offered for sale at my local garden center. Ridiculous, I thought, to buy beans the way one might buy petunias. I'd never thought of seeding beans indoors and then setting them out as started plants. Somebody else obviously had, though, and, as I thought more about it, I could see why. Gardeners want early crops, with no skips in the row, and started bean plants give them those advantages. With just a little extra effort, it's possible to have beans 2 weeks earlier than direct-seeded crops — without those gaping empty spots in the rows. I start my bean plants indoors about the first of April, using peat strips filled with soilless medium. The seeds are planted 2 to a pot about ½ inch deep, bottom-watered until all the medium is moist, and then set onto the heat pad at 75 degrees. The sprouts will be up in a week or so, thinned to the stronger seedling, and moved to a sunny windowsill, where they'll grow until it's time to harden them off in the cold frame. When they're planted out, the peat strips will go right into the ground, so the beans will suffer no transplant shock. Just as important, they'll start life outdoors undaunted by still-cold soil. In the past, I might have endured a 30-percent loss of the earliest direct sowing of bush and pole beans. The seeds of some varieties just would not germinate fully in soils below that 60-degree mark. With this new approach, there are far fewer casualties.

My favorite bush bean varieties are Contender, Provider, Bush Blue Lake, and a French variety called Triomphe de Farcy. The best wax variety I've grown is called Beurre de Rocquencourt. The pole beans I keep coming back to are Kentucky Wonder, Scarlet Runner, and Blue Lake. And a friend recently sent seeds of a variety called French Crystal, which I tried and which indeed turned out to be exceptionally tasty.

Beets   I don't know how many times I've opened a gardening book to the beet section and read the following: "Beets are one of the easiest vegetables to grow." Perhaps they are in the utterly controlled environment of the laboratory or experimental garden, but I have found beets to be a much tougher real-world customer than those nice book entries would indicate, especially in cool April soils. Just getting the seeds to germinate is often difficult when they've been sown directly in the garden, for instance. And that's not the only problem. For several years when I first came to the Victory Garden I was rewarded by good luck with just about every crop — except beets. Though the tops were lush and lovely, the beets themselves were puny. Thinking that soil nutrients might have been lacking, I doubled the amount of fertilizer I'd been using, then sat back and waited for my crop of superbeets. Imagine my surprise when I found, beneath still more magnificent tops, pencil-thin and sadly anemic beet globes. Exasperated, I sought a beet-expert friend, who finally revealed the error of my ways. I'd been *too* kind to those beets, which rebel at overzealous feeding. Improving soil *composition*, the beet aficionado suggested, would produce better beets than pumping up their diet. My expert friend was correct. These days, I make sure that the beets' soil is stone-free and heavily laced with copious amounts of rotted manure or compost and any other organic matter I can work in — but *not* extra fertilizer.

After soaking them overnight to speed germination, I plant beet seeds in soil that's enriched with compost or well-rotted manure and lightly fertilized.

Before I plant beet seeds outside in mid-April, I speed their sometimes reticent germination by soaking the seeds in tepid water overnight. Then, outside, I string a line the length of the beets' raised bed and use my planting board to make furrows ½ inch deep the length of the bed. I plant the seeds in the furrows with a foot between each row and 1 inch between seeds, then cover them with ¼ inch of soilless medium and give them a good watering-in.

My favorite beet varieties are Pacemaker II and Warrior, hybrids that have performed well. Burpee's Golden is a yellow-orange globe variety that produces excellent greens, which I enjoy just as much as the beets themselves. Since most beet seeds produce several seedlings per seed, I've recently tried a variety, Mobile, which seedsmen have developed to produce only a single sprout. This promises to eliminate the annoying chore of thinning the beets when they first emerge. It's an interesting new direction and, though Mobile won't replace my tried-and-true favorites like Pacemaker II, it adds variety while saving a bit of labor at the same time.

Broccoli The broccoli seedlings I started indoors in March will be ready, in mid-April, for their trip to the cold frame. I give them 5 days there, and then make ready for planting them in the garden. First step is to select a raised bed in which brassicas have *not* grown the previous season. This rotation is a defense against clubroot, which can linger in the soil all winter after plants have been pulled in the fall. Next, I work in 1 cup of 10-10-10 fertilizer for every 10 feet of row, as a last-minute amendment to provide adequate nitrogen and phosphorus, both of which are typically unavailable in cool soils. When I dig the planting holes for the broccoli plants, I add and blend with the

Broccoli and lettuce seedlings make good interplanting neighbors. The lettuce will be harvested before the broccoli grows large enough to need the extra room.

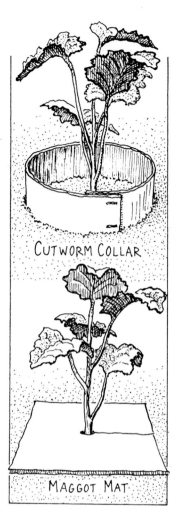

CUTWORM COLLAR

MAGGOT MAT

soil half a handful of lime per hole. This will elevate the pH to about 7.5, which is yet another safeguard against clubroot. Then, at last, it's time to set the broccoli plants into the soil. They'll be 4 to 6 inches tall by now, and I set them into the ground an inch deeper than they were growing in their cell-packs. Broccoli, like tomatoes and certain other crops, will root all along their stems, and setting them in a bit deeper each time they're transplanted lets them develop the strongest possible root systems. Spacing for broccoli is 18 inches between plants and 24 inches between rows, which leaves plenty of room for big, healthy plants to grow and room, as well, for the interplanting of lettuce. Finally, I water the seedlings in with water-soluble fertilizer diluted to half strength and then turn my attention to protecting them from insect invaders. At one time, I fiddled with all kinds of antibug alternatives: cutworm collars, maggot mats, organic insecticides. Now I've found a one-stop bug stopper: spun, bonded polyester fabric. I cover the broccoli beds with this fabric these days, supporting the fabric with hoops of #12 wire, the ends of which are pushed into the soil about 6 inches. Some sources advise laying the spun, bonded fiber right down on the soil, and letting the growing seedlings push the fabric up as they enlarge. I prefer to support the fabric with hoops, so that the seedlings are spared even that little bit of extra effort at this early stage in their development. The fabric protects against all the insects that pester broccoli — cabbage moths, flea beetles, aphids, and root maggots. In addition, it traps heat, which is an advantage with this early planting. Watering is no problem, because moisture passes right through the porous polyester fabric. Any way you look at it, this fabric is a big breakthrough for the home gardener. The stuff is even reusable from season to season.

Cabbage One week before my last expected frost date — April 20 — I move the cabbage seedlings into the cold frame for 5 days of hardening-off. While they're making the transition, I put the finishing touches on their beds. Cabbage, like the other brassicas, is a heavy feeder. To accommodate that appetite, I work in 1 cup of 10-10-10 fertilizer per 10 feet of row. My fall soil amendment program has provided for a different pH in the cabbage bed than the rest of the Victory Garden enjoys. My standard throughout the garden is 6.5, in which most vegetables thrive. A higher pH seems to inactivate the clubroot organism, however, which has been troublesome in my cabbage beds. Thus I lime the beds in fall to produce a pH of 7.5 for the cabbage plants, and work in another half-handful to each planting hole.

When I set the plants into the garden soil, I allow 18 inches between the small-headed varieties and 24 inches between the larger. The plants will need all this room eventually, but now it lets me interplant lettuce. I set the cabbage seedlings into the ground so that their seed leaves are just above the surface (they'll root all along the stem, producing sturdier seedlings),

Cabbage seedlings look like this when they're ready for 5 days of hardening-off in the cold frame.

and then I give them a watering-in with soluble fertilizer diluted to half strength. Finally, I cover the seedlings with polyester fabric supported on hoops of #12 wire. The fabric will protect against cabbage moths and cabbage loopers.

A final word of warning: Cabbage, like broccoli, is susceptible to clubroot infestation. To minimize this, I plant my cabbage in beds where other brassicas have not grown for several seasons.

Carrots I learned a lot about carrots when I was a youngster working on a farm, and one of the first things I learned was weeding. That was my task, and I crawled along the endless sandy rows doing the job by hand. As I grew taller and stronger, I was allowed to push a wheel hoe between the rows. That was better than toiling on hands and knees, but it required sharper concentration — the price for failure was greater. Those rows were close together, and a moment's inattention could easily wipe out a whole swath of young carrot plants.

I'm even less fond of weeding and thinning today than I was then, so it's fortunate that I've learned a much easier carrot routine: pelleted seed. I've also learned to avoid a few "accepted" practices. Take planting out, for instance. Many sources will tell you to sow carrots outside as soon as the soil can be worked. Don't. Carrots are very sensitive to cold, and there's no better shortcut to carrot catastrophe than too-early sowing. They're slow germinators anyway, and that recalcitrance is aggravated by cool conditions.

The real key to superb carrots, though, is superb soil. Carrots most appreciate loose, deep, sandy soil that will present no obstructions to the tiny, developing taproot. To achieve that fine soil, my initial bed preparation for the carrots included the addition of 2 inches of coarse builder's sand, and a very careful culling to remove stones, clumps, or anything else that might get in the way of those taproots.

Carrot germination rates increase rapidly when soil temperature rises above 55 degrees, so I wait until the ground is at least that warm before planting seeds outside. Usually, the soil will be that warm as soon as the last expected frost date in my region — April 20 — is past. When that times comes, I rake the prepared bed smooth and make ¼-inch-deep furrows with my planting board, spacing the rows 1 foot apart. I usually plant 3 to 4 rows, about one bed's worth. I used to fuss with the terribly fine carrot seed in an effort to achieve very regular spacing, knowing that much later work could be avoided if I could sow one seed every ½ inch. Memories of those long days on hands and knees made me wary of the thicker sowings recommended in some catalogs. No matter how careful I was, though, sooner or later I found myself down on hands and knees for extended sessions of thinning. Now I've taken to pelleted seeds, and thinning is almost a thing of the past. Several of the major catalogs carry pelleted carrot seeds, and the cost is quite reasonable — about $1.25 for 1000 seeds. The increased ease of handling (each pellet contains one seed and is about the size of a buckshot) makes the slightly higher cost more than worthwhile. Seed tapes are yet another alternative to sowing straight from the packet. The tapes are 15 feet long, with seeds spaced every ½ inch, and cost about $2. The tape itself dissolves after planting, leaving behind a furrow filled with well-spaced seedlings that need little, if any, thinning.

Whether I'm using loose seed, pellets, or tapes, I cover the seed with ¼ inch of soilless medium, which reduces weed growth in the new bed and means still less work after the seedlings sprout. I gently water the seeds in well, and keep that covering of soilless medium moist. It's a thin layer, and thus can dry out quickly in full sun. Carrots can take up to 3 weeks to germinate, and those seeds need constant moisture the whole time.

Because overzealous watering can actually wash away freshly planted loose seed, I've occasionally resorted to covering the seed rows with cheesecloth in very dry weather. This permits frequent watering without disturbing the seeds. It also breaks the force of heavy rains.

Although superbly groomed soil really is necessary to grow foot-long carrots like Imperator, breeders have recognized that not every gardener will be able to create such favorable growing conditions. To help gardeners, they have produced varieties like Danvers Half-Long and Short-and-Sweet expressly for heavy,

A cheesecloth covering keeps newly sown carrot seed from washing away in heavy spring rains.

stony soils. In those bygone days when I was trudging along on hands and knees, there really were only a few varieties for carrot growers to choose from. They had to take the time and do the work necessary to produce perfect soil. Now, with the new varieties, gardeners have the option of suiting the carrot to the soil, rather than vice versa.

Carrots can be bothered by wireworms, which tend to inhabit freshly opened ground and then disappear after several years. Wireworms will bore little tunnels through the carrots. The brownish worms are about ¾ inch long and are much less active in established garden beds. A friend recommends burying half a potato in the garden if wireworms become troublesome. The worms, so he claims, will be attracted to the potato, which can be pulled out in several days. I've not tried the technique, but it was so intriguing that I decided to include it here anyway.

In addition to Danvers Half-Long and Short-and-Sweet, which I mentioned above, I like Pioneer and Trophy. And I'm especially fond of the new variety, A+, which has a very high vitamin A content and a wonderfully sweet taste.

Cauliflower   I can't think of cauliflower without remembering one trip I took with the "Victory Garden" television crew to an international gardening exposition, the I.G.A. show, in Munich, West Germany. The Germans had provided an immense hall for exhibitors to display their prize vegetables, and we spent hours shooting exhibit after exhibit. Toward day's end I thought I'd seen just about everything — giant vegetables and ingenious displays — until I turned a corner and confronted the Germans' ultimate cauliflower extravaganza. There before me was a full-sized lifeboat, filled to the gunwales with broccoli and adrift on a foaming sea of cauliflower. There's nothing like an international gardening exposition to help one see vegetables in new ways.

In late April, after the last expected frost date (April 20) has passed, I move my cauliflower seedlings out into the cold frame for 5 days of hardening-off. I am cautious about that date, because cauliflower is the most weather-sensitive brassica. Too much cold too early in life will cause an undersized curd or premature flowering. Too much heat later on may simply prevent any curd at all from forming. It's a narrow "window of opportunity" to slip through, but the reward is one of the garden's tastiest vegetables.

Chinese Cabbage   The Chinese cabbage seedlings started back in March will be 3 to 5 inches tall by mid-April, and it's time to move them out to the cold frame for 5 days of hardening-off. While the seedlings are doing that, I prepare their beds by working into the soil 1 cup of 10-10-10 fertilizer for every 10 feet of row. With the bed raked smooth, after the seedlings have had their 5 days in the cold frame, I peel back the tops of the peat pots (to keep them from wicking away moisture and drying out roots) and set them into the soil at the same depth they were growing. Plants are spaced 12 inches in the rows, with 24 inches between rows. When the peat pots are all in, I water the seedlings with a solution of complete liquid fertilizer diluted to half strength. Finally, I cover them with hoop-supported fabric to protect against root maggots and any other insects that might develop a hankering for this tasty crop. And as with broccoli, cabbage, and cauliflower, I try to maintain a crop-rotation schedule that avoids placing Chinese cabbage where other clubroot-prone crops have grown in the past several seasons.

Corn   Corn used to be a problem in the Victory Garden — and lots of other places. In the first small garden behind the WGBH-TV studios, I was always short of room. Also, the early varieties that I tried were disappointing. When I finally did produce a decent crop (and here's the problem that corn growers everywhere shared), I had to rush the ears from plant to pot with great urgency because corn's sugar converted to starch so quickly after picking. Moving out to the suburban garden solved

Growing Chinese cabbage in individual peat pots can be the critical difference for this temperate member of the brassica family.

my space problem, but corn's tendency to lose its sweetness so quickly continued to frustrate me. Even more frustrated, I knew, were the millions of people who had to buy their corn in supermarkets. I loved the taste of corn, but was dismayed by the amount of work required to produce so fragile and unstable a crop.

Then, several years ago, corn breeders responded to the bad reputation of supermarket corn. They delivered from their laboratories a genetic advance designed to vastly improve commercial corn's eating quality. In short, they produced varieties of corn that would hold their sweetness for a long time — up to 2 weeks. This, of course, delighted supermarket shoppers, who can now avail themselves of corn that tastes almost as though it came from the plants moments ago. And even those of us who grow corn in our own gardens appreciate the new "supersweet" varieties, as they're called. I do like to eat my vegetables fresh, as I've often said on the air and in this book, but I resent having to behave like the Marx Brothers in a Chinese fire drill in order to eat a vegetable before it degrades. Now I'm spared that indignity by the supersweets.

There are two supersweet genotypes available to home gardeners these days. "Sugary enhanced" varieties include Burgundy Delight and Platinum Lady, as well as all varieties that carry the designation "SE" or "EH." These are somewhat more tender and a bit sweeter than standard varieties, and their sugars do not convert to starch as quickly after picking. They do not need to be isolated from standard sweet corn varieties when planting.

"Shrunken gene" types (also called sh_2 varieties), on the other hand, should be isolated from both standard and sugary enhanced corns. Cross-pollination will produce disappointing ears with woody, starchy kernels in both crops if shrunken gene corn and standard or sugary enhanced types are planted closer than about 25 feet in home gardens. That's a minimum spacing, and 40 feet is better, if the room is available. The reward for this extra care, in the sh_2 corn, is *much* higher sugar content and slower conversion to starch after picking. Varieties of this type include Starstruck, How Sweet It Is (a 1986 All-America Selection), and Florida Staysweet.

Corn, once it's up, does very well in cool weather, but the seeds will just not germinate in soil that is too cool — below about 45 degrees. Growers used to get around corn seeds' tendency to sit in the soil and rot by applying a fungicide to the seeds. That fungicide has now fallen into disfavor, and may soon be banned in a number of states. I much prefer the natural alternative anyway, by which I mean sowing the corn seeds indoors and letting them develop while waiting for the soil to warm to about 60 degrees.

In early April, therefore, I soak corn seeds overnight to help speed their germination. This is particularly important with the true supersweet, or sh_2 varieties, which must absorb twice as much water as normal corn to germinate. I sow the seeds 2 to the cell in peat strips filled with soilless medium, bottom-water to moisten the medium all the way through, and then set the pots on my 75-degree heat pad. The seedlings will appear in about 5 days, and then they go to a sunny spot to grow until their move to the cold frame in early May.

A word about my Victory Garden experience with early corn varieties: I've never had much success with any of them. They gave me poor ears that turned out woody and tasteless, and I've decided that — in my growing area, anyway — there's a pretty strict relationship between taste and days to maturity: The more days, the better the taste. Now I use a midseason variety like

Corn-growing has been revolutionized by the introduction of supersweet varieties, which lose their sugar content much more slowly than standard types.

Burgundy Delight for my early spring corn planting. Given an indoor start and warm soil, this and other midseason varieties have worked very well for me.

I do grow a mixture of standard varieties and supersweets these days. Silver Queen and Butter and Sugar are among my standard favorites. In addition to the supersweets mentioned above, I like Early Sunglow, Kandy Korn EH, Pearls 'n Gold EH, and Snow Queen EH.

Cucumbers I love fresh cucumbers, and for some time I had heard stories about the Dutch, whose tables sport fresh cukes all year round. Those stories made me very curious, and several seasons ago I had a chance to investigate. I arrived in Holland a day or two ahead of the "Victory Garden" television crew, and struck out on my own to the Floriade, a vast international horticultural exhibition on the outskirts of Amsterdam. Ostensibly, my mission was to scout the exhibits and single out those that would be suitable for inclusion in the show. Secretly, though, I was on the trail of the year-round cucumber I had heard so much about.

Trellised cukes form up perfectly, have added protection from insects and rot, and are a snap to harvest.

After hours of fruitless hunting, I sought refuge from a driving rain in one of the exhibition's greenhouses. I expected to find flowers inside. When I stepped through the door, though, I was confronted by rows of vegetables: eggplant, pole beans — and cucumbers! The wily Dutch were growing their cukes in large tubs something like sawed-off whiskey barrels. A simple drip irrigation system watered the plants. Two parallel rows of tubs, spaced 4 feet apart, ran the length of the greenhouse. The tubs were separated by only a few inches in the rows. From a horizontal rod 8 feet above the tubs hung nylon netting with 4-inch-square openings. The netting stretched downward in two sheets and was fastened to a frame on either side of the tubs, forming a large A-frame.

Cucumber vines grew up both sheets of netting, completely covering them with leaves and blossoms. Some cucumbers formed on the netting itself, but most hung through, dropping down vertically between the two angled netting sheets. Harvesting was a snap, and productivity was far above average, as it should have been in such ideal greenhouse conditions of temperature, humidity, spacing, and circulation. Perhaps most impressive of all, though, was the cucumbers' perfect shape. Cucumbers grown on the ground — even on black plastic — would rarely achieve such perfection.

Having discovered the Dutch secret for supercukes, I rushed home and tried the netting A-frame idea in the Victory Garden. With some modifications, which I'll get to in May, the trellising system has produced supercukes on this side of the Atlantic, too. (Though not, alas, year-round cukes!)

I can't set cucumbers out until mid-May, and to have 6-inch plants ready by then I start my cucumber seedlings indoors in mid-April. I fill 3-inch peat pots with soilless growing medium and plant the cucumber seeds 2 to a pot, ½ inch deep. (I use the peat pots because cucumbers are very sensitive to transplant shock, and peat pots, which go right into the ground themselves, minimize that trauma.) The pots are bottom-watered until the medium is completely moist, then set on the heat pad at 75 degrees. I'll have sprouts in about 3 days. After they've been up a week, I pinch out the weaker seedling in each pot, give them a day out of full sun, and then move them to the greenhouse or a sunny, south-facing windowsill.

I've come to like Sweet Success, a 1983 All-America Selection, as well as Dasher, Green Knight, and Euro-American. Pickling varieties that have done well in the Victory Garden include Peppi, Liberty (another AAS), and Country Fair.

Eggplant The English use a French word — *aubergine* — for eggplant, which is an Asian crop. That kind of diversity is reflected in eggplant's various forms, too. Out at the Peto Seed Company in California, for instance, horticultural expert John Waterson showed me literally dozens of varieties of eggplants they were "trialing." When I asked him why so many kinds were being cultivated, he explained that disease resistance was one of the company's goals. Just as important, though, was the desire to develop varieties that would satisfy differing cultural expectations of what an eggplant should be. National preferences, apparently, place more emphasis on size and shape than on taste, which explained the golf balls, tennis balls, softballs, eggs, and other odd configurations he showed me. Given the chance to taste-test half a dozen very different shapes, however, I had to confess that I couldn't tell them apart!

All of which does not mean that I am not a lover of eggplant. I am, and to ensure a good supply later in the summer, I start my eggplant seed indoors on April 1 — 3 weeks before my last expected spring frost. Eggplant is susceptible to fruit rot and wilts, with verticillium wilt being especially troublesome in my cool growing area. Once it gets into the soil, it is there forever. Thus I've selected dependable Dusky, which is resistant to this wilt, as the Victory Garden eggplant variety. I sow 12 to 15 seeds in a 4-inch pot filled with soilless medium. I keep the heat pad set at 75 degrees, and in 5 to 7 days my sprouts are up. They reside on a sunny windowsill until I see true leaves — about the middle of April — when I transplant them to individual cell-packs.

Dusky, which resists verticillium wilt, is my eggplant variety of choice. In April I start seedlings indoors, planning for a May move to cell-packs.

Kohlrabi   One warm summer day a few years ago I was sitting in the Victory Garden, jotting down notes for an upcoming TV show. It was a drowsy afternoon and I was deep in thought until a small voice broke the silence — and my concentration. I'd thought I was alone, but a little girl stood not five feet away. Right behind her stood a big brother and a set of parents.

"Excuse me, sir, but aren't you Bob?" she asked me again, and I admitted that I was, and we had a talk. It turned out that they were from Iowa, visiting New England for the first time. Back home, they had a large kitchen garden in which they grew most of the vegetables I grow, but in much larger quantities. We talked gardening for a while, and then they told me how excited they'd been by things they had never seen before: the ocean, Bunker Hill, *Old Ironsides*. As we strolled through the garden, their eyes went wide when we encountered something else they'd not seen before: kohlrabi. "Looks like a space station," the brother said. The little girl just shook her head: "It's *funny!* I bet I wouldn't like it!" Dad, however, said he'd like to try it back home, so I told him what I'd learned about growing and harvesting this unusual member of the cabbage family. He went on his way determined to grow a crop or two, but I imagine he had a tough time convincing his daughter that such an oddity could be worth eating.

Perhaps because of that odd appearance (it *does* look like Sputnik), kohlrabi has never achieved wide popularity in the U.S. My travels have shown me that it is quite popular in Ger-

Kohlrabi is a short-term crop (45 to 60 days) that adapts to a variety of climates and soils. Though the English feed kohlrabi to cattle, I eat it as a gourmet snack.

many and India, though in England gardeners are more likely to feed kohlrabies to their cattle than to their families. While it may never be the darling of chic eateries, I certainly think kohlrabi deserves better treatment than that. One of my favorite tricks, for instance, is to cut the raw globes into slices like potato chips and then scoop up hearty dollops of dip — a tastier and less fattening way to snack when the urge hits.

Kohlrabi is rugged enough to grow in a variety of climatic conditions and soils, so I direct-seed my crop in the Victory Garden soil in mid-April. Because kohlrabi, like other members of the brassica family (which includes broccoli, cabbage, cauliflower, and Chinese cabbage, among others), is prone to clubroot infestation, I try to plant it where members of this family of plants have not grown in the last few years. It's a heavy feeder, so before planting I work in 5 pounds of 5-10-5 fertilizer for every 100 square feet of bed. Then, a week before our last expected spring frost date — April 20 — I sow the seeds, placing them ¼ inch deep and 2 inches apart in the rows, which are 12 inches apart. I cover the seeds with ¼ inch of soilless medium, water thoroughly, and wait for the seedlings to appear in a week or two. When they're up and growing, I thin them to the final spacing of 6 inches.

Kohlrabi, which matures in 45 to 60 days, is a short-term crop. Like all fast growers, it needs consistent watering for unchecked growth. My Victory Garden regimen of 1 inch per week ensures that regular supply of moisture.

Grand Duke is the variety I've come to favor. It's an improved hybrid and, unlike its predecessors, will not turn woody if left too long in the ground.

Lettuce   I've been growing lettuce indoors since early March, and by early April there are seedlings all over the place. I have them growing in many stages. One generation is emerging — just — in the 4-inch pots. Another is farther along in cell-packs, and a third has just been planted. My oldest seedlings will be ready in early April for 5 days of hardening-off in the cold frame.

With one exception (the lettuce I grow in a cold frame, which we'll discuss in a moment) most Victory Garden lettuce is interplanted, meaning that it is set in between already established plants of crops like broccoli, cauliflower, and cabbage. Interplanting is one of the best ways to increase my yield from limited garden space and, while some gardeners may claim to have "invented" the practice, it's really nothing more than copying nature. In the wild, many different types of plants with different growth patterns and nutrient needs commonly share the same space quite amicably. The trick is to keep in mind that plants that don't compete with each other for light and soil nutrients can be most successfully interplanted. Lettuce, for instance, will be ready earlier, and will be out of the ground before the brassicas mature, thus offering them no competition for moisture and nutrients.

Wherever I have 18 inches between plants, as is the case with broccoli, I set one lettuce plant equidistant between the two broccoli plants. If I have 24 inches between plants — in the Savoy cabbage rows, for instance — I tuck two lettuce plants in. The lettuce seedlings are planted exactly to the same depth they were growing in their cell-packs, as planting them too deeply will slow their growth and can kill the growing points of the plants. I give them all a welcome watering-in with my balanced

It's my standard Victory Garden practice to give newly transplanted seedlings (broccoli and lettuce, here) a drink of water-soluble fertilizer diluted to half strength.

water-soluble fertilizer diluted to half strength, and that's all they need for now.

That's half the drill for April lettuce. At the same time I interplant my lettuce seedlings in the garden proper, I prepare a cold frame bed. This cold frame crop will back up my other lettuce plants in two ways. One, it will give me the earliest possible fresh lettuce. Two, the cold frame crop is insurance. Come what may — hurricanes, Easter blizzards, rabbit attacks — my cold frame lettuce is safe and sound.

To make the cold frame bed, I mark off a 4x4-foot plot in the garden's sunniest spot. Then I enrich the soil by forking in 1 pound of 10-10-10 fertilizer for the bed. I rake the soil smooth, then cover it with the cold frame, allowing several days for the soil to warm. Leaving the cold frame in place, I plant lettuce seedlings 9 inches apart, spacing the rows 12 inches apart. In each row I transplant 5 seedlings of the same variety. The seedlings are watered-in with balanced water-soluble fertilizer diluted to half strength and the cold frame lid is lowered. When the April sun is very bright, bringing the temperature in the cold frame to 75 degrees or higher, I vent it to prevent the seedlings from being cooked.

Melons The comprehensive Thomson taste test is applied to virtually every Victory Garden contest selection, and no part of this examination pleases me more than the melon assessment. I've sampled some truly super fruit, but the very best melons in memory grew in Jeanette Hanson's Grand Island, Nebraska, garden. We traveled there to record footage for the "Victory Garden" television series, and after we'd taped from one end of Jeanette's garden to the other, she said, "Bob, I've saved the best for last. Follow me!"

I did, and I could tell by the rich scent that Jeanette's melons were perfectly ripe. Awaiting us there were 15 or 20 cantaloupes, a cutting board, and a sturdy knife. "Try a slice," Jeanette invited me, and for a moment all thoughts of taping were forgotten as the whole crew moved in for their share of the harvest. Those melons were the sweetest I've ever tasted, with tender orange flesh and a melt-in-your-mouth quality. Two factors enabled Jeanette to grow such superb melons. One was the rich Nebraska soil, and the other was the strong Nebraska sun, shining down hour after hour on the flat, treeless countryside.

In the Victory Garden region I don't have that strong Nebraska sun, nor do many gardeners in the United States. I've found, though, that I can give melons the growing season they require by covering the soil they grow in with black plastic, which heats it up sooner and keeps it warm longer than bare soil. Rich, sandy soil is just as important for successful melons, so my initial soil preparation for the melon bed included 2 inches of coarse builder's sand. Every season thereafter, the standard Victory Garden soil amendment program adds 2 inches of compost or manure to the melon bed, as well as the green manure cover crop of winter rye, which is turned under in the spring. Finally, I know that melons are especially heavy feeders, and I keep them happy with slow-release 14-14-14 fertilizer and periodic applications of water-soluble fertilizer. I'll give specific instructions for all these melon tasks as they come due, month by month. In April, I start melons from seed indoors.

During the last week of the month, I sow 2 melon seeds per 3-inch peat pot filled with soilless medium. I cover the seeds

To have beautiful melons like this ready for harvest in August, I start the seeds indoors, in peat pots, in April.

with ½ inch of the medium and then bottom-water the peat pots to moisten them from bottom to top. They're set onto a plastic tray with all the pots touching, which keeps them from drying out too quickly, and the plastic tray goes atop my heat pad, which I set at 75 degrees. I'll have seedlings up in about a week. Then they're moved to full sun. After another week, I thin to the stronger seedling in each pot by snipping or pinching off the weaker seedling at soil level. Then I set the survivors in a sunny spot, still in their tray, where daytime temperatures will be consistently 75 degrees or higher. They'll grow there 4 to 5 weeks, after which I'll move them to the cold frame for 5 days of hardening-off.

I've experimented with a lot of cantaloupe varieties in the Victory Garden, and have come to favor both Ambrosia and Marble White. Ambrosia has produced exceptionally sweet fruit that average 4 to 5 pounds and are mildew resistant as well. While I favor cantaloupes, it's possible to grow other kinds of melon — Crenshaw, honeydew, and watermelon — using the same procedures I've described above.

Okra   Whenever I mention okra to friends, I think of the spicy crab gumbo I was once served down in New Orleans (or "Nawlins," as my Southern friends call their hometown). That gumbo was magic, bubbling in a huge pot from which wafted the aromas of bayou, open sea, and exotic spices — and that Cajun stew tasted every bit as good as it smelled.

In the minds of most gardeners, okra is exclusively a Southern crop. It's true that okra thrives under the conditions of heat and humidity characteristic of Southern gardens. Probably the finest okra I've ever seen, in fact, flourished in the North Carolina garden of Chuck and Marian Brackett, contest finalists. Their okra stood a good 6 feet tall, with stems at least 2 inches thick, and the plants were festooned with bright red and yellow flowers. It was an impressive display made possible by the long days of bright, hot sunlight, high humidity, and by Chuck's copious applications of a rich manure tea that he brewed using an oak whiskey barrel and a minnow can.

I can't claim to have grown okra that spectacular in the Victory Garden, but we have turned out some perfectly respectable crops. In early April, I start the okra indoors by planting 2 seeds in each 3-inch peat pot filled with soilless medium. The seeds are covered with ¼-inch of medium, bottom-watered, and then put onto the heat pad. Okra seeds will germinate within a 2-week period at 75 degrees. After the seedlings have grown a week in full sun, I thin out the weaker in each pot by snipping it off at soil level. Then the plants go to the sunniest, warmest windowsill or greenhouse shelf I have for the remainder of April and all of May. They'll be set out into the garden in June, but only after the soil has warmed to a consistent 60 degrees.

Blondie, a 1986 All-America Selection winner, is more compact than other varieties and does well in limited space like the Victory Garden's. Clemson Spineless is another of my favorites, and both have done well — though not spectacularly, as I said — in our cooler Northern climate.

Onions   In early April, the onions that have been growing indoors since February are set into the cold frame for 5 days of hardening-off. I prepare the beds in the same way I did for the onion sets in March: 5 pounds of 5-10-5 fertilizer for every 100 square feet, forked into the soil.

I plant the started seedlings outdoors after our last frost date, April 20. They're set in at the same depth they were growing in their container, with a spacing of 2 inches in the rows and 1 foot between rows. Here's a planting tip I learned the hard way. Despite the fact that I use raised beds for onions in the Victory Garden, and despite very conscientious soil amendment every year, I noticed for several seasons that the outermost row of onions was never as vigorous as other rows. It took me a while to understand that I was planting the outside rows too close to the edge of the raised beds. Onions have shallow root systems that

Heat-retaining black plastic mulch helps me grow respectable crops of okra, a hot-weather-lover, in my cool New England climate. ▶

April's onion seedlings. I've learned to set the shallow-rooted onions at least 6 inches from the bed's edge to prevent damage by foot traffic. ▼

branch out laterally, rather than penetrating deeply. Those outside rows were suffering foot damage from traffic along the adjacent walkways. Now I plant my first row at least 6 inches from the edge of the bed. I also give the onions a watering-in with complete water-soluble fertilizer diluted to half strength.

I used to recommend using some of these seedlings as scallions, but have come to realize that green onions (bunching onions from seed) are much better to eat in salads. The flavor is milder, the outer skin is thinner, and the edible white sections longer than is true with bulbing varieties. Given all this, my strategy in the Victory Garden has been to create a separate scallion row, where I plant scallion seeds every ¾ inch, allowing 16 inches between rows. The scallions will never grow large enough to need the extra room that bulb-onion spacing provides, but the extra 4 inches between the rows allows me to hill around the scallions for pale, blanched bases. Soil preparation and other planting methods are the same for my scallion seedlings as for the bulb-onion seedlings.

Parsnips I am always surprised when I hear people say that parsnips are not a very popular crop. They are hardy enough to survive the coldest regions, and frost actually improves their flavor by converting starches to sugar. That sugar content, in

Eighteen-inch-deep planting holes for parsnips are easy to dig with a pointed crowbar. Each hole is filled with a blend of soil and compost.

fact, is the sweetest of any root crop. Sliced like potato chips, then sautéed in butter, they are really superb eating. They're nutritious, as well — full of B vitamins, vitamin C, and potassium. They do require a long growing season, though. The parsnips I plant in April will not achieve maximum size and sugar content until October, a full 7 months later. And parsnips, like all the long-rooted crops, must have deep, loose, rich, well-drained soil.

In early April, I go out to the parsnip beds, located at the edge of the garden so that they won't be disturbed by the care of short-term crops. I take with me my seeds and a tool that is called, in the building trades, a crowbar. This is a steel bar, 6 feet long, with a chisel-like point on its business end. I use the crowbar to make planting holes for my parsnip seeds. I thrust the bar 18 inches deep, then rotate it several times to create a cone-shaped hole 6 inches in diameter. I space these holes 9 inches apart, and fill each hole completely with a mixture of soil and an equal amount of sifted compost. Three *fresh* parsnip seeds are pushed ½ inch deep into each hole. I stress "fresh" here because parsnip seeds are notorious for losing vitality if stored over time. I cover the planting hole with soilless growing medium, which helps keep weed growth down. And because the parsnip seeds will take a minimum of 2 weeks to emerge, I interplant radish seedlings to mark the row. In several weeks, long before the parsnips will need the space, I will harvest the radishes and thin the parsnips to one healthy plant per hole.

Peas In April I will have pea seedlings several inches tall in my peat strips, and they go into the cold frame for 5 days of hardening-off on April 15. Then I plant them in the garden, pre-spaced in the peat strips, peeling off the tops of the peat cells to prevent undue moisture loss from wicking action. The plants are set in to the same depth they were growing in their cells, and watered in with water-soluble fertilizer at half strength. I watch them carefully after this to make sure that the quick-growing plants are not wanting moisture. Usually my 1-inch-per-week ration in the Victory Garden is sufficient, but these peas really are fast movers and may outstrip even that generous water supply. I'm also prepared to rush in with a drink of balanced water-soluble fertilizer at full strength if the leaves begin to look a bit yellow. That can happen in early spring, when cold soil retards nutrient uptake.

The peas that were direct-seeded will be grabbing the trellis by now, and they also receive careful watering and a boost of water-soluble fertilizer if the need arises.

Peppers In the April 1981 issue of *Horticulture* magazine, a gardening expert wrote, "Nothing presents the gardener with a greater challenge than green peppers. Every season this member of the nightshade family frustrates thousands of North

There's still plenty of indoor work in April. Pea seedlings grow in the greenhouse until mid-April, then go to the cold frame to harden off.

American gardeners." In the April 1982 issue of *American Horticulturist*, another expert wrote, "Sweet peppers are one of the most popular home garden vegetables because of their easy culture." Who's a gardener to believe?

My own experience has shown that peppers are not really that much more difficult to grow than tomatoes or potatoes. It's important not to set them out too early, because the best growing temperatures are from 70 to 75 degrees (air temperature) during the day. I don't set out peppers into the garden until June, but I start them indoors in early April. I sow 12 to 15 seeds per 4-inch pot filled with soilless medium and cover the seeds with ¼ inch of the same material. The seeds are bottom-watered, and the ideal germination temperature of 75 degrees provided by my heat pad produces seedlings in about one week. As soon as they're up, I move the seedlings to full sunlight in a location where daytime temperatures will remain at 70 degrees or higher. By April 30 the seedlings show their first true leaves, and I transplant them to individual cell-packs filled with soilless medium.

Big Bertha, an old standby, is still my favorite variety for a large, thick-skinned stuffing pepper. Ace is another excellent stuffer, but Gypsy, a thinner-skinned, white and yellow pepper, was a 1981 All-America Selection that has grown very well in the Victory Garden. It produces heavily and tastes like the champion it is.

Potatoes Like most people, I never thought of the potato as a colorful crop, but when I visited the Chelsea Flower Show in England, I saw something that changed my mind. Peter Seabrook, the English television gardener, introduced me to a kilted Scotsman who was a potato specialist. The fellow's exhibit of more than 300 potato varieties included specimens that were not only white but blue, purple, yellow, and other shades as well. His potatoes were as colorful as his kilt.

I think I am not the only gardener who has made the mistake of considering potatoes too prosaic for home cultivation. In fact, potatoes are excellent candidates for the backyard garden. The taste of fresh, homegrown potatoes far surpasses anything that the supermarkets can offer. In addition, potatoes are prolific, yielding half a bushel from a 20-foot row.

Traditional wisdom holds that to start potatoes, one should bring home a bag of seed potatoes from the garden center, cut them into pieces, treat the pieces with a fungicide, dry them on a windowsill for 3 days, and then, finally, plant them in prepared trenches. All of which illustrates that traditional wisdom is sometimes more traditional than wise.

My own approach is different and much easier, and derives from my Victory Garden philosophy of achieving maximum yield with minimum effort. It's not that I object to putting in my time in the garden. I do that virtually every day, and have done so

for over thirty years, and have loved every minute of it. But every ounce of energy I can save by being more efficient with potatoes, to take one example, can go to the good of other crops or to the garden as a whole. Anyway, here's how I grow potatoes.

First, I buy only those seed potatoes that are "certified," meaning that they have been grown specifically for use as a seed crop in soil guaranteed to be free of the fungi and other diseases that plague potatoes. I buy early in the season to get a good selection of varieties and sizes. That's important because the U.S., unlike Europe, has not yet standardized the grading of seed potatoes. Egg-sized potatoes are perfect — easy to handle and economical, since they are sold by the pound. If I'm forced to buy larger potatoes, I'll plant them whole rather than go through that time-consuming cut-dust-dry-wait routine. Planting a 40-foot row with cut and treated potatoes may save $2, but it costs a lot more than that in my time. Even more important, planting whole, certified seed potatoes greatly reduces the risk of disease.

In mid-April, I open a trench 6 inches wide and 6 inches deep. Potatoes don't like a richly organic soil, so I do not add manure or compost at this point. Recent studies have shown that pota-

I save time and effort by planting whole certified seed potatoes in the Victory Garden. Egg-sized potatoes are perfect for handling and 9-inch spacing.

toes are quite sensitive to variations in pH, and actually prefer an acid soil, around 5.7 on the scale. Much below that, and yields will be reduced. Much above, and the crop is more likely to succumb to scab. Since 5.7 is more acid than the 6.5 that prevails throughout other areas of the Victory Garden, I set aside a patch of ground early on, and make sure *not* to treat that patch with limestone. This seems to work well, because I always get great potatoes, but it would be possible to lower that pH with agricultural sulfur (see "Steps to Victorious Gardening" for amounts to use) if I had to.

In the bottom of the trench, I loosen the soil and scratch in 1 cup of 5-10-5 fertilizer for every 10 feet of row. I then toss the seed potatoes into the trench, leaving about 9 inches between potatoes. Rows are 24 inches apart. Finally, I return about 3 inches of soil to the trench, so that the potatoes will be covered by a full inch of dirt.

Because potatoes are susceptible to many diseases (wilts, mosaics, blights, blackleg — to name a few), disease resistance is important when selecting varieties. Red Norland is excellent, a very early variety that produces high yields and resists scab. Kennebec, a late-season white variety, produces big tubers that are among the finest tasting I've grown. This variety is also resistant to mosaic and blight, which makes it a favorite of mine. Irish Cobbler and Red Pontiac are other varieties I've tried and liked.

Radishes   Easy to sow, murder to grow. That *used* to be my line on radishes. Flea beetles and other bugs attacked their tops. Root maggots assaulted the bottoms. If grown too slowly into hot weather, they turned into four-alarm fires. They could also suffer from clubroot, a disease that is very hard to eradicate once it gets a foothold. Nowadays, though, my line on radishes is softer. I've discovered spun, bonded fiber, which holds the bugs at bay — a major victory in the Victory Garden. And I grow very-fast-maturing varieties to ward off the bad case of hots that plagues radishes which grow on into summer weather. I'm now able to focus on radishes' undeniable assets. They grow quickly to maturity (anywhere from 21 to 45 days), making them a great crop for those of us who love instant gratification. They're amenable to less than superior soil, too. And they happily take up residence among other garden crops, making them perfect for my Victory Garden regime of interplanting.

Probably my favorite variety is Easter Egg, a blend of seeds that produces a colorful harvest of red, white, pink, and purple radishes that are as much fun to hunt as they are to eat. Champion is a fine traditional radish, bright red and round, about 1 inch in diameter when ripe. And Cherry Belle, an All-America Selection, can mature in *3 weeks* under the right conditions!

Radishes are a shallow-rooted crop that grow well in the standard Victory Garden pH of 6.5. They like loose soil, and to give

Colorful Easter Egg radishes.

them that I fork up the radish bed to a depth of 6 inches in early April, working in at the same time 5 pounds of 5-10-5 fertilizer for every 100 square feet of bed. I rake the soil smooth, then string lines to make my rows in the raised bed. With the planting board I make furrows ¼ inch deep, then sow the radish seeds 1 inch apart in the rows, with 6 inches between rows. I cover the seeds first with ¼ inch of soilless medium, water in, and then set in place the fabric row covers supported by #12 wire hoops. With soil temperatures between 50 and 60 degrees, I'll have seedlings in 7 to 10 days. When they're 1 inch tall, I

My fast-maturing spring radish varieties are planted in April and harvested in May. Bug problems are largely a thing of the past, thanks to protective spun polyester fabrics.

thin every other seedling, leaving a final spacing of 2 inches for these early varieties. This sowing may well be ready for harvest early in May, and I'm careful to take the radishes as soon as they're ready. They remain in top eating condition for only a few days.

Spinach   The spinach I planted in March is ready for thinning in April. My rule for thinning is simple: When the leaves touch, I thin. The thinned seedlings will be about 2 inches tall, and are perfect in salads. Spinach this tender one just can't buy.

After thinning, I erect hoop-supported covers of fabric over the spinach rows. This barrier will prevent flies from laying eggs that would eventually turn into the dreaded leaf miners. At one time, this insect was the bane of my spinach crop, but no more.

Summer Squash   Summer squash is the darling of gourmets these days. They like the blossoms as well as the tiny, immature fruit. The blossoms are prepared tempura-style or sautéed, and they are delicious indeed. At the Mayfair Hotel in Miami recently, the "Victory Garden" television crew was treated to tiny crookneck squash, lightly sautéed. I won't soon forget their delicate flavor.

The only problem I've had with squash in the Victory Garden is overabundance. I seem to end up, always, with more zucchini than I can use for the combined demands of television taping, cooking, and demonstrations. That means the neighbors are assured, each year, of fresh Victory Garden squash. Then again, I guess that's not such a horrible fate.

I want to plant my squash seedlings outdoors in May, so I start them indoors in late April. I sow 2 seeds per 3-inch peat pot filled with soilless medium, cover the seeds with ½ inch of soilless medium, and bottom-water. They receive a germination temperature of 75 degrees over my heat pad, and give me seedlings in about 5 days. After another week, I thin to the stronger seedling in each pot, and leave them growing in full sunlight where the daytime temperatures will remain between 65 and 70 degrees. On May 1 they'll go to the cold frame for 5 days of hardening-off.

My favorite varieties include Elite, a green zucchini; Sunburst, a yellow scalloped 1985 All-America Selection; and Peter Pan, a green scalloped summer squash that took an All-America award of its own in 1982. Finally, Sundance is a fine crookneck variety that I like.

Swiss Chard   There are mentions of chard by Greek writers as early as A.D. 400, but most of the references include warnings that the growth is indigestible and fit only for the common people. Thankfully, that attitude no longer holds sway and Swiss chard now takes its place in the Victory Garden with no apologies whatever.

I have seen lots of good chard crops, but none finer than that grown by Peter Abbot, our first Victory Garden contest winner. I remember that we arrived at Peter's house very late, after a hectic day of travel and taping elsewhere. Surveying his garden by the glare of our car headlights, we picked it as a regional winner at once. When I asked him about the secret of his success the next day, he pointed toward a couple of big concrete towers, which had served as shore fortifications that protected Boston during World War II. When the military abandoned those towers, pigeons and gulls moved in. Peter used their nitrogen-rich guano to fertilize his garden, and no crop responded as handsomely as his Swiss chard, which also received doses of rinsed, ground seaweed. His plants grew 18 inches tall, and were brilliantly colored ruby and green.

I don't plan to move my seedlings outdoors until the first week of May now, which means that I start them indoors in the first week of April. I sow the seeds in 3-inch peat pots — 2 seeds per pot — cover them with ¼ inch of soilless medium, and bottom-water. The seeds germinate in 5 or 6 days over the heat pad at 75 degrees and as soon as they're up I move them into full sunlight where the daytime temperatures will stay at 65 to 70 degrees. After a week or so in full sunlight, I'll give them a drink of complete water-soluble fertilizer diluted to half strength.

I have grown Fordhook Giant, an old standby, with consistent success. Ruby Red has done well in the Victory Garden, too. Both varieties will mature in 50 to 60 days and will provide a continuous supply of leaves all the way through to fall frost.

Tomatoes Tomatoes are the most popular home garden crop, bar none. *Everybody* loves tomatoes nowadays. That wasn't always the case, though. The tomato's botanical name, *Lycopersicum*, is Greek for "wolf peach," a reflection of the belief, once held by many, that tomatoes were poisonous and to be avoided.

Not so today, of course, and gardeners know that there is no tomato like that grown and ripened in the home garden. Supermarket varieties, grown for commercial use, must be picked when green and then gassed into ripening. Mechanical harvesting and shipping require a tough skin, not the most desirable eating characteristic. Seed catalogs these days overflow with tomato varieties. There are standards, hybrids, cherries, orange tomatoes, yellow tomatoes, giant tomatoes . . . on and on. To make sense of all this diversity, it helps to know that all tomatoes fall into one of two categories: determinant or indeterminant. These terms describe the plants' growth habits. Determinant varieties set a certain number of flowers, grow to a certain height, and produce a certain, predetermined number of fruit. This is a plus in some growing conditions — container culture, for instance. Indeterminant varieties, on the other hand,

Swiss chard is a long-bearing crop that supplies leaves from June until frost. I start the crop indoors in peat pots in early April. ▶

will keep on growing, flowering, and fruiting until frost kills them. In frost-free climes, indeterminant varieties actually become perennial plants.

Tomatoes are also imbued with varying degrees of resistance to diseases and insects. Four of the most common and dangerous tomato afflictions are verticillium wilt, fusarium wilt, tobacco mosaic, and nematodes (not a disease, but a destructive worm that lives in the soil). Better Boy VNF, for instance, is resistant to verticillium and fusarium wilts, and to nematode infestation. Some varieties are bred to resist all four: Celebrity VNFT is such a tomato, and it's a favorite of mine. Not only disease resistance figures into my varietal selection with tomatoes, though. I also like Sweet 100 and Gardener's Delight, both cherry types. Though not particularly disease resistant, Sweet 100 will beat any other variety for sheer production — the cherry tomatoes hang like bunches of grapes from those fragrant, green vines. And Gardener's Delight is my personal flavor favorite, blending just the right combination of sweet and acid elements. My full-sized main crop picks are Celebrity, Superfantastic, Jet Star, and Better Bush. The latter is a strong determinant variety (something of an exception that really gives the best of both types: good continuous production on a compact plant with indeterminant flowering habit), sturdy and potato-leaved, that produces a very healthy crop of 6-ounce tomatoes. It's an excellent choice for small spaces. Big Boy is the one to pick for dependable production of large tomatoes. It will give a steady supply of 1-pound fruit. For what it's worth, though, the largest tomato ever grown (look it up in *The Guinness Book of Records*) was a 6-pound, 7-ounce monster of the Delicious variety.

On April 1, I sow the seeds, indoors, for my main crop of tomatoes. The seeds are planted in 4-inch pots filled with soilless medium, covered with ¼ inch of the mix, and bottom-watered thoroughly. I sow early, midseason, and late varieties — all at the same time. The pots go onto my 75-degree heat pad, producing seedlings in a week. They're moved to a sunny, warm spot and left to grow until true leaves show, later in the month. Then the seedlings are transplanted to individual cell-packs filled with soilless medium, bottom-watered with water-soluble fertilizer at half strength, and given a day out of full sun to recover from transplant shock. Then, I set them back into full sun, water consistently, and wait for warmer weather.

Turnips   I'm afraid that turnips have received something of a bum rap. I've heard them called tasteless, and peasant food, and a few other unpleasant things. Not true. Spring turnips steamed with butter are an elegant dish indeed. To have those ready for harvest by late May or early June, I sow turnip seeds directly into the garden when the soil has warmed to at least 50 degrees — usually by mid-April. I prepare the bed by turning it

Sweet 100 is the champion producer among my tomato varieties, giving up fruit clusters like bunches of grapes.

A month from now I'll be harvesting small, tender turnips from this bed. For now, shallow cultivating lets the tender seedlings develop free from competing weeds.

over with my spading fork and then raking the soil smooth. I use the planting board to make furrows, and then plant the seeds ¼ inch deep, ½ inch apart, with 12 inches between the rows. When the seedlings are 3 to 4 inches high, I thin them out to their final spacing of 3 to 4 inches in the rows. In a month or 6 weeks, I can expect to have small turnips ready for harvest. The pungent greens are good in salads.

CONTAINER GARDENING

Growing vegetables in containers is both satisfying and a lot of fun. Container gardening is the perfect solution for apartment and condominium dwellers, or for any gardeners who are short on growing space. Even gardeners who do have ample space are not always blessed with perfect growing conditions. In some yards, for instance, the sun may not shine on plantable areas, but blazes down, instead, on driveways, decks, and other service areas. With container gardening culture, it's possible to take the plants to the sun. Container gardening is as versatile as it is helpful, too. Just about any vegetable — even sweet corn — can be grown in containers.

Some of the gardening guidelines for growing good vegetables also hold true for those grown in containers. First of all, they must be in a location that receives at least 6 hours of sunlight each day — *direct* sunlight. In addition, the soil must be good, one that holds water but drains well, supplies plenty of nutrients, and breathes. And like plants in the garden, plants in containers must be fed.

There *are* some differences between conventional culture and container gardening. The

Container culture makes vegetable gardening possible for urban apartment-dwellers and anyone else who's short of space. As you can see at left, there's no shortage of varieties suited to container growing. ◄

Container-grown plants need more frequent watering than those grown in garden soil. A hose-end attachment that creates a superfine spray is ideal.

biggest, I think, is that container-grown plants need more water. Because their pots are exposed to sun and air, plants in containers dry out more quickly than those in the soil. They need more frequent watering, and I often water my container crops daily during peak growing. This frequent watering washes away fertilizer and other nutrients in the soil, so feeding must also be more frequent. I feed plants in containers with slow-release fertilizer at the time of planting, and continue feeding weekly through the growing season with a complete (20-20-20) water-soluble fertilizer.

Soil, of course, is as important to plants in containers as it is to those in the ground. Filling many containers with soil can be both troublesome and expensive if you have to buy every pound from a garden center or nursery. I've learned to make my own mix for container culture, both because I plant a lot of container crops and because I like the satisfaction of creating my own "special blend." To make the mix, I blend in a wheelbarrow equal parts of sifted garden soil (run through a ½-inch mesh), sphagnum peat moss, and coarse builder's sand. The peat moss holds moisture. The sand assures good drainage. The soil brings a host of nutritious organic matter to the mix. This is a good, heavy mix that will support heavily fruited crops like tomatoes, peppers, and squash. For vegetables like lettuce, chard, and any others in containers that might be moved around often, I substitute perlite for the builder's sand. The perlite is much lighter, and serves the same function as the sand, promoting good drainage. A tip here that I've learned the hard way: Fill large containers where they will ultimately be positioned. If you have to move them after they're full, they'll be pretty heavy. Finally, with certain crops that are prone to diseases — eggplant, say — I use a commercial soilless growing medium.

When choosing containers, I let my creative urges run free. Some are utilitarian, some are beautiful, some economical. All have a place. Terra-cotta is the classic choice, for good reasons. It's elegant, with a natural look that blends with any environment. Terra-cotta is practical, too. It's heavy enough that it won't blow over in a strong wind with a heavy load of fruit. It also breathes well, and that is good for the plants. Terra-cotta does have a few drawbacks, though. Its breathability means that the rate of water loss is increased, and *that* means more frequent watering. Terra-cotta is brittle, too, and can break easily if dropped, whacked with a hoe, or subjected to a cracking frost.

I also like whiskey barrel halves for container culture. Their rustic good looks appeal to me, and they hold a lot of soil. They're readily available from garden supply houses, nurseries, and hardware stores, and they'll last almost as long as terra-cotta. I've discovered, by the way, that they're considerably less expensive when bought whole, rather than cut in half. It's no chore at all to snap a line around their middle with a chalked string and then saw them in half, using either a power saw or a handsaw. I especially like whiskey barrels placed in the garden at the ends of rows, with vegetables and flowers planted in them.

Recently, I discovered fiberglass containers. The best of these are richly adorned with nice detailing and, even better,

Whiskey barrels make excellent vegetable-gardening containers. Place large containers like these where you want them *before* filling with soil!

Zucchini grown in a container can be just as vigorous and healthy as that grown in the garden itself, as this Burpee's Hybrid shows.

are *very* light. Fiberglass being what it is, they'll last for years. They're a bit expensive, but their longevity should offset that initial expense. They're just the thing to dress up formal areas like decks and porches.

I've also collected, over the years, a number of nursery cans of both metal and plastic. These make fine pots for vegetables, too, when I recycle them after they've held a shrub or tree. No matter what kind of container I choose, I make sure that there are several holes at least ½ inch in diameter in the bottom, to assure good drainage so that the plants won't drown. And I'll admit that I don't really have a favorite type of container. Each has its place in the yard or garden, and I make use of them all, as the location requires.

Size is as important as type when choosing containers. I think that most gardeners err by not giving their plants enough soil volume in which to grow and mature. It's hard even for the veteran gardener to remember just how large a 6-inch tomato seedling will become. When I select containers, I'm perfectly content to err on the side of excess. I like containers that will hold at least 5 gallons of soil, and, because I like to mix flowers with the vegetables, most of my containers are even larger than this. It's true, too, that a large container means less frequent watering and fertilizing.

After I've drilled the holes in any new pots that don't have them, I fill them with my soil mix or soilless medium to within 1 inch of the top. When the plants are in place and watered, the soil level will drop another inch, and that will leave plenty of room for future watering.

Breeders have devoted a lot of attention in recent years to developing varieties that are suited to small-space and container culture. Thus we now have cucumbers and squash that grow on short vines. Those are only two examples, and I study the catalogs every year to keep up with the latest advances in container varieties. One new tomato variety that's pleased me in containers is Park's Better Bush. It's well named because it does have a very compact bush habit but fruits heavily. One plant, alone, will fill a half whiskey barrel.

Container cauliflower, thriving in half a whiskey tub. A key to successful container culture is giving plant roots sufficient room. Too big a container is better than too small.

Champion is another good tomato variety for container growing. I stay away from the cherry types and the beefsteak tomatoes because the plants just grow too large. Peppers are great in containers, too. I've been happy with Gypsy and Ace, and I ring the pepper plants in their containers with annual flowers that will cascade over the rims: alyssum, nierembergia, browallia, petunias, and dwarf small-flowered zinnias. A single stake for the pepper plant in each container keeps it standing tall under a heavy fruit set. Eggplant also shines in pots, especially with soilless growing medium, which assures they'll be spared the ravages of verticillium wilt. Eggplants are beautiful dressed with purple alyssum. I'm never afraid to show my vegetables off, displaying them as proudly around the yard as if they were ornamentals. Their colors and textures enhance any piece of land.

Most of the brassicas, especially broccoli, cauliflower, and cabbage, will do well in containers. I've grown combinations of Premium Crop broccoli and Little Gem lettuce in the spring garden with excellent results. White Sails cauliflower, grown with a decorative fringe of Red Sails lettuce, is another striking combination. And a bold planting of Brussels sprouts with hardy kale at their base will last right through the cool of fall.

Cucumbers also do well in containers, and we benefit now from the breeders who have shortened cukes' vines and given us bushlike behavior. Because they trail out over the pot (you could stake them upright, but why bother?), I like to grow an upright, strong an-

Strawberries have long been a favorite of container gardeners. The berries are easily protected from birds, and, kept off the ground, are less prone to rot.

nual like large-flowered zinnias to add a strong vertical contrast. The same arrangement works beautifully with summer squash.

Have you ever thought of okra in a container? A recent All-America winner called Blondy is a dwarf variety well suited to container culture. It's beautiful, too, with its hibiscuslike flowers. Lettuce and Swiss chard do well in pots, and carrots will, too, if you give them a tailored, stone-free soil.

Here are two last tips for growing vegetables in containers. If plants are positioned against a wall, make sure to rotate the pots so that the growing stems don't start leaning toward the sun. And consider putting *very* large containers on dollies, which makes turning and moving much easier on the human back.

The gardener's bench for overseeing the vegetable garden is highlighted by brilliant red azaleas. A bit too much time sitting has given the weeds a chance to grow, but they'll soon be looked after.

MAY

MAY

If forced to choose my most satisfying gardening month, I would probably pick May. Everything growing is still young, vigorous, and unblemished, at least in the beginning of the month — living proof of that old saw about hope springing eternal. The weather has stabilized nicely by now, and shirtsleeves are the uniform more often than not. And in May, *everything* needs attention. I have plenty of crops up and growing in the garden. The greenhouse and windowsills are filled with seedlings. Cold frame lettuce needs watering and venting. Most important, perhaps, is the warming soil, which by midmonth will support my most delicate crops.

May is also the month in which I take the first spring harvests of asparagus, lettuce, radishes, and spinach. With planting and harvesting going on at the same time there is a symmetry, a bringing together of beginning and end, that appeals to me very much. I don't lose sight, though, of my goal of season-long productivity. Thus I'll be keeping tabs on my succession plantings of lettuce, and making sure that long-season crops like leeks and winter squash receive careful attention.

Rewarding though it is, May is not totally carefree, being the month when pests come on strong. Leaf miners and Colorado potato beetles can gain a foothold in May, as can aphids and flea beetles. I pay very careful attention to all the crops when I'm in the garden at this time of year. My use of physical barriers, varietal selection, and black plastic mulch has greatly reduced insect problems. A few bugs always manage to sneak in, though, and I deal with these by removing them manually or with organic pesticides. Four-legged pests will also visit in May. During the 1985 season, in fact, I had fine early crops of peas, cabbage, and broccoli nibbled to nubbins in *one night* by woodchucks. A whole family of the toothy creatures burrowed under my chain-link fence and devastated the garden. Now I make sure that the fencing extends down at least 12 inches into the ground.

Start Indoors
Brussels sprouts
Pumpkins
Winter squash

Transplant
Brussels sprouts
Eggplant
Lettuce

Plant in Garden
Beans
Cauliflower
Corn
Cucumbers
Leeks
Lettuce
Melons
Summer squash
Tomatoes
Winter squash

Fertilize
Carrots
Chinese cabbage
Kohlrabi
Peas
Potatoes

Screen
Beets
Cauliflower
Cucumbers
Potatoes

Harvest
Asparagus
Lettuce
Radishes
Spinach

Mulch
Asparagus

By early May, this asparagus is almost table ready.

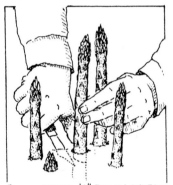

SLICE SHOOTS ½" BELOW SURFACE

Asparagus The whole "Victory Garden" crew was dining at a fine Liverpool restaurant one evening after a long day's shooting at a nearby gardening exposition called the Garden Festival. Our host this night was a representative from that exposition, and, while the staff served our meal, he explained to us how very important asparagus growing was to this particular part of England. He launched into a detailed description of how meticulous asparagus farmers lovingly blanch the already-tender stalks by hilling up soil early on in the spring as shoots appear, causing the stems to stretch and stretch, creating unique, pale stalks at least 12 inches long. So involved did he become in extolling the virtues of English asparagus that he failed to notice, on the plate at his elbow, half a dozen superb examples of that very crop. It was hard to keep from smiling, because we had all been munching contentedly on our own asparagus throughout his explanation.

May is the month when I begin harvesting spears from my own established bed in the Victory Garden. I look for shoots that are as thick as a piece of chalk (about ½ inch in diameter), 6 to 12 inches tall, and in tight bud. I use a sharp penknife to slice the shoots off about ½ inch below the soil surface — a trick I learned from my English asparagus-growing friends. Leaving the exposed cut protected by the soil lessens the likelihood of later disease or insect damage.

Asparagus loses its sweetness quickly after harvesting, but it is possible to slow that loss somewhat by setting the freshly harvested shoots stem-down in a dish of water in the refrigerator. I almost hesitate to pass on that advice, however, because one of my reasons for gardening is to enjoy the taste of vegetables when they are *fresh*. I much prefer to hustle the shoots from plant to pot, steam them lightly, and dine like a king.

The new asparagus bed planted in April will need hand-weeding in May. It must be done with caution, so that the delicate crowns and shoots are left undisturbed. When the weeding is complete, I mulch the sprouts with salt marsh hay, shredded wood bark, or 2 inches of grass clippings to suppress weeds and conserve moisture. Two inches of grass is the maximum, by the way. A thicker layer invites matting, which can allow too much heat to build up underneath, damaging or killing the tender young plants. If I do any further weeding or cultivation, I'm very careful in this bed, because the crowns' delicate rootlets can radiate as much as 2 feet from the central plant and they're only 4 to 6 inches down. Easy does it!

Beans I direct-seed varieties of both bush and pole beans in late May, only after I'm absolutely sure that the soil has warmed to at least 60 degrees. This is important enough for me to use and refer to my soil thermometer before sowing the beans. If the soil is too cool, the bean seeds will lie there and rot. Before planting, I treat seeds of both types with legume

inoculant, using the same method described for peas in March. I prepare their raised beds a little differently than most other crops', forking in 5-10-5 fertilizer at the rate of 2, rather than 5, pounds for every 100 square feet of bed. This reduction is made possible by the beans' nitrogen-fixing ability.

For pole beans, I plant a single row, spacing the seeds 2 inches apart and 1 inch deep. For bush beans, I use wide-row planting, scattering the seeds 1 to 2 inches apart, 1 inch deep, in a row 6 inches wide. I cover all the freshly planted seeds with 1 inch of soilless medium and water them in well. If the early growth of either variety appears slow, it's probably because the cool soil is retarding intake of nutrients. This problem is easily remedied with a dose of balanced (20-20-20) water-soluble fertilizer at full strength.

I've tried all kinds of support systems for pole beans in the Victory Garden: single poles and stakes, A-frames, and so on. After all is said and done, I've come to like wide-mesh nylon netting with 4x4-inch or 4x6-inch openings strung between 8-foot metal snow-fence stakes driven 18 inches into the ground. The stakes and netting go up quickly and are easy to remove

With a well-used hoe, I'm opening a wide row for seeding bush beans. A casual 1- to 2-inch spacing is fine.

and clean come fall. The netting's large openings make harvesting simple. I erect this netting above my row of pole beans at planting time. No thinning of these seedlings is necessary, and in 2 weeks I'll have small plants getting their first grip on the bottom of my netting.

Beets The beets I sowed in April will have produced healthy seedlings by May. I like to thin the seedlings now, before they get too large, leaving 2 to 3 inches between plants. If I have gaps elsewhere in the garden that I'd like to fill, I can use these seedlings. They'll transplant just fine if I moisten the soil and then lift them out carefully with a plant label. After thinning, I water the beets with liquid fertilizer, and then I erect protective screening.

Don't think May is too soon for screening. May is the month when leaf miners make their first appearance, and they like nothing better than to feast on the young, tender beet leaves. The first sign of miners is white egg case clusters on the backs of the foliage. Later on, the symptoms show up as fine tunneling that soon turns to limp, gray, mushy leaves; the miners are there chewing their way through the inner tissue of the leaves. I've found it best to screen early, before any signs of the miners

These young, well-spaced beet seedlings are almost weed free thanks to salt marsh hay mulch.

appear. Having experimented with various systems, I've settled on supporting hoops of #12 wire with polyester fabric draped over them. I make the hoops long enough to give 12 inches of clearance over the plants at their highest point, and I bury the borders of the netting all the way around the edge of the bed. This barrier system has several advantages over chemical applications. For one thing, once the barrier is in place, my plants are protected — period. No repeated application required. Perhaps more important, the barrier is hazardous to no one's health.

Brussels Sprouts There is nothing I love more than a plate of freshly steamed Brussels sprouts anointed with golden, dripping butter. They're a superb vegetable for the Thanksgiving feast, and my affinity for them was frustrated somewhat by my early experience in the Victory Garden. For several seasons I started the Brussels sprouts as early as possible. When this produced less than satisfactory harvests, I began starting them much later. That approach worked no better. It took a visit to northern California, where I saw Brussels sprouts thriving in cold, coastal regions, to put me on the right track. I know now that the key is to have healthy plants with established sprouts by the time cool fall weather arrives. That means (in my region) starting the plants indoors in mid-May. I plant the seeds in 4-inch pots filled with soilless medium. The seeds are covered with ¼ inch of the medium and bottom-watered until thoroughly moist. Seven days over the heat pad at 75 degrees produces seedlings, which I keep on a sunny windowsill until their true leaves appear. This is usually in early June, and that's when I transplant them to individual cell-packs and bottom-water again with half-strength water-soluble fertilizer.

I have grown Jade Cross E, Prince Marvel, and Achilles with success in the Victory Garden, but Jade Cross E has been the most consistent performer of all the varieties.

Carrots The seeds I sowed in April will have produced, by now, wispy, grasslike carrot seedlings. I thin those seedlings before they are 2 inches tall. If they're allowed to grow any larger, removing them will disturb the threadlike taproots that are left behind. My strategy is to water or wait for a good rain and then thin when the soil is still wet and loose. Because I use pelleted seed most of the time now, my thinning chores are greatly simplified. If I've sown a variety that is not available in pelleted seed or in seed tapes, though, it's back to the tried-and-true methods from the old days. This work must be done with two hands, and, if the seedlings are very close together, it's a matter of holding one delicately with the fingers of my left hand while I pluck out a neighbor with my right, leaving a final spacing of 1 inch between seedlings. I'm careful not to compress the soil around the stems of the remaining seedlings.

A well-grown Brussels sprout plant in late summer. ▶

Carrots at just the right stage for thinning. ▼

After thinning, I side-dress the beds with 5-10-5 fertilizer at the rate of 5 pounds per 100 square feet of bed. I spread a band of fertilizer by hand on either side of the carrot rows, then scratch it into the soil with a three-pronged cultivator, taking care to keep the fertilizer from coming into contact with any of the seedlings.

Cauliflower   After 5 days of hardening-off in the Victory Garden cold frame, my cauliflower seedlings are ready for planting in the garden during the first week of May. Because cauliflower (like broccoli, Brussels sprouts, cabbage, kohlrabi, and certain other brassica family members) is susceptible to clubroot, I try to rotate this crop so that it's planted in a bed where other likely clubroot victims haven't grown for three or four seasons. In the Victory Garden, clubroot has been a major problem, and this rotation is one of my primary defenses (along with liming the planting holes) against the disease. I recognize that it's not as critical a problem in all parts of the country as in mine, but for those who are victimized as I've been, rotation and liming have proven effective safeguards.

The seedlings are planted an inch deeper than they were growing in their cell-packs, and before setting them into their holes I work in half a handful of ground limestone per hole to keep the pH up around 7.5 and stave off the dreaded clubroot. Spacing for the cauliflower seedlings is 18 inches between plants and 24 inches between the rows. When they're in place, I give all the seedlings a watering-in with balanced water-soluble fertilizer diluted to half strength. To protect them from the variety of insect pests that can attack cauliflower seedlings, I set up hoop-supported netting now. This one-time task takes the place of maggot mats and chemical insecticides.

Chinese Cabbage   In May, the Chinese cabbage crop needs fertilizing, weeding, and watering. The idea is to keep the plants growing fast to provide a June harvest before sizzling weather sets in. I fertilize the plants twice this month with complete liquid fertilizer at full strength. I make sure that they receive at least 1 inch of water per week, too. But the water or rain brings its own problems: hungry slugs. The first symptom is a number of dime-sized holes in the outermost leaves. Checking the plants and hand-picking these slimy vegetarians is the safest way to protect the crop. This means a night patrol or two, because that's when the slugs are most active. Weeding is another effective defense, because a neat, well-weeded bed leaves them fewer places to hide.

Corn   The corn I started indoors in April will be ready for planting in the garden after 5 days in the cold frame for hardening-off. Corn is planted in blocks, by variety, and I make each block 8

On the labels: CHINESE CABBAGE Nagoda 50 / CHINESE CABBAGE 2 Seasons Hybrid

Getting to the weeds among the Chinese cabbage is a necessary chore to ensure a good harvest — I also keep my fingers crossed for cool weather.

feet square. The blocks are located on the north or west side of the garden so that the plants, which eventually grow to 6 or 8 feet, will not shade other crops. Block planting also allows for wind pollination (corn is a wind-pollinated crop), which would occur less efficiently or not at all if the corn plants were set out in single rows. With the advent of the new supersweet sh_2 varieties, I have had to adopt new spacing techniques. Various catalogs recommend different spacing requirements between supersweet and standard varieties, but I've found that 25 feet is really a minimum to keep the two types from cross-pollinating. If cross-pollination between supersweet and standard varieties does occur, *both* are spoiled, so it's worth working hard to avoid contact.

Corn is one of the few crops, by the way, for which I revert to flat-bed culture. Before laying out the beds, I work in 5 pounds of 10-10-10 fertilizer for every 100 square feet of bed — corn is a very heavy feeder. Then I string an 8-foot line every 2 feet for the 4 rows that will make up each bed. I mark each row by sprinkling limestone over the smooth-raked soil. When I have

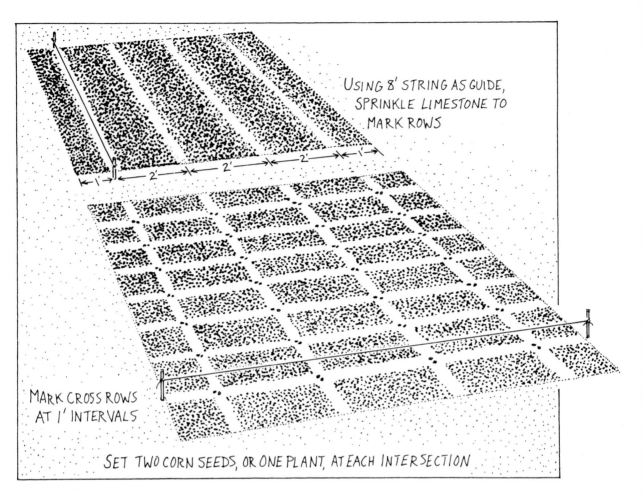

USING 8' STRING AS GUIDE, SPRINKLE LIMESTONE TO MARK ROWS

MARK CROSS ROWS AT 1' INTERVALS

SET TWO CORN SEEDS, OR ONE PLANT, AT EACH INTERSECTION

the rows marked out, I go back and string my 8-foot lines across the row markings at 1-foot intervals. (This is easier drawn than written, so see the accompanying illustration.) I mark this second set of lines with limestone, too, thus ending up with a design like a tic-tac-toe diagram. Wherever two lines intersect, I set in a corn plant. This gives me a spacing of 1 foot in rows and 2 feet between rows, which is more real estate between rows than you'll find recommended in some sources. But I have discovered over the seasons that corn — as well as a good many other crops in the Victory Garden — does much better if the plants are given ample elbow room. For a time I did experiment with extremely close spacing (1x1 foot) but ended up with stunted plants and frayed nerves — hilling-up and other work was inconvenient. The crowded plants seemed to be fighting for light, water, and nutrients, and I found it hard to do the necessary cultivation with them jammed in too tightly. I've come to favor the more spacious 1x2-foot spacing, which has produced happier plants and, in this case at least, a happier gardener.

In early May, after the corn seedlings have spent 5 days hardening off in the cold frame, I set them into the ground. Because

The corn seedlings I started in peat strips are hardening off in the cold frame before their move to the garden. ▶

May   139

the peat pots will dry out if their tops are left exposed to air, I peel the tops off.

In mid-May, I sow a second generation of corn outdoors, using varieties like Butter and Sugar, Butterfruit, Silver Queen, Kandy Korn, and Symphony. I sow 2 seeds 2 inches deep every 1 foot along the row, and thin to the stronger seedling in a couple of weeks.

Cucumbers The cucumber seedlings I started in April will be moved into the cold frame for 5 days of hardening-off in mid-May. While they're doing that, I prepare the cucumber beds. Cucumbers are heavy feeders, and they like richly organic soil, so I work in 2 inches of compost and augment that with 5 pounds of slow-release 14-14-14 fertilizer for every 100 square feet of bed. After those amendments have been turned in and the soil raked smooth, I cover the raised bed with black plastic, burying the borders under the soil all around. The plastic warms the soil, saves moisture, and cuts weeding.

After their stay in the cold frame, I plant cucumber seedlings through 4-inch squares cut in the plastic every 12 inches. I peel the tops off the cucumbers' peat pots (to keep the porous peat pots from wicking away moisture from the soil), and set them into the soil at the same depth they were growing.

People with large gardens can grow cucumbers on the ground without difficulty, but the same crop can be grown in about one-fifth the space with some kind of vertical support. After a good bit of experimenting, I've settled on an A-frame support made of redwood, secured with staples and weatherproof glue, and covered with galvanized dog wire stapled to the frame. The wire has 4x6-inch openings. The frame is 8 feet long and 6 feet high, and is anchored into the raised bed with long steel reinforcing rods that extend 16 inches into the ground. There's another advantage to growing cukes vertically, by the way: They grow nice and straight. Whenever I grow cukes on the ground, many will curl. That has no effect on flavor, but who really wants bent cukes? More important, perhaps, keeping the fruit off the soil reduces the likelihood of rot.

Though I don't do so, it's possible to sow cucumber seeds directly in the soil. Timing is very important. The seeds won't germinate at all in soil cooler than 50 degrees, and will germinate very slowly in soil that's 68 degrees. Seventy degrees or warmer is best, and that's not usually found until early summer. If I were to direct-seed cukes, I'd fortify the beds and lay the black plastic down 2 weeks before I wanted to plant, then monitor the soil temperature with a thermometer to be safe. When the soil was at least 70 degrees, I would sow the seeds through 4-inch squares cut out of the plastic. The seeds would be sowed in pairs, 2 inches apart and 1 inch deep, spaced every 12 inches. I'd cover them with ¼ inch of soilless medium, water well, and keep moist until germination.

Space-hungry cucumber seedlings are kept in bounds on the Victory Garden A-frame trellis — one very good way to get the most out of the garden. ◄

Early tomatoes are warmed with plastic-wrapped cages and spun polyester fabric temporarily pulled off PVC tubing. Letting tomatoes sprawl like this is not my preferred method, but was suggested for early determinate types, which crop early and then die off.

Cucumber beetles have been somewhat troublesome in the Victory Garden, and I've found an effective defense. It is a weekly dusting with the organic pesticide rotenone.

Eggplant My seedlings will be at least 2 inches high by now, and showing their first true leaves — the sign that it's time to transplant them into individual cell-packs filled with soilless medium. I bottom-water with water-soluble fertilizer diluted to half strength, protect them from full sun for a day, and then move them to my sunniest windowsill. In June I'll set them into the cold frame for 5 days of hardening-off before moving them into the open ground or into containers.

Kohlrabi My kohlrabi seedlings will be up by now, and it's time to thin them down to a final spacing of 6 inches in the rows. They are heavy feeders, and to make doubly sure that they receive all that they require, I give them a generous drink of complete water-soluble fertilizer around the middle of the month.

Leeks In early May, I move my leek seedlings into the cold frame for 5 days of hardening-off. While they're doing so, I excavate the leek trench. The key to good leeks is blanching, and the key to good blanching is trenching. I *have* seen it done other ways. At the Royal Horticultural Society's Harvest Show in London, gardeners produced 4-foot leeks with 18 inches of beautifully blanched stalk by growing them in flue tiles — the kind used to line chimneys. Superrich soil filled the tubular tiles, and the resulting leeks were indeed spectacular. They also required a great deal of TLC, as do most of the eye-popping specialty crops grown for such international shows. Trenching is a more traditional method of blanching leeks, and I've been perfectly satisfied with it.

I dig my trench 9 inches deep and as wide as my spade, about 8 inches. I put half the soil I remove on one side of the trench, and half on the other. Into the bottom of the trench goes 2 inches of compost, which I blend with an equal amount of soil. When I set the leek seedlings into the trench, I use a trick I learned from master gardener Peter Chan, certainly one of the most knowledgeable small-space gardeners on earth and a keen observer of how plants perform. Peter showed me that leeks send leaves out from their stalks in only two directions. Thus it is possible to align the seedlings so that all the leaves extend the same way. This keeps them from interfering with the growth of neighboring plants, provides maximum exposure to sun and air, and allows for a close spacing. Over the seasons, I've found that orienting the leaves about 15 degrees off the parallel line of the row makes maximum use of space and still keeps the leeks from touching. I space them 9 inches apart in the rows, and plant them to the depth of the union between the roots and leaves.

Excavating my leek trench against a string line helps keep the bed neat. ▶

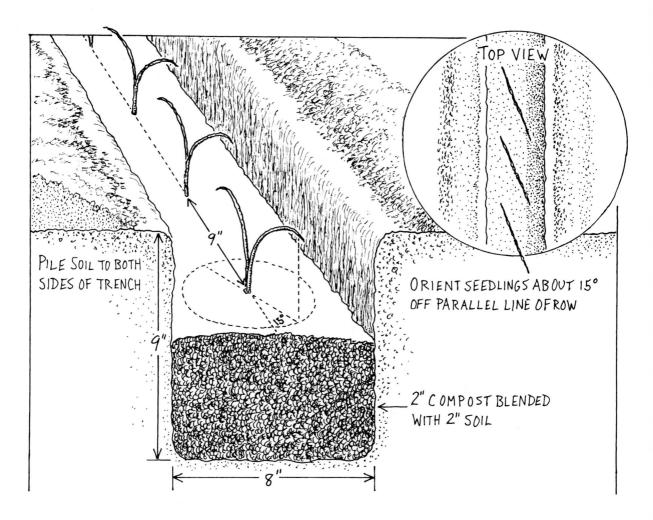

TOP VIEW

PILE SOIL TO BOTH SIDES OF TRENCH

9"

9"

8"

ORIENT SEEDLINGS ABOUT 15° OFF PARALLEL LINE OF ROW

15°

2" COMPOST BLENDED WITH 2" SOIL

Finally, I water the seedlings in with complete water-soluble fertilizer (20-20-20) diluted to half strength. The remaining soil standing beside the trench will be used to hill-up around the leeks as they grow in subsequent months.

Lettuce   In May I'll be harvesting the lettuce from my cold frame, and, a little later, from the garden itself. I pop in lettuce seedlings whenever a space appears between tomatoes, peppers, and eggplants, thereby assuring a steady supply of succulent, delicious greens all month long. All the lettuce that I plant now will be cell-pack seedlings 3 to 4 weeks old that I have been growing indoors, using hot-weather-tolerant varieties like Slowbolt, Summer Bibb, and Webb's Wonderful.

Melons   No description of melon planting would be complete without reference to "Victory Garden" contest finalist Reverend Ralph Miller and his "zoodoo" melons. Reverend Miller lives up north in New Hampshire, not generally considered prime melon country. From his garden, though, come some of the sweetest,

Dinner for two grows happily between cabbage and broccoli. ▶

juiciest melons I've ever tasted. This clergyman, you see, lives not far from a petting zoo that houses zebras, antelopes, and many other species of exotic fauna, all of which produce a steady supply of high-octane manure. The Miller melon patch receives hearty doses of this "zoodoo," and that, according to the reverend, is responsible for the super melons he grows in a decidedly less-than-super climate. The story points up an important fact about melon culture, namely that this crop requires a very rich soil to thrive.

In early May, I move my Victory Garden melon seedlings out to the cold frame for 5 days of hardening-off. While they're toughening up, I prepare their raised bed. I amended the soil the previous fall to bring the pH in line, and added 2 inches of manure or compost for a rich, organic composition. Now, before planting the seedlings, I fork in 2 inches of compost and 5 pounds of slow-release 14-14-14 fertilizer for every 100 square feet of bed space. I rake the bed into shape, then cover it with black plastic, burying the borders all around. When I'm ready to plant the melon seedlings, I cut 4-inch squares out of the plastic, spacing the squares every 2 feet. After peeling back the tops of the peat pots (to keep them from wicking away moisture), I set them in at the same depth they were growing. Then they're watered in well with half-strength water-soluble fertilizer.

That's how I do it in the Victory Garden, but it is possible to sow melon seeds directly in the soil. With that method, I would wait until the soil was 70 degrees or higher. Two seeds would be spaced 24 inches apart, and sowed ½ inch deep through 4-inch squares in the black plastic mulch. I would water them in and, when the seedlings were 2 to 3 inches tall, thin to the stronger seedlings, leaving a final spacing of 2 feet.

Peas   About this time in their growth cycle, my peas' nitrogen-fixing ability may be impaired by cool soil. If I see yellowing leaves, I give them a drink of complete water-soluble fertilizer.

I also watch the tall Sugar Snaps to make sure they're getting enough support. If they seem to be wandering around, I'll tie extra string at 12-inch intervals parallel to the ground. This will help to tuck the vines into the netting and keep weak clingers securely attached to my supports.

Potatoes   My potatoes are ready, in May, for their first hilling-up. The foliage will be at least 6 inches tall by now, and the very young potatoes forming on the roots need protection from the sun. If they're exposed to light, they will turn green, and a poisonous substance called solanine will be produced in their skins.

Hilling-up is easy. I begin by side-dressing each plant with half a handful of 5-10-5 fertilizer. Then I fill their trench with 4 inches of soil, mixing in the fertilizer at the same time and being

In May the Sugar Snap peas are well up on their 6-foot nylon trellis against an old, sweetly fragrant lilac backdrop. ◄

The row of potatoes on the left has been filled in and hilling-up will begin shortly. The row on the right will be filled to level when the plants get a few inches taller.

careful not to cover the growing points. The soil cover keeps roots deep and cool, and the tubers forming up are completely protected from harmful sunlight.

I'm also keeping an eye out for the Colorado potato beetle. If I see just a few of the beetle's bright orange eggs under my leaves, I'll pick them off by hand or remove the affected leaves. This ravenous insect is the bane of all potato growers. A friend of mine on Nantucket Island grows potatoes for the restaurant market. He simply has given up trying to control the Colorado bugs. "So what if they get the foliage?" he reasons, "I only want small potatoes anyway."

I suppose giving in to these nasty little creatures is one way of dealing with the problem, but I don't lose gracefully here in the Victory Garden. An idea that shows promise is covering potatoes with the spun polyester fabric that I use to protect other crops from insects. Although a few bugs emerge from the soil under the covering, the fabric protects against flying invaders. One interesting side effect of this tactic, however, is that the beetles move on to their second-favorite meal in the garden — eggplant. Thus I have to be very vigilant after I put the fabric in place, to make sure that one crop's gain is not another's loss.

Pumpkins When I was a child, I would go out into our family's pumpkin patch and walk among the pumpkins, which seemed huge. They weren't real giants — probably in the 10- to 20-pound range — but my vantage point was a lot lower then. Giant pumpkins did not disappear when I outgrew the family patch, though. Not long ago I saw a pumpkin grown by Howard

With luck, May's seeding of pumpkin will produce the perfect candidate for the Halloween jack o' lantern.

Dill of Nova Scotia that weighed nearly 500 pounds! Giant-pumpkin-growing has become quite a craze, in fact, and 400-pound monsters are common sights at contest weigh-ins. The gardeners who produce these giants work up superfertile soil, and allow each plant to produce only one pumpkin by plucking all other flowers from the vines. Variety selection is also crucial: Atlantic Giant is the one that produces the real monsters.

I haven't room in the Victory Garden for giant pumpkins. In fact, I barely have room for the normal varieties. This long-season crop takes up a lot of space, and is really better suited to very large gardens than to compact operations like mine. I get by, though, with varieties like Spirit Hybrid, New England Pie, and Jackpot, all of which produce shorter vines and 7- to 10-pound fruit.

In May, I start the pumpkin seeds in 3-inch peat pots, sowing 2 seeds per pot early in the month. It's possible to direct-seed pumpkins in the garden in May but, as with many Victory Garden crops, I prefer to start the seedlings indoors. This gives me better control over temperature, moisture, and light early on. The seedlings are protected from pests and diseases, and critical garden space is left free for spring crops like lettuce and radishes. I use my heating pad to give the seeds their ideal germination temperature of 75 degrees, making sure that I don't let their growing medium dry out. Consistent watering right from the start is very important to pumpkin development.

If I were to sow pumpkin seed directly into the soil, I would warm it up by laying black plastic down several weeks before my June 1 planting date. Then, come June, I'd cut 4-inch squares 24 inches apart in the plastic, and plant 2 seeds 1 inch deep in each square. They'd be watered in and then left alone for 2 weeks, when I'd thin to the stronger seedling.

Radishes In May I enjoy an excellent radish harvest, taking the radishes from the soil as soon as they're large enough to eat. I like to pluck them out by their greens, rinse with the hose, and munch them right there. I know that spring radishes won't hold their peak quality very long, so I harvest the whole crop when they're ready, even if the result is more than I can use right then. Stored in plastic bags, they'll keep nicely in the refrigerator for days.

In August, I'll plant my fall radish crop. Until then, the weather will just be too hot for successful radish growing.

Spinach I'm harvesting beautiful, mature spinach from the Victory Garden by now, and I use a technique that leaves the grit in the garden, where it belongs. Instead of yanking out the spinach plant root and all, I cut the plants off at ground level. This gives me the leaves, which I want for salads and cooking, but does not shower sand and soil over the remaining plants.

This month the spinach is ready for harvest — just waiting to be snipped off. ▶

White Icicle radishes. ▼

Summer Squash   During the middle of May, I move my summer squash seedlings into the cold frame for 5 days of hardening-off. While they're doing so, I add 5 pounds of slow-release 14-14-14 fertilizer to their bed. Squash are heavy feeders and will need every bit of nutrient material I can work into that soil. Next, I stretch black plastic over the bed and bury the edges of the plastic sheet. Then I cut 4-inch squares in the plastic, giving a single row of plants spaced 4 feet in the bed.

Summer squash and zucchini seeds can be planted directly in the soil, though my practice is to start the seedlings indoors. For direct sowing, I'd plan on waiting at least a week after the last spring frost date, and on making sure that soil temperature is at least 60 degrees. Black plastic, laid down 2 weeks before planting day, will warm the soil much more rapidly. For planting, I'd cut 4-inch squares in the plastic and sow 2 seeds per hole, 4 feet apart. When the seedlings were up, I'd thin to the stronger plant.

Tomatoes   I aim for a late-May planting of my main-crop tomato seedlings. That timing puts a month between them and the last expected spring frost, and gives them 60- to 65-degree soil temperatures as well. Air temperatures will be relatively stable in the 70- to 75-degree range — ideal for tomato seedlings.

On May 20, I set my seedlings into the cold frame for 5 days of hardening-off. While they're adjusting, I work 5 pounds of 5-10-5 fertilizer for every 100 square feet of area into their raised beds. For planting in the raised beds, I make 2 staggered rows with 2 feet between rows and 3 feet between the plants themselves. I set the plants in the soil right up to their true leaves, to encourage root formation all along the buried stem. They get a drink of balanced water-soluble fertilizer diluted to half strength, too.

If May or June weather turns inclement, I protect the seedlings with Wall O' Water towers. These are flexible polyethylene multichambered constructions that provide the last word in outdoor microclimate control. The Wall O' Water's tubes are filled with water, which gains heat during the day, creating a warmer miniclimate for the tomatoes. That heat is retained at night, moderating the cooler evening temperatures as well.

Now is also the time to consider support systems, and I will tell you that in my years of gardening, I've tried them all. I've let tomatoes sprawl on the ground, over hay, and on black plastic. I've trained them up single stakes. I've trained them up elaborate string trellis affairs, and along both single and multiple string runners to overhead wires. And I've used cages. Before I say which I like best, let me pass on a few lessons learned the hard way.

One thing I can confirm is that pruned, vertical tomato plants (using, say, two leaders on string to wire overhead) do ripen faster than those left to sprawl. They also suffer a reduced

At lilac and tulip time when most folks are just thinking about putting their tomatoes in, the pampered Victory Garden early crop is 3 to 4 feet tall and in flower.

yield. Even in the Victory Garden, I don't get something for nothing. In general, it's true that pruning hastens ripening at the expense of yield, and tomatoes are no exception to this rule. In very short season areas, it might make sense to use this method to avoid loss of late ripeners, but I don't use it in the Victory Garden.

I've also found that sprawling tomatoes on black plastic produce unequaled yield, but commandeer more real estate than I can afford to surrender. This method will cause some increase in fruit rot, too.

Another conclusion based on years of trial: Single stakes with single leaders are undesirable. This system reduces foliage cover too drastically, with poor production from each plant resulting.

After all is said and done, I have come to favor tomato cages. They make the very best use of available space by promoting vertical growth. The fruit, when it appears, is held aloft and thereby protected from feet, slugs, pests, and rot. Harvest from a cage is easier, requiring less bending and stooping. And cages create a neat garden that is visually pleasing. I think this is not

unimportant. A garden that creates a sense of order and beauty will be doubly rewarding, certainly more so than one that is only half a step removed from the weed patch.

I've tried the cages available from garden supply centers and seed catalogs, but they're too short. Most are only 4 feet tall, and my indeterminant varieties would routinely cascade up and over the tops of these cages. Now I make my own cages, 5 feet tall, from steel reinforcing wire with 4-inch openings. I buy the wire from masonry supply houses. For detailed tomato cage directions, see the feature titled "Victory Garden Structures." I put these cages in place as soon as the weather allows me to remove the Wall O' Water towers once and for all.

Winter Squash   Winter squash take twice as long, on average, to mature as summer squash, but in other ways they're quite similar. Both gobble up garden space with their long vines, and both are very heavy feeders. I tried solving the space problem by training vines up trellises, but supporting the very heavy fruit was just too difficult. More recently, I've been experimenting with bush varieties of winter squash that require

Concrete-reinforcing-wire cages will last a good many years and are my favorite way for training tomatoes. ◄

In this system, I've trained each tomato plant to a double leader and woven them in and out between sturdy twine strung on 8-foot-high snow fencing. ▲

about half the 10 or 20 square feet occupied by each plant of standard-vining varieties.

I want to set my winter squash seedlings into the garden on June 1, so I start them indoors on May 1, sowing 2 seeds per 3-inch peat pot filled with soilless medium, covering the seeds with ½ inch of medium, and then bottom-watering. (I use the peat pots because winter squash are very sensitive to transplant shock.) On the 75-degree heat pad the seeds will germinate in about 7 days. Once they're up, I move them to the sunniest, warmest spot I have, keeping the peat pots moist but not soaking. After 2 weeks, I'll thin to the stronger seedling in each pot, then let them grow in peace until the last week of the month, when they're moved to the cold frame for hardening-off.

It's also possible to direct-seed winter squash now. When the soil has warmed to at least 60 degrees, I prepare the squash beds by adding 2 inches of compost and 5 pounds of slow-release 14-14-14 fertilizer per 100 square feet of bed. Black plastic goes down next, and I bury the borders all around. I cut 4-inch squares out of the plastic, spacing every 5 feet for larger varieties and 3 feet for the smaller, bush varieties. Into each square cutout I plant 3 seeds ½ inch deep, allowing about 2 inches between seeds. They're covered with soilless medium and watered in well. The seeds in each cluster will germinate in about 7 days, and a week later I'll thin to the strongest seedling in each spot.

As far as varieties go, I'm very fond of Waltham Butternut, and not only because it was developed by Bob Young at our nearby suburban experiment station in Waltham, Massachusetts. This winter squash comes ready in 90 days, producing manageable 12-inch fruits with wonderfully sweet flesh. Waltham Butternut also peels easily, and is even somewhat resistant to vine borers. That's a lot to recommend it! Sweet Mama hybrid and Jersey Golden Acorn are more modest in their demand for space, and Jersey Golden Acorn has a fine, sweet flesh. Blue Hubbard, the classic New England squash, is — to me, at least — the tastiest of them all, and I grow a crop every year. Turk's Turban is a dramatic decorative addition to any garden, with flying-saucer-shaped fruits that mature into bright shades of red, yellow, white, and green.

Waltham Butternut — a real winner!

VICTORY GARDEN HERBS

Not surprisingly, herbs are some of the more enduring plants cultivated by man over the ages. They improve the subtlety of food, sweeten the air with beautiful fragrances, and for centuries have been used as healing agents. Their presence is long-lasting when dried and used in sachets and potpourris. They can decorate wreaths, and add graceful touches to table arrangements. My particular fondness is for those which supplement vegetables from the garden, so in the Victory Garden I grow herbs chosen for their usefulness in cooking. Sweet basil is an indispensable complement to tomatoes. Dill goes perfectly with cucumbers. Tarragon is a must for roast chicken. And chives brighten the taste of eggs.

I've reserved a small area for my culinary herbs, just off the back door of the house and literally steps away from the kitchen. I fear that if the herbs were 150 feet away in the main garden, their impromptu use would decrease dramatically. Herbs love sunshine, and this location gives them at least 6 hours of full sun. The best and most fragrant herbs are grown in full sun, under somewhat drier conditions than in the

The culinary herb garden just outside the kitchen door. ◄

A selection of sweet basil ready to be set in the garden.

vegetable garden. That's another reason why I think it's a good idea to give them their own spot, where water can be meted out more sparingly. The herbs in my kitchen garden do well with a pH of 6.5, and in fact will be content with a pH anywhere from 6.0 to 7.5. Good drainage is essential, so I ensured that with 2 inches of sand and peat moss when I prepared their bed. I also worked in compost (a couple of inches), because there will be both perennial and annual herbs in the bed and I want to get it in good shape at the time of creation. Any deficiencies will be harder to correct later on.

My herb garden is divided in half, and each bed measures 6

feet by 5 feet. I wanted a formal look to this garden, in part because it's traditional but also because it's next to the house. Herbs, by the way, enjoy a reputation for being a bit rank, and some do grow vigorously. But an untidy look is more the result of poor maintenance than any innate unruliness. There's no reason for an unattractive herb garden. Frequent "pinch-pruning" (the reason we grow these little wonders in the first place!) is usually enough to keep them in line.

To give the herb garden a sense of history, I planted a hedge of boxwood on the front border. The boxwood can't be used in the kitchen, but it is lovely to behold. I keep the hedge neatly trimmed at 1 foot high, and it is a very attractive first layer in my planting. The two beds are separated by a 2-foot-wide gravel pathway that provides easy access to all the herbs.

Sweet basil is an annual grown from seeds sown indoors in April. I follow the same indoor-seed-starting procedures for herbs that I use for vegetables (see the chapter titled "Steps to Victorious Gardening" for details). Basil will not tolerate any frost and even resents a chill, so I don't set it out into the garden until the middle of May. This 6-week jump indoors produces sturdy transplants for the garden. The thing to bear in mind with basil is that it will try very hard to go to flower and seed. While this is attractive, it shortens the herb's productive life, so I cut basil frequently, or use my forefinger and thumb to pinch off its topmost, succulent growth. Dark Opal is a handsome, deep-colored variety that is ornamental as well as useful. It will get stiff competition now from a 1987 All-America winner named Purple Ruffles. Another excellent, new variety that makes a wonderful edger to the herb garden and produces heavily for the table is Spicy Globe. This variety has a dwarf habit and most of the plants will hold to a tight ball shape that looks finely clipped but is, in fact, the herb's natural habit. As is the case with all the herbs I'll mention, basil can be purchased as started plants at garden centers or, as mentioned above, started from seed.

Chervil, an annual, is parsley's exuberant first cousin. It grows quickly and comes easily from seed. I sow seed directly in the ground at the end of April, and have harvest-ready plants in June. Chervil has a delicate, anise-licorice flavor that is best appreciated right after harvest. I make another sowing in a month because the plants tend to be short-lived. It's lovely and graceful in flower, and chervil will reseed if left to itself. I prefer to choose its location myself (the middle of the bed), so I keep the plants under control. Chervil does well in cool weather and, unlike most of the herbs, will do well in a bit of shade.

Chives' colorful bloom adds a pleasing touch to this perennial member of the onion family.

Chives are a hardy perennial, whose flowers add a rich purple color to an otherwise basically gray and green herb garden. Chives produce that mild onion flavor so indispensable for omelettes and chowders. The plants are started from seed indoors in March, for set-out in late April. About 15 to 20 seeds are sown in a 4-inch pot filled with soilless medium. I use one pot for each clump of chives I want. They're transplanted to their spot, where they grow together afterward. I sow 6 pots of garlic chives and 6 of regular chives as well. They're all harvested by cutting the tops with a knife or, better still, with scissors. If the plants go too long without harvesting, they'll form flower heads which are quite beautiful and do not affect the flavor in any way. They're a fine ornamental addition to the herb garden and, with their 12- to

14-inch height, are good edging plants. Harvest will last well into fall. Old clumps may need to be divided and set into newly enriched ground if they begin to decline or crowd out their neighbors.

Dill (or dill weed, as it is sometimes called) is a wonderful annual in the kitchen but short-lived in the garden, requiring successive sowings. I start a first generation in the greenhouse in mid-March for a late April set-out, then plant a few seeds in the open ground at the same time and also at monthly intervals through the season. Dill is a must when cucumbers come in, and beyond succession plantings, it's of easy culture, requiring only a single stake per tall plant to hold the seed head up.

Marjoram is a mild, sweet-flavored herb related closely to oregano. Though people don't

As delicate as it is desirable — dill coming into flower.

always distinguish between the two, the flavors are different. Marjoram is an annual easily raised by seed that I sow in mid-March for set-out in the garden in early May. Six plants provide well for the whole season.

Mint relieves the heat of summer and cools many a dish and drink. There are many flavored mints — spearmint, peppermint, pineapple, and apple. They make fine iced teas, and their strong flavors carry through well, but they can be terribly invasive in the garden. Thus I like to contain these rock-hardy perennials, especially in a small space. I grow several flavors, and each is set in the ground in a 5-gallon container with the top rim of the pot 1 inch above the soil. This keeps these spreaders from taking over the garden, and a 5-gallon container will give them all the root they need and me all the

mint I can use. Seeds can be started indoors in March for garden set-out in April. The garden center can also supply one or two different flavors, which prevents having to buy whole packets of seeds that will never be fully used.

Oregano is stronger and more pungent than its close relative, marjoram, and is the herb people think of when they think of pizza pie. I start oregano plants from seed in mid-March for set-out in early May. Unlike marjoram, oregano is a hardy perennial, and 6 plants will suffice. Both of these herbs can spread 1 foot, and get to be about as tall. Frequent pinching of both for table use will keep a fresh supply of leaves coming and produce a bushier plant.

Parsley, though tough once started, is not easy to get going. The trick to sowing parsley is to get the seeds to germinate. I often soak the very hard seeds overnight in warm water before sowing a dozen or so in a 4-inch pot. An alternative is to nick, or "scarify," the seeds with a file to hasten sprouting. I sow indoors in mid-March to have young plants ready for the garden in May. Parsley has different leaf textures, one being more savoyed, or crinkled, than the other. The smoother varieties clean more easily, but are not as rich-looking. Besides putting half a dozen plants in the garden, I always grow a few in pots that will come indoors after the growing season to provide a garnish into winter. They do have large root systems, so I use 8-inch pots and give regular liquid fertilizing through the season.

As useful as it is beautiful, parsley benefits from frequent snippings.

Rosemary is a tender perennial. In mild areas of the country it will become a handsome, long-lived, woody shrub, but for most of us it needs indoor wintering-over, and thus lives in a large terra-cotta container that travels in and out with the seasons. One choice plant of rosemary suits me, because this marvelously pungent herb requires a chef's gentle touch. I buy rosemary plants as I need them in the spring from a good garden center. I use a soilless mix for planting in the pot, because it's light and makes transporting in and out easier. Rosemary needs watering only once a week, except in midsummer, when I double that. Feeding every other week with water-soluble fertilizer will keep this herb in good health. Generally pest-free (as

Oregano backed up by sage — find room for it too if you can.

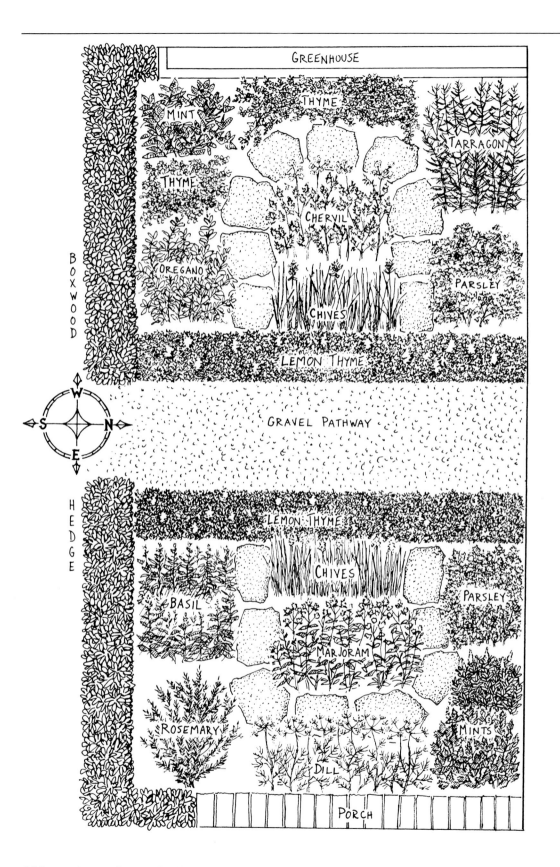

GREENHOUSE

THYME

MINT

TARRAGON

THYME

CHERVIL

OREGANO

PARSLEY

CHIVES

LEMON THYME

BOXWOOD

W
S — N
E

GRAVEL PATHWAY

HEDGE

LEMON THYME

CHIVES

BASIL

PARSLEY

MARJORAM

ROSEMARY

MINTS

DILL

PORCH

162   **Victory Garden Herbs**

This rosemary is a veteran of many moves into the garden and back indoors for winter protection.

are all the other herbs), it can be troubled by spittle bugs, which conceal themselves under a white, frothy bubble on the stems of the plant. I simply wash them off. If the demand on leaves is not heavy for the kitchen, rosemary will often flower with small, blue-violet blooms that sparkle among the green, needle-like leaves.

Tarragon *must* be French. Any other is banished from the kitchen. This is a slow-growing but hardy perennial, and I need several plants to supply the table. The best tarragon for table use is propagated from cuttings, and will not come true from seed. Thus I avoid seeds altogether, and buy plants from good garden centers. I was reminded of one way to distinguish French from Russian (the unwanted) tarragon by a delightful passage from the writing of herb matri-

arch Adelma Grenier Simmons: "The best way to tell with Tarragon (meaning French) is to pick a piece and bite it and it will bite you back. It stings your tongue. It must taste of anise." I give tarragon plenty of room to grow, as it will come 2 feet high or more, and spread to that dimension. It's a good choice for the back of my basically low-growing culinary garden. It's also one of the few herbs that I dry for winter use. In the fall, I gather several 12-inch braids of this pungent herb and keep the stems together with an elastic band. As the stems wither, the elastic retains a tight hold. I hang the bunches away from the sun in a warm location with good air circulation, and use them as needed.

Thyme is a moody perennial that will last many years if treated kindly and watered carefully. It needs very good

A favored spot in the herb garden is reserved for French tarragon.

drainage to prevent winterkill, and I can't guarantee that it will come back year after year. I look on thyme as a short-lived perennial. It's welcome and useful, despite this tendency to come and go, for it begs to be touched to release its memorable scent. It softens garden edges nicely, adding a bit of free form to otherwise formal areas, so I let thyme spill freely out into the walkways, where passing feet will bruise the leaves and release that delicious scent. There are many varieties of thyme, and it pays to sniff them all at a good garden center or herb farm. Lemon thyme smells remarkably like real lemons, and makes a fine edger. I use it on both sides of my kitchen herb garden. Woolly thyme is almost a pet, and golden thyme adds rich color to the bed. Common thyme serves the table best. I plant all these wonderful, ground-hugging varieties from started plants, because thyme is hard to start from seed.

As I mentioned earlier, all the herbs in my garden do well with minimal care, my standard pH of 6.5, and about half the water I give to the vegetables. Herbs do need to be weeded, and my three-pronged cultivator does this nicely. Actually, I minimize this task by applying a 2-inch mulch of cocoa bean hulls. This is an attractive, brown mulch of small hulls that blends nicely with the reserved textures of the herb garden. Once it's settled down, the mulch — despite being very light — doesn't blow around. The hulls are slow to decompose, and serve several years before requiring replacement.

In June, I keep an eye on more than a dozen crops, waiting for the moment of perfection to harvest. Peas, one of my favorites, will be ready by midmonth.

JUNE

JUNE

With its long, warm days and frequent, torrential showers, June is an exciting month in the Victory Garden. Lush foliage is flowing over the garden's raised beds as the effort expended over earlier months pays dividends. I've already completed the spinach harvest, and will be making quite a few more this month: broccoli, cabbage, turnips, cauliflower, radishes, peas, beets, and chard. Early tomatoes will be ready, and so will scallions. I'll take lettuce, too, and the leeks, planted in open trenches 6 inches deep back in April, will now be backfilled to the level of surrounding soil. The wispy green shoots, with their leaves all perfectly aligned, stand guard over their territory as neatly as a platoon of soldiers with shouldered arms.

Of all the June events in the Victory Garden, none pleases me more than the harvest of peas. Later in the month I will be strolling through the beds, plucking those tender beauties from the vines — and eating quite a few of them right there. I'm not distracted, though, from succession plantings of lettuce, nor from the careful attention to watering that June crops often need.

Weeding and cultivating actually help offset some of those watering demands, by reducing the competition for moisture in the beds. I don't look upon either of these as hard labor, because the little time I spend weeding and cultivating produces so much reward for the crops. My black plastic mulch, of course, drastically reduces the amount of weeding and cultivating I have to do. I use that mulch wherever possible, and it's one of the greatest time- and labor-savers in the garden. Where it can't be applied, I use salt marsh hay or do the weeding and cultivating by hand, always aware as I'm grooming the soil that this activity is really my first line of defense against insects. In addition, the dust mulch that cultivating creates actually slows evaporation from the soil. Even as I'm performing this summery care, though, I have one eye on the fall crops of pumpkins, winter squash, broccoli, cabbage, and Brussels sprouts.

Start Indoors
Broccoli
Cabbage
Kale
Lettuce

Transplant
Broccoli
Brussels sprouts
Cabbage
Kale
Lettuce

Plant in Garden
Beets
Cabbage
Lettuce
Rutabagas

Fertilize
Asparagus
Kohlrabi
Leeks
Melons
Onions
Swiss chard

Screen
Cauliflower

Mulch
Asparagus

Harvest
Asparagus
Beets
Broccoli
Cabbage
Cauliflower
Chinese cabbage
Kohlrabi
Lettuce
Onions
Peas
Shallots
Summer squash
Swiss chard
Tomatoes
Turnips

Asparagus   Since planting the asparagus crowns in their trench, I have been adding the rich mixture of topsoil and compost or manure around the shoots as they grow taller. By late June, the trench will be filled in and level with the surrounding soil. When that happens, it's time for me to scratch in a side-dressing of 1 cup of 10-10-10 fertilizer per 10 feet of row all along both sides of the trench, and then to refresh the mulch of salt marsh hay or grass clippings that I laid down in May.

After I've finished harvesting asparagus from the established beds, I side-dress them, too, scratching in 1 cup of 10-10-10 fertilizer per 10 feet of row and then mulching with 2 inches of grass clippings or salt marsh hay to suppress weeds and conserve moisture.

Beans   The bush beans and pole beans that I started indoors can be set out with safety during the first week of June. After hardening them off for 5 days, I separate the peat strip seedlings into individual cells, and space them 3 to 4 inches apart in a 10-inch-wide row. I set them in as deeply as they were growing in their peat cells, and peel off the tops of those cells so that they won't wick away soil moisture. I water the seedlings in with balanced, water-soluble fertilizer diluted to half strength, and then tend to the bush limas. I've been growing varieties like Fordhook #242 and Henderson Bush Lima since April, and they can go out, too, using the same hardening-off and planting procedures described above. Even more than standard bean varieties, limas were very chancy in cold soil. The new setting-out of started seedlings greatly reduces my lima mortality rate.

From now on, I can plant a new row of bush beans every couple of weeks to ensure a steady harvest throughout the season. I seed them directly in the soil now, and continue this successive planting of 10- to 15-foot rows through the season.

The key to my easy-growing, easy-harvesting Victory Garden beets: loose, friable soil, sifted to remove stones and amended with compost or well-rotted manure.

Beets   My April planting of beets will have produced 2-inch globular roots that are ready for harvest in June. I like to get them out of the ground before they are any larger because the increased size and age can bring a tough woodiness to the beets. Some of my recommended hybrid varieties do stand a bit longer in the garden, but even these I prefer to harvest young. Harvesting is a breeze. With the Victory Garden's loose, friable soil, I'm able to grasp the beets by their tops and gently pull them right out. If I notice any leaf miner damage at this point (sometimes a few manage to circumvent even my careful screening — don't ask me how!), I cut the leaves and discard them. They do *not*, of course, go into the compost pile. I've found it easier to clean beets outside by just washing them down with the garden hose. After I've done that, I trim the tops off, leaving about 1 inch of stem attached to the globe to minimize bleeding.

It's also time to sow another crop of beets, using the same steps described in April. Because the weather is so much warmer, this June crop will need more careful attention to watering, and the seed bed must be kept moist until germination occurs.

Broccoli In June I harvest the first of my spring broccoli planting. Broccoli heads are made up of hundreds of individual flowers, and with this vegetable we're actually eating the flowering part of the plant. Thus it's important to take it when the flowers are tightly wrapped and just at or before the individual flowers show any yellowing. Flowering can be triggered by several factors: a warm or cold spell, or aging. This means I keep a vigilant eye on the plants as their time approaches.

When I harvest from side-shooting varieties, I do so in a way that lets the plants keep producing for several weeks. I remove the main head with a cut across the stem a couple of inches below the point where the head and stem meet. This will allow the plant to develop many more smaller heads on side shoots, which are just as tasty as the big head. After the primary harvest from any of my broccoli plants, I side-dress by scratching in half a handful of 10-10-10 per plant.

Even though there is no danger of frost, I'll start my fall crop of broccoli indoors to give the plants every possible benefit from the controlled conditions of watering, temperature, and an insect- and disease-free environment. I sow the seeds in 4-inch pots filled with soilless medium, then bottom-water. With a germination temperature of 75 degrees on my heat pad, I will have seedlings up in about 7 days. Then I move them to full sun and wait for the true leaves. When those show, I transplant the seedlings to individual cell-packs filled with soilless medium and bottom-water with a balanced water-soluble fertilizer diluted to half strength. They receive a day out of full sun to ease transplant shock, and then they go back to a sunny spot to grow for a week or so. Finally, I give them 5 days in the cold frame for hardening-off before setting them into the garden soil.

I'm an advocate of indoor starting, but it's possible to sow broccoli seeds outdoors, too. If I were to do so, I'd sow 4 seeds in a cluster at 18-inch intervals, cover them with ¼ inch of soilless medium, and water in well. Later I'd thin to the strongest seedling in each cluster.

Brussels Sprouts Brussels sprouts fit very nicely into the Victory Garden scheme of things because, despite being a long-season crop that requires 3 months or more to mature, they grow vertically and make excellent use of available space. I'm so fond of their taste, though, that I'd probably grow them regardless. In early June, I transplant my seedlings from their 4-inch pots into individual cell-packs. Given a drink of half-strength water-soluble fertilizer, they'll grow happily on a sun-bathed windowsill or in the uncovered cold frame while I prepare the raised bed for their arrival. (To ward off clubroot, I plant them

Slicing off only the main broccoli head stimulates the development of side shoots, which will continue to produce for weeks.

in a bed where other brassicas haven't grown for the last several seasons.) Like the other brassicas, Brussels sprouts prefer a slightly sweet soil, and I add enough lime to their beds to raise the pH to around 7.5. Because of my problem with clubroot, I like a pH of 7.5 for Brussels sprouts. I'll also add 2 inches of compost to the soil of their bed, working the compost in well with my spading fork. Toward the end of June the seedlings will be about 6 inches tall, and ready to be set out into the garden. I space them 24 inches apart, and I plant only one row of Brussels sprouts, because each plant of Jade Cross E. will produce 75 to 100 sprouts. The seedlings are set in the ground a little deeper than they were growing in their cell-packs, and I water them in with water-soluble fertilizer diluted to half strength.

Aphids seem to have a particular fondness for Brussels sprouts, and have given me fits in the Victory Garden. Once the tiny insects find their way onto the undersides of leaves and into the sprouts themselves, they're just about impossible to

The indoor start always gives me superb Brussels sprout seedlings in June, ready for transplanting to the garden by month's end.

Cabbages with interplanted lettuce. This technique lets me make maximum use of available space — an important consideration in any garden. ▶

dislodge. My best defense against this kind of invasion has been careful vigilance. At the first sign of aphid presence, I spray the leaves with a strong blast from the garden hose, hoping the force of water will flush most of them off. If that doesn't dislodge them, I'll dust with rotenone or spray with pyrethrum.

Cabbage Cabbage heads are ready for harvest when they're well formed and solid, and it's important to take them when they're ready. Cabbage that stays in the ground too long is likely to split. Splitting heads can also be caused by overly generous or irregular watering, or from excessive water uptake after heavy June rains. To minimize this problem, I use my spade to trim the roots of any cabbages that will stay in the ground longer. I cut down through one side, just outside the lower leaves.

To take the heads, I cut just above the soil level and then, as with all the brassicas, pull and discard the roots. This helps prevent the spread of clubroot.

In early June, I start the seedlings for my fall crop of Victory Garden cabbage, following the same indoor-planting techniques I used in April. Come July, I'll transplant the seedlings to cell-packs, harden them off, and set them into the garden. Savoy Ace and Ice Prince are my favorite fall varieties.

Though I prefer starting the seedlings indoors to give them the best possible growth, it's acceptable to sow the seeds of a fall crop directly into the soil. Were I to do it this way, I'd cluster 3 seeds at 24-inch intervals, cover with ¼ inch of soil-less medium, and water in well. I'd keep the seed bed moist until germination, then thin to a single strong seedling in each cluster.

Cauliflower   In the late 1940s I was a fledgling in the nursery business — a budding entrepreneur — and on purchasing trips I traveled the length and breadth of Long Island, home not only of beautiful nurseries but of thriving truck farms as well. Those truck farms devoted much of their acreage to cabbage, broccoli, Brussels sprouts, and especially cauliflower. Stopping one day for lunch at a roadside diner, I got into a conversation with a grizzled old fellow who'd obviously been farming for a long, long time. Why, I asked him, was so much cauliflower grown on Long Island? Perhaps thinking that I was some kind of spy, he ignored my question and spoke, instead, about trucks and tractors and the weather. As I was leaving, I told him that I was in the nursery business, and left him a card to prove it. Then I headed for my truck. After looking at the card he called me back. I came eagerly, thinking that he'd treat me to the secrets of this region's spectacular brassica crops. I was all ears as he glanced at my card once more and said, "Well, we grow cauli-flower 'cause we're near a damned good market!" And that was it. Well, not quite. After I'd thanked him again and was about to go, he said, "Stay in the nursery business. It's interestin' work. Growin' cauliflower is too damn monotonous."

In the ideal climate of Long Island, with its rich soil and moisture-laden air, growing cauliflower may have been so easy that it *was* monotonous. In the Victory Garden, unfortunately, the culture of this finicky crop has been more of an adventure. The most common problem has been the root maggot, which attacks the plants' water delivery system, making them droop and wilt on warm days. The repeated wilting triggers early maturing of the plant, and usually results in very small heads. The maggot is the offspring of an egg-laying fly, however, and I reasoned that tenting the crop with polyester row covering would discourage the insects. It worked, and now I routinely protect the cauliflower rows with fabric supported on hoops of #12 wire.

Yellowing heads is another cauliflower problem. To prevent the plants from discoloring, it's necessary to blanch the heads — shield them from sunlight. This is done by tying leaves up over the emerging heads, by breaking the leaves over the heads, or

Cauliflower heads must be protected from direct sunlight, which causes yellowing. I tie the leaves into a cover, using garden twine, as soon as white heads begin to form.

by growing varieties that are self-blanching. I like the tying technique best, because the self-blanchers produce somewhat smaller heads and the broken-leaf method seems to weaken the plants a bit.

Once the blanched cauliflower is 8 to 10 inches in diameter, snow white, and tightly grained, it's ready for harvest. I pull the whole plant out, cut the head free, and discard the roots. No composting for these or any brassica roots — too much risk of spreading clubroot.

Celery Now that our weather has stabilized and I'm sure that the celery seedlings will not be subjected to temperatures below 50 degrees (which would cause them to bolt), I'll plant the seedlings in the garden. First they'll go into the cold frame for 5 days of hardening-off. While they're getting used to the weather, I'll prepare the celery bed by working in 2 inches of compost or well-rotted manure with my spading fork, taking care to loosen the soil very deeply — a full 12 inches. I'll also work in 10-10-10 fertilizer, allowing 5 pounds per 100 square feet of bed. When the seedlings are ready for planting, I set them into the soil with a spacing of 6 inches in the rows and 12 inches between rows, then water in with water-soluble fertilizer.

At one time, most celery was blanched by hilling-up, but blanching, which does rob the stalks of some nutritional value, has become less popular. Blanching also means more work, even if you use an ingenious method like that of Delbert Thompson, described in March. My own preference now is not to blanch celery, but to let it grow green and crunchy, full of all the vitamin

It used to be common practice to blanch celery, but unblanched celery is actually more nutritious. For the few plants I do blanch, 12-inch planks laid against the celery do the job neatly. ▶

A and nutrients that exposure to sun will create. If I *were* to opt for blanching, though, I doubt if I'd use the hilling-up method. It's a lot of extra work, for one thing, but I've also found that hilling-up allows soil to fall down between the plant's stalks, making them not only gritty when harvested but more susceptible to rot. Instead of hilling, I'd probably plant the celery in 9- or 12-inch blocks, creating a "self-blanching" bed. It's also possible to lay 12-inch-wide planks up against the plants, with stakes on the outside to keep the planks from tipping backward away from the plants.

Chinese Cabbage   In June, my crop of Chinese cabbage will be ready for harvest. I keep an eye on the thermometer throughout this month, watching for several days of temperatures above 80 degrees. If 3 such days come back-to-back, I go ahead and harvest the Chinese cabbage plants — even though they may not be completely mature — to get them before they bolt.

This panorama of the June garden shows off several of my favorite Victory Garden techniques: raised beds with spacious walkways, black plastic mulch, A-frame trellises, and protective spun polyester fabric supported on PVC hoops.

In June I plant the eggplant seedlings through 4-inch squares cut out of the black plastic mulch covering their bed. I'm careful to handle the seedling by its root ball rather than by the fragile stem and leaves.

To harvest, I remove the whole plant from the soil, then cut the top growth off with a sharp knife. I discard the roots and, as with all the brassica roots, avoid putting them into the compost bin because of the danger of spreading clubroot.

As soon as possible after harvesting the Chinese cabbage, I plant a crop of beans in the same bed. The beans, with their nitrogen-fixing talent, will help replenish the soil that the heavy-feeding Chinese cabbage has depleted.

Eggplant During the first week of June, I begin final soil preparation for my eggplant seedlings. While they're hardening-off, I work in 2 inches of compost and 5 pounds of slow-release 14-14-14 fertilizer for every 100 square feet of bed. I rake the bed into shape, then place the black plastic, burying its borders all the way around. I cut 4-inch squares in the plastic 24 inches apart and plant the seedlings through these when they're ready, setting them in to the same depth they grew in their cell-packs.

Verticillium wilt has become a problem with my Victory Garden eggplant crop. Commercial farmers fumigate their soil to defend against wilt, but I prefer to outrun the problem with a disease-tolerant variety like Dusky and a fertile soil that helps keep healthy plants growing fast, one step ahead of the disease.

Kale Kale is the toughest customer in the Victory Garden. Extremely cold tolerant and resistant to most bugs and diseases, kale is rich in both vitamins A and C and in iron as well. Six ounces of kale, in fact, deliver twice the vitamin C contained in 6 ounces of orange juice. As if that were not enough, kale supplies as much calcium as an equal volume of milk! And

when all else has been harvested out of the Victory Garden, kale remains. It's become a must in my winter garden.

I start my kale seeds indoors in early June, sowing them in 4-inch pots filled with soilless growing medium and covering the seeds with ¼ inch of that medium. Over the 75-degree heat pad, I will have seedlings in 5 to 7 days. When they're up, I move them to full sunlight, and at the first appearance of true leaves I transplant the seedlings to individual cell-packs. After that, they're given a day's break from full sun while they recover from transplanting shock and are then set back onto a very sunny windowsill or into my versatile cold frame. Kale is a fast grower, so I'm careful not to let that medium dry out while the seedlings are growing in containers. In July I'll set seedlings into the open ground, being sure first to harden them off for 5 days in the cold frame.

Kohlrabi Short-term crops like kohlrabi enjoy rapid growth, so I side-dress the plants with 1 cup of 5-10-5 fertilizer per 10 feet of row in the first week of June.

Good kohlrabi is *young* kohlrabi, so I harvest them at the end of this month, when they're about golf-ball-sized (and definitely before they're as big as tennis balls). If allowed to grow beyond 2 inches in diameter, they quickly lose dinnertime appeal. Grand Duke, my variety of choice, won't go woody, but it will toughen a bit. I harvest by breaking off the leaves, then cutting the stem about 1 inch below the ball.

When the bed is vacant, I work in 5 pounds of 10-10-10 fertilizer for every 100 square feet of bed space and then plant lettuce seedlings or beans in that space. Legumes are a particularly good follow-up crop for the heavy-feeding kohlrabi, as their nitrogen-fixing roots will help replenish the soil.

Leeks Leeks are very heavy feeders, so I side-dress them in June with 1 cup of 10-10-10 fertilizer for every 10 feet of row, keeping the fertilizer at least 2 inches from the leek stems. I also weed now, carefully, with my short-handled three-pronged cultivator. And I'm not disheartened by the wispy, grass-blade appearance of the June seedlings. They *will* develop.

Lettuce The lettuce just keeps on coming. By this time of the season, I'm planting only varieties that are heat tolerant: Red Sails, Mission, Great Lakes. Whenever a space opens up — in the kohlrabi bed, for instance — I pop in lettuce seedlings. They appreciate some shade now, and the taller crops — peas, beans, trellised cucumbers — give them just that. Careful attention to watering is important, too, now that the hot days are here to stay.

As far as harvest techniques are concerned, I've read about, listened to, and tried a good many. Some gardeners like to pick only the outer leaves at first. Some take only the tender inner leaves. Some actually "crew-cut" the loose-leaf types down to within 2 inches of the soil, hoping that the plant will produce more leaves. I'll tell you what I've concluded: It doesn't make much difference *how* I harvest lettuce. One way's as good as another. The important thing is to use the lettuce I've harvested as soon as possible. The fresher the better, and *that* is the crux of lettuce harvesting! Equally important, in June's heat, is to watch for evidence of pre-bolt. At the slightest tinge of bitterness in the outer leaves, or hardening or knobby formations in

It's time to side-dress the leek seedlings with 1 cup of 10-10-10 fertilizer for every 10 feet of row. My plant labels, clearly marked with waterproof pens, are withstanding summer showers to keep me informed.

Use number 1,421 for the trusty Victory Garden knife. I've had good success growing small icebox-type watermelon in the cool Northeast.

the center, I rip the plant out and replant with new lettuce. The old has gone by when those signs appear.

Melons In June I water the melons regularly, making sure that they receive at least 1 inch of moisture per week. I don't have to worry about weeding or cultivating because the black plastic mulch eliminates those chores, but I do make sure that the vines are kept on the beds and out of the aisles. In June and July, I will give the melon plants a nutrient boost of complete water-soluble fertilizer, and then bide my time until August harvest arrives. There is simply no comparison between store-bought and homegrown melons. The store-bought variety are generally picked green to allow for shipping and storage time. Contrary to popular belief, though, melons don't ripen to full flavor once they're off the vine, so if you've never taken a crop all the way in the home garden, chances are you've never tasted what a melon can *really* accomplish.

Okra Down in the Victory Garden South, Jim Wilson is able to produce a veritable forest of okra. Thriving in the heat and humidity, the plants grow at least 6 feet tall, and I just can't grow beauties that size up north. Okra needs 100 days of very warm soil and air temperatures, and can be stunted badly by cool temperatures in June. But if the weather is benign, I can depend on a decent, if not spectacular, okra harvest in August.

The plants that I started indoors in April will be ready for 5 days of hardening-off in early June. Before planting the seedlings, I'll work in 5 pounds of 14-14-14 slow-release fertilizer for every 100 square feet of bed, and then cover the soil with black plastic, burying the edges just as I did for the cucumber and melon beds. I plant the seedlings through 4-inch squares cut into the plastic, 24 inches apart, setting the plants in the same depth they were growing. And I peel off the tops of those peat pots, to keep them from wicking away moisture.

Onions The very nice thing about onions is that they can be harvested throughout the growing season, as they are needed. My scallion patch will be ready for harvesting throughout June. In my main bed, the onions planted from sets will be ready first. I can take onions at this point if I wish, and I usually harvest a few now. I'll keep on harvesting throughout July and August, and the foliage tops of the main-bed onions will turn brown and wither during these months, indicating storage-ready onions underneath.

This is a good time to watch for root maggot damage, which will be revealed on top by discoloring at the onions' tips. There's not much to be done except watch carefully and pull the afflicted at once. I tried spreading wood ashes to discourage these egg-laying insects by creating a gritty barrier around the plants, but any appreciable rainfall washed them right away (the ashes, not

Onions planted from sets
come ready first, and I'll
harvest them any time af-
ter the first week in June.
The fallen tops indicate
that the onions' storage
mechanism has begun to
work.

the insects, alas). Now I just follow my watch-and-pull strategy
if the maggots appear, but they've never really been a serious
problem.

The onion beds will need cultivating this month, and I do it —
carefully — with my three-pronged cultivator. Onions have shallow roots and are easily checked if those roots are disturbed.
This is also the time to side-dress with 1 cup of 5-10-5 fertilizer
for every 10 feet of row.

Peas The pea harvest has never been earlier, now that I
plant seeds in peat strips and set out seedlings in the open garden in mid-April. The first year I tried this technique, I was as-
tonished by the results, and continue to be just as pleased. That
year, I got first peas (the variety was low-growing Sugar Anne)
on June 1, or *3 weeks* earlier than ever before. Other,
later-maturing varieties followed closely.

Harvesting various types of peas is not without its subtlety.
Snow peas can be harvested any time before the pods swell. So
can sugar-podded types, though their flavor is vastly improved if
one waits until the pods are about to burst from their skins.
With standard garden peas (which I rarely grow any longer),

the key is not so much in harvest as it is in use thereafter. These, like corn, lose their sugar content very quickly after being picked. That means being ready to shell and cook these old-fashioned types within minutes of the harvest. The pea harvest will last 3 to 4 weeks, and when the plants have finally produced their last I pull them up by hand, taking as many roots as possible, and add them to the compost bin. With these legumes there's no danger of spreading disease (the case with brassicas and clubroot, for example), and the peas are a rich source of nitrogen in the compost.

Peppers Rather than use a specific date for planting peppers, I keep my eye on the weather forecast. When I'm satisfied that the nighttime temperatures won't fall below 55 degrees, I feel safe in setting the peppers out. Sometimes that's as early as the middle of May in my region, and sometimes I have to wait until early June. Each year has its own personality, and I try to be sensitive to that. The real key, though, is to err on the side of caution, because peppers love warm weather and loathe cold. At one time, when it was standard practice to rush all crops out into the garden as early as possible, I had quite a few pepper crop failures. One year the peppers produced their usual two flushes of blossoms, but no fruit. They'd been set into the garden too early, and a spate of cool, rainy weather forced the blossoms before the plants were ready to bear fruit. Later, another unexpected blast of cool weather did the same thing, after it was too *late* for the plants to fruit. The key, I think, is waiting until the soil is at least 60 degrees and nighttime temperatures won't go below 55 degrees. If, despite my thermometer-watching and cautious scheduling, an untimely set of cool days threatens the peppers, I'll protect them with Wall O' Water towers.

Peppers *love* growing under black plastic, which conserves heat and retains moisture. *I* love the plastic because it eliminates weeding and greatly reduces watering chores.

Peppers are heavy feeders that produce a long harvest, so I give them a thorough job of soil preparation. In addition to the standard Victory Garden fall soil improving, I work up the peppers' soil while they're hardening-off in the cold frame for 5 days (after those temperatures have stabilized). I add both 2 inches of compost and 14-14-14 slow-release fertilizer (5 pounds per 100 square feet of bed) to their soil. Then I lay down the black plastic mulch and bury its borders. The 4- to 6-inch seedlings are planted through 4-inch squares cut out of the plastic every 18 inches, with 24 inches between the rows. After the seedlings are in, I water them with half-strength liquid fertilizer.

I've found that in the Victory Garden I have few problems with insects or diseases with the pepper crop. For a while I used cutworm collars, but neglected to do so one season with no damage at all. Nor have I ever staked my pepper plants, though I know some gardeners who do. Adequate, consistent watering is much more important, and I am careful about that all season long.

Pumpkins June is pumpkin-planting month in the Victory Garden. It's always hard to believe that the 6-inch seedlings I set out now will eventually grow into plants with 8-foot vines and 10-pound fruit — but they always do!

The planting procedure for pumpkins is similar to that for squash and cucumbers. I move the seedlings to the cold frame on June 1 for 5 days of hardening-off, and while they're doing that I prepare the pumpkin-bed soil. The standard Victory Garden pH of 6.5 is ideal. Pumpkins like a rich, highly organic soil, so I work in 2 inches of well-rotted manure or compost to give them that, and at the same time add 5 pounds of 14-14-14 slow-release fertilizer for every 100 square feet of bed space. Then I cover the beds with black plastic, burying the edges all the way around and cutting out 4-inch squares every 24 inches. When the seedlings have completed their 5 days in the cold frame, I set them into the ground at the same depth they were growing in their peat pots, first tearing the tops off those pots so that they will not be exposed to air and dry the seedlings out. Last of all, they receive a drink of complete water-soluble fertilizer diluted to half strength.

Woodchuck neighbors have demonstrated a real affinity for my Victory Garden pumpkins, and I tried several defenses before finally resorting to chicken-wire fencing, 4 feet high and buried a full 12 inches beneath the surface. That buried border is important. Woodchucks aren't great climbers, but they can burrow like mad.

Rutabagas Rutabagas, also called Swede turnips, or just plain "Swedes," have an image problem. Too many gardeners make the mistake of thinking of them as food fit only for starving armies. I once believed that, remembering my grandmother's Thanksgiving table and the inevitable yellow lump of overcooked mush she said was good for me. But rutabagas allowed to grow into fall weather and harvested the day before Thanksgiving are a different — and very rewarding —experience. Started this month in the open garden, the seeds will quickly germinate. Once they're up, I can almost forget about them until harvest time. They're not particularly finicky about soil, so I don't even bother working extra compost or manure into their raised bed. They do like my standard pH of 6.5. I plant the seeds in mid to late June in ¼-inch-deep furrows, with 6 inches between the seeds and rows 12 inches apart. I group 3 seeds in each spot, cover them with soilless medium, and water them in well. Seedlings will be up in 5 to 7 days, and I'll thin to the strongest seedling in each group a week later. This is a long-term crop that won't be ready for harvest until early October, and the rutabagas need two more things for proper growth: cool weather and plenty of moisture. The Victory Garden climate provides the former, and I take care of the latter, giving them at least 1 inch of water per week.

A gourmet's delight, my shallots are ready for harvest when their tops wither and fall over. After harvesting, they should be cured in a dry, cool area.

Shallots My March-planted shallots can be harvested any time now. I watch the tops, and I know that the bulbs are ready for use when the tops wither and fall over, which usually occurs in early June in the Victory Garden. There's nothing easier than digging or pulling out these gourmet bulbs, and they'll store very well for a long time in any area that's reasonably dry and no warmer than 40 degrees.

Summer Squash Summer squash develops quickly from its bold yellow flowerings. My squash rule is to harvest young and frequently. For me, gardening is a way to get vegetables at the peak of perfection, the way they *aren't* in all too many grocery stores. Summer squash that is allowed to sit too long on the vine overgrows its maturity, loses flavor, and develops tough skin. I like to get these delicacies when they're small enough to hold in my hand, 6 to 8 inches long. And I keep picking them throughout the season, because this stimulates the plants to keep producing more fruit. As soon as the blossoms have turned

Summer squash the way I like to harvest it: young and tender. The blossoms are eminently edible.

brown and dried, the little squash have reached prime picking condition. Don't be surprised if some of them are thumb-sized when this happens — that's when they're at the peak of flavor.

Occasionally I'll see some blossom-end rot (caused by incomplete pollination) at the first flowering of my summer squash crop, and this is usually the result of unsettled weather. I'm never overly alarmed by the rot, because I know that when the weather settles down the plant will be just fine. I just discard any mushy-ended fruit that results.

Swiss Chard In June I harvest Swiss chard, when the outer leaves are 6 to 12 inches long. It's the outer leaves I take, snapping a few from each plant all the way down the bed. Cutting for once, is not recommended, as the plants seem to recover better from having the leaves snapped off cleanly. By taking the mature, outer leaves only, I stimulate the plant's inner-leaf growth. This continual regeneration will provide a steady harvest of foliage throughout the summer and into the early fall.

After harvest, I give the plants a side-dressing of 10-10-10 (a half-handful per plant), scratched in well with my cultivator. That and conscientious watering will be all this sturdy crop needs.

I harvest only a few outer leaves from each Swiss chard plant in June, snapping the leaves cleanly at the plant's base. ◄

A super-healthy winter squash seedling, ready for transplanting. My use of sterile soilless growing medium eliminates disease and provides plenty of nutrients during the plants' critical early growth phase. ▼

Turnips If June stays cool and moist, the turnip harvest can be spread over the season. If the forecaster predicts an early hot spell — a week of weather over 80 degrees, say — I'll go ahead and harvest the whole crop. They'll taste just fine after a week or two in the refrigerator, but that hot weather can put their fine flavor off if they're left in the ground. As with most Victory Garden vegetables, I like to harvest the turnips when they're small and tender, no more than 2 inches in diameter. And the tops will add a body punch to a fresh garden soup.

Winter Squash The seedlings I started back in May are ready for planting out now, in early June. While they're hardening off in the cold frame for 5 days, I prepare their raised beds. I add 2 inches of compost and 5 pounds of 14-14-14 slow-release fertilizer for every 100 square feet of garden space. When these have been forked in well, I rake the soil smooth and then spread black plastic over the raised bed, burying the borders all the way around. I cut 4-inch squares in the plastic, spacing them every 36 inches for bush varieties and 5 feet for the larger, long-vining types. After peeling the tops of the peat pots back (to keep them from wicking away soil moisture), I set them into the soil and water in with a welcoming drink of balanced, water-soluble fertilizer at half strength.

PESTS AND PLAGUES

Insect pests and diseases are both inevitable parts of gardening. Their impact can be minimized by following the sound cultural practices outlined in "Steps to Victorious Gardening," but there comes a time when every gardener must deal with insects and diseases. In this chapter, you'll find descriptions and pictures of the most common pests and plagues, along with my specific solutions for each.

Aphids are troublesome everywhere. What they lack in size (1/10 inch) they make up for in quantity, reproducing with a fervor that would make rabbits blush. Aphids suck juices from leaves and transmit diseases in the process. The many species of aphids come in a variety of colors. They can reproduce with or without a mate, and give birth to eggs as well as living young. Ants frequently live with aphids, because the latter secrete honeydew, which is a food source for the ants. It's a nice symbiosis: Ants do their part by protecting the aphids, and even moving them to lusher pastures. Aphids are present throughout the growing season, and my first line of defense is to keep a clean garden and to buy plants that are insect-free. I keep the perimeter of the garden weeded, thereby reducing areas where they can hide. And I compost all refuse immediately. Early, small infestations of aphids can be sprayed off with a strong stream of water. If they begin to accumulate, I dust the plants with fast-acting rotenone.

Leaf miners destroy leaves by tunneling between leaf surfaces. There are many species, and adults will lay eggs on leaf surfaces of a variety of vegetables. These eggs are usually yellow, making them easy to spot, and they appear to be lying at right angles to the undersides of the leaves. The eggs hatch and the larvae then tunnel in between the leaf surfaces, eventually creating leaves that resemble topographic maps and that are

Leaf miners

also rendered inedible. Miners are particularly troublesome on spinach, Swiss chard, and beets. They do tend to come in cycles, being most troublesome in spring because that's the season of lush, green, leafy growth. In days past, this was a very difficult pest, because the best control was a systemic insecticide that would be absorbed by the plant and then ingested by the miner. Contact insecticides were ineffective because the larvae were protected by the leaves. In those days, I watched carefully for the eggs, and crushed them whenever I found any. That reduced, but never really controlled, a leaf miner invasion. Now I cover miner-susceptible crops with spun polyester fabric at planting time. This barrier prevents adults from laying eggs. It's nontoxic and very effective.

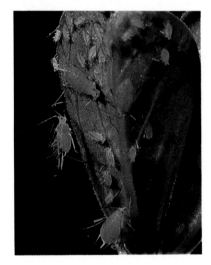

Aphids

I no longer use chemical insecticides in the Victory Garden. Spun, bonded polyester fiber offers chemical-free protection while admitting both sunlight and moisture. This late-June potato foliage, which would have been riddled by the Colorado potato beetle, is untouched and growing beautifully. ◄

Imported cabbage worm

Adult form

Cabbage looper

Adult form

Cabbage moths produce two harmful pests: the imported cabbageworm and the cabbage looper. The former is a green caterpillar produced by a moth with white and black spots. The green looper crawls with a distinctive looping motion, and is produced by a brownish moth with a silvery spot in the middle of each wing. Both caterpillars eat the leaves of all brassicas. Control these days is easy and safe: agricultural fabric, which keeps the moths at bay. *Bacillus thuringiensis* kills any that manage to slip in. *Bt* is an effective control alone — without the fabric. *Bt* must be ingested by the caterpillars to kill them, so some leaf damage results while the sprayed leaves are eaten. The change is insignificant, especially if *Bt* is sprayed while the caterpillars are small. Both types of caterpillars produce several generations through the season, so I watch for them all summer long.

The Colorado potato beetle was once a restricted and little-known bug. Now that potatoes are widely cultivated, this insect is troublesome everywhere. It's become a national nuisance, and has been dosed with more than a fair share of DDT. The adult is yellow with black stripes on the wings and black dots on its orange head. It will lay yellow-orange eggs on the undersides of leaves. The eggs hatch into fat red grubs, which chew ravenously through potato foliage. They can completely destroy the leaves, preventing tuber formation or causing poorly developed spuds. They *must* be controlled. My favorite method is to cover the crop (having ro-

Colorado potato beetle

tated the bed, because adult beetles winter-over in the soil) with polyester fabric draped over tall hoops of #12 wire. Dusting with rotenone is another approach, but it's difficult to get complete coverage. Hand-picking is practical on small patches of potatoes.

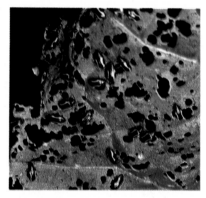

Flea beetles

Flea beetles are spring pests, often feeding on newly set-out and young plants. They are small, about 1/10 inch, and hop like fleas when disturbed. Their chewing riddles leaves. There are a number of species, all of which feed on brassicas, eggplant, and potatoes. Their damage is unsightly (it looks like dozens of tiny buckshot holes in the leaves) but not usually fatal. Agricultural fabric will keep many out, and a rotenone dusting should control the rest.

Squash vine borers are worrisome pests east of the Rockies. The borer is the caterpillar of an orange and black, clear-winged moth that also has coppery forewings. It will lay eggs at the base of summer and winter squash, pumpkins, cucumbers, and melons. The eggs hatch a white grub that enters the soft, succulent stems of these plants. Left unchecked, the grubs will kill plants. Breeders have produced some borer-resistant varieties with toughened stems, but the borers continue to be a problem. My solution is to drape agricultural fabric over the vines, with the ends of the fabric secured with stones or pieces of wood, leaving plenty of slack. As the plants grow, they'll push up the feather-light fabric, which keeps moths away from the plants. An alternative is to dust the base of the plants weekly with rotenone. Once infestation occurs, surgery is the only remedy, and I describe the procedure in detail in the July summer squash entry.

Spotted cucumber beetle

Striped cucumber beetle

Cucumber beetles feed not only on cucumbers but also on squash, melons, beans, and peas. There are two varieties of beetles, striped and spotted. Both are about ¼ inch long. The striped beetle has a pale yellow or orange body, with three black stripes running the length of its body. The spotted cucumber beetle is greenish yellow, with a small black head and 11 (count 'em) black spots on the back. Beetle larvae live in the soil, feeding on roots and stems. Of greater concern is the fact that they spread bacterial wilt and cucumber mosaic, which can lead to total vine collapse. Netting is very effective, as is a weekly dusting with rotenone, if the plants are grown in the open.

Cutworms are the larvae of night-flying moths, and can wreak havoc in the garden. The larvae emerge from below the soil surface, girdle the young stems of plants, and chew them off at ground level. There are few more dispiriting sights than a cutworm-devastated garden after an evening foray. Frequent cultivation will unsettle the bugs, and bring them to the surface, where birds will rejoice over the easy pickings. There are many species and, among them all, the cutworms can remain active through the season. Individual plants can be protected easily with cardboard collars 3 inches in diameter. I cut 9-inch strips, fold them into circles, and staple the ends together. Then I slip the collars over individual tomato, pepper, and eggplants — if it looks like a bad cutworm year. The Victory Garden, fortunately, hasn't suffered greatly from cutworms, so I haven't

Cutworm

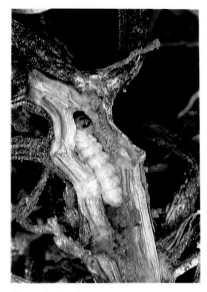

Squash vine borer

included this collar defense in any of the monthly vegetable entries, but it *is* effective. Cutworms will not climb over the collars and, if they're pushed 1 inch deep into the soil, the worms can't burrow under, either.

Root maggots have bedeviled me in the Victory Garden. They can attack all members of the brassica family, as well as onions. The adult fly lays eggs at the bases of the cabbage, broccoli, cauliflower, Brussels sprout, radish, and turnip plants. These eggs hatch into maggots that chew and suck on the roots. They can easily kill plants or, in the case of broccoli and cauliflower, stress the plants into premature heading or flowering. They are more damaging in the Victory Garden in spring, but they are also present with fall crops. Control is by barrier — agricultural fabric. A rotenone dust applied weekly to the base of the plants will offer protection, too. Individual plants can be protected by placing 4-inch tarpaper squares at the base of each plant. A slit from one side

Corn earworm

of the square to its center allows it to fit around the plant's stem. Because it requires less work and no chemicals, I favor the use of fabric.

Corn earworms are the worst corn pests in the U.S. and can visit any patch. The adult is a night-flying moth that lays eggs on corn leaves. The larvae chew leaves and thereby stunt plant growth. As the corn ears develop, they enter through the silk and work their way from top to bottom, eating kernels as they go. Breeders are working on very tightly wrapped cobs that make it difficult for the larvae to enter, but that development seems a few generations away just yet. That said, it's also true that damage in the Victory Garden has never been severe. My solution is to cut

out the small affected areas with my pocketknife. I've also sealed the silks with several drops of mineral oil from a medicine dropper, which prevents the worms from crawling down into the ears. The time to do this is just when the corn ears are beginning to fill out.

Tomato horn worms are among the most frightening garden pests. If they were bigger, they'd fit perfectly into a grade-B Japanese monster film. They can grow up to 5 inches long, and they blend in frustratingly well with tomato foliage. They have orange antennae, which they extend when disturbed. With these "horns" showing, the creatures can be rather daunting. Fortunately, there are several effective controls. Hungry birds love them. They're easily hand-picked. *Bacillus thuringiensis* kills them. Certain parasitic wasps will also destroy them. Without control, however, they have an insatiable appetite for tomato foliage and fruits. Their name is a bit misleading, because they'll also go after the leaves and fruits of peppers, eggplants, and potatoes.

Tomato horn worm

Root maggot mat

Most vegetable diseases are caused by fungi, bacteria, or viruses. Most viruses and some bacteria are transmitted by insects, and can be minimized by controlling insect populations. Of the three types of disease, fungal problems are perhaps the most common. Disease damage from all three types can range from minor cosmetic damage to total plant collapse.

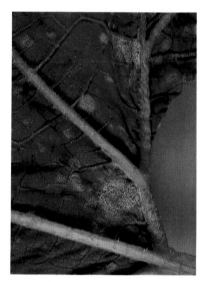

Powdery mildew

Powdery mildew manifests as a white powder on leaf surfaces. The infestation can be limited to the surface only, in which case it's not severe enough to weaken or kill the plant. The disease commonly afflicts squash, melons, cucumbers, and beans. If infection is severe, plants can be killed.

My defense is to space plants adequately for good air circulation, and to avoid late-afternoon waterings that send plants into evening with wet foliage. In areas where powdery mildew is very troublesome, a fungicide may be in order.

Damping off affects seeds and newly emerged seedlings, and is caused by soil-borne fungi. Under ideal conditions — excess moisture, primarily — a whole crop can be lost. Seedlings may fail to emerge, or after growing 2 inches, may simple topple over and die. I have solved this problem by starting seeds in sterile, soilless growing medium. Good cultural practices like adequate spacing in the seed flats or pots and careful — not excessive — watering are also important.

Damping off

Anthracnose

Anthracnose is quite common, unfortunately, though it occurs primarily in the eastern U.S. It commonly affects beans, peas, cucumbers, and melons. Black, sunken spots appear on fruits, and the veins on the undersides of leaves turn black. The disease spreads easily in wet weather, and can be distributed throughout the garden by an unwitting gardener walking about when foliage is wet. Control involves watering early in the day, so that foliage can dry before nightfall. It's also wise to avoid working with anthracnose-susceptible crops when their foliage is wet.

Leaf spots

Leaf spots, though sometimes caused by bacteria, are most commonly caused by fungi. Leaves develop spots, sometimes turn yellow and die. Humid weather in summer encourages the development of this disease. Tomatoes are sometimes affected, but virtually any plant can develop leaf spots. I try to control this by avoiding excessive watering, and by working in the garden when plants are dry. Good garden sanitation is also important.

Clubroot has been devilish in the Victory Garden, and it's troublesome on brassicas throughout the U.S. The causative organisms live in the soil, and have been variously classified as slime molds and fungus. They're very long-lived, and extremely hard to control. They can cause severe wilting during the day. Mature leaves turn yellow and drop, and roots become swollen and distorted. The plants are usually stunted, and may often die. The disease attacks all members of the brassica family throughout the country. It's impossible to dig out clubroot once it's established, as the organisms can survive in the soil for years. Rotation in new gardens is one important control. Beds, once planted to brassicas, should not be replanted with them for at least 5 years. In all but the very largest gardens,

Clubroot

this is hard to put in practice, however. In the Victory Garden, I've managed to grow decent brassica crops despite widespread clubroot infestation by heavily liming the planting holes of the most susceptible brassicas (I include this measure in the appropriate monthly vegetable entries for specific crops). A pH of 7.5 in brassica beds seems to check the growth of clubroot. It's also important to keep plants growing vigorously, with ample nutrients and consistent watering.

Fusarium and verticillium wilts are both caused by soilborne fungi. They are difficult to tell apart.

Fusarium wilt plagues cucumbers, tomatoes, asparagus, peas, peppers, and potatoes. The plants' lower leaves will yellow and curl up during the hottest part of the day, and then will recover — for a while — during the night. After a bit, the whole plant withers and dies. There is no chemical control for this wilt. Instead, I plant disease-resistant varieties, and pull and destroy infected plants at once.

Wilt on eggplants

Verticillium wilt can afflict many plants, including tomatoes, eggplants, peppers, and potatoes. Symptoms include yellowing of lower leaves, poor fruit production, and curling leaves at the tip of the plant. It's possible to fumigate or drench the soil with certain chemicals to control this disease, but I prefer to keep the Victory Garden as chemical-free as possible. To that end, I plant disease-resistant varieties of vegetables and destroy any infected plants as soon as I find them.

Bacterial wilt of cucurbits is, as its name implies, caused by bacteria rather than fungi. It can occur anywhere in the U.S., and most commonly affects melons, cucumbers, pumpkins, squash, beans, potatoes, and onions. Leaves will wilt during the day and, at first, recover overnight. Eventually the vine dies. There's an easy way to test for this disease. If you cut through a wilted stem and squeeze out white, sticky sap that forms a thread when you touch a plant label to it and draw the label away, you've got bacterial wilt. Since the disease is spread by cucumber beetles, the best way to control it is by keeping the beetles at bay, as described in their entry in the "Insects" section.

Bacterial wilt

Viruses are numerous, and affect many plants all over the United States, including tomatoes, peas, peppers, corn, beans, cucumbers, and celery. Symptoms may vary widely, but the most common include mottling, streaking, puckering, and curled leaves. To minimize the incidence of virus infection, I always select disease-resistant varieties. Good garden sanitation — prompt clearing of trimmings and refuse — is also important. And since many viruses are spread from plant to plant by insects that suck — aphids, for instance — insect control is another primary defense.

The disease list above is not exhaustive, but it does include the most common and damaging maladies that may strike the home vegetable garden. An invaluable source of information and advice is the oft-mentioned county extension service agent, both for insect and disease problems. Don't hesitate to call up these helpful men and women whenever you encounter a bug or illness that baffles you. A list of county extension offices, with addresses and phone numbers, is included in the appendix at the end of this book.

Mulched pathways keep the garden accessible in all weather and let me pick the day's harvest without tracking mud back into the house.

JULY

JULY

July is payday. Hot summer weather and warm soil are urging all the crops into high-gear growth. The corn harvest, certainly one of the gardening season's high points, will begin in mid to late July. My first main-crop tomatoes will be ready in July, too, and their appearance causes just as much excitement as the corn. Bush and pole beans will be at their tender best and need frequent picking during this busy month. In fact, I'll be harvesting over a dozen crops, and planting quite a few more, with an eye on the fall season just ahead.

As July's heat settles in, I prefer to move my gardening time to the cool of early morning. Watering, weeding, and thinning are quite pleasant in the freshness of the new day. If I've provided well for feathered friends, I'm often rewarded this time of year with their early-bird feeding on garden pests. Speaking of which, my routine of checking for pest presence continues (see "Pests and Plagues"). Vigilance is the first line of attack. I'm ever ready to wash some off, and to use organic sprays to deal with the few that penetrate the fabric barriers.

Because the soil in the Victory Garden has been producing so intensively for several months now, it's time to pay particular attention to side-dressing and, as each bed is harvested, to replenish it with compost or well-rotted cow manure, and fertilizer. This midseason rejuvenation allows me to keep every square yard of real estate producing intensively all season long.

Here's how I accomplish it. First I broadcast fertilizer (5-10-5 or 10-10-10, depending on the crop that's coming next) at the rate of 5 pounds per 100 square feet of bed, then add 2 inches of compost or well-rotted manure to the cleared bed. I go to work with my spading fork or small tiller, turning over the soil and mixing the ingredients into the top 6 inches. With my raised bed system and emphasis on shorter rows, this task is never overwhelming — a comfort in the midsummer heat.

Start Indoors
Cauliflower

Transplant
Cauliflower
Cabbage

Plant in Garden
Beans
Beets
Broccoli
Carrots
Cucumbers
Kale
Peas
Summer squash

Fertilize
Celery
Leeks
Parsnips
Peppers
Tomatoes

Screen
Broccoli
Cabbage
Cucumbers

Harvest
Beans
Beets
Carrots
Celery
Corn
Cucumbers
Peppers
Potatoes
Summer squash
Tomatoes

Mulch
Beans
Beets

Beans I came across a wonderful assortment of beans at a community garden near Pearl Harbor in Hawaii. Among the gardeners were recent Asian immigrants who took particular pleasure in beans. Glenn Tanaguchi, a county extension agent, was especially enthusiastic about winged beans, a legume with long flaps extending out along their length. Every part of the plant was edible — leaves, stems, even roots. There were also yard-long beans, thin as a pencil but actually stretching up to 3 feet long. As I mentioned in an earlier entry, the diversity of beans is truly amazing. And in pointing out this great variety, I'm getting around to a picking point. With all these, including those I grow in the Victory Garden, it's a good idea to pick young and often. In July my May bean planting will begin to

Tender snap beans complement summer squash and sweet basil.

come ready, and I look for quality, not size, when harvesting. Keeping the harvest picked actually extends the bearing time, too, as the plants are urged on to continued production by the removal of mature beans.

It's also time to plant another generation of bush beans, and to keep planting new short rows every 10 to 14 days for continuous harvest. Planting directions are similar to those of the earlier spring bush beans. I do tend to be more vigilant in my watering during these warm summer months, because I don't want the germinating seeds to dry out. I've found that a light mulch — just enough to cover the ground — of salt marsh hay or grass clippings spread right on the seed bed is an excellent way to keep the beds from drying out under that July sun.

One caution that I've learned the hard way: I do not travel through the bean plants when they are wet. To do so is an excellent way to spread leaf diseases like anthracnose, so when there's water on the foliage, I tend to other projects.

Beets I'll finish harvesting my first planting of beets this month. My second generation is coming along, and now it's time to think of September with a July seeding. I always look forward to this sowing because I know that, in the Victory Garden region at least, the dreaded leaf miner will be much less troublesome from now on. Why that is I'm not sure, but I've observed that insect invasions seem to come in cycles with predictable rhythms.

Planting procedure for the beets this month is no different from the methods used in April. I soak the seeds overnight in tepid water to hasten their sometimes reluctant germination, then plant them outside in the loose, stone-free soil of the Victory Garden's raised beds. That carefully prepared soil is the key to good beets. In hard or stony soil, the beets just won't grow into the moist-fleshed, globular beauties that are so prominently featured in all the seed catalogs. Spacing is 1 inch between seeds and 12 inches between rows. After I've covered the seeds with ½ inch of soilless growing medium, I'm careful to keep the rows well watered in this warmer summer weather. Any seeds that dry out simply won't germinate. The best beets are those that have grown quickly, so my end-of-the-month thinning to 3 inches is followed by a good watering with a balanced water-soluble fertilizer. The beets will produce harvestable tops in early August. The globes themselves should be ready by Labor Day.

Broccoli The seedlings that I started indoors in June are ready for planting in the garden now. I plant this fall crop in the bed that grew a spring crop of peas. I lime the planting area and scatter 10-10-10 fertilizer at the rate of 1 cup for every 10 feet of row. This is turned in and raked smooth. I also blend in half a handful of lime to each planting hole. A slightly alkaline soil (at pH 7.5) seems to inhibit the spread of clubroot. The seedlings are set in so that the seed leaves, their lowest set of leaves, are just above the surface of the soil. Broccoli will root along the stem and this will help produce a sturdier seedling. Plants are spaced 18 inches apart in the row, with rows 2 feet apart. With a double-row planting, if I set the first plant in the second row between the first and second plants in row one (i.e., stagger the planting), I will get the most out of the space. After planting, I water the seedlings in with a complete, water-soluble fertilizer, diluted to half strength. Because cabbage moths are still active, I protect the seedlings with fabric.

Cabbage   Cabbage is one of the real stalwarts of the fall Victory Garden. My June-sown seedlings will supply the table well into October, and they're ready, in early July, for transplanting to individual cell-packs filled with soilless medium. They're hardened off for 5 days, then planted outside in the soil. Procedures are the same as those used in the spring, except that spacing is

The July harvest includes cabbage, sweet peppers, and mild onions. This month I'll set out my cabbage destined for fall harvesting.

Picture-perfect reds: beets and onions.

Well-spaced, carefully weeded, and soon-to-be-harvested carrots. Sow now for a fall harvest.

more generous (24 to 30 inches) because fall varieties produce larger plants. Row covers, supported by wire hoops, will keep cabbageworms and root maggots at bay. If any caterpillars manage to sneak in, I spray with *Bacillus thuringiensis*.

Carrots New England is known for its "bony" soil, of course, and in the old days settlers had to work hard before they could plant. The stones they took from the fields were plentiful enough to build walls all around those fields, and anyone with 8 inches of topsoil was considered very lucky indeed. I think of those rugged farmers often when I harvest carrots in the Victory Garden, not because the soil in my beds is that bad, but because it's so very different. I've worked hard on the Victory Garden's raised beds, adding sand, peat moss, and compost, amending with fertilizers, and testing for pH and nutrient content. Nowhere has the effort paid off more handsomely than with my carrots. And at no time is this more apparent to me than when I harvest the carrots: All I have to do is grasp a handful of lush green tops and pull gently. The soil is so deep and friable that the carrots pop right out.

In July, I plant the fall crop. I don't really do anything different from what I did in April except covering the newly seeded rows with salt marsh hay to keep them from drying out and watering the rows twice daily, rather than once.

Cauliflower Although I start the seedlings of most other fall brassicas — broccoli, cabbage, Brussels sprouts — in May and June, I delay starting cauliflower until July. Earlier sowings have often yielded disappointing results if the cauliflower headed in August heat. Cauliflower likes to mature in the cool of fall. Breeders have made considerable progress in tempering cauliflower's intemperance for heat, but fall is still the best season.

I sow the seeds in 4-inch pots filled with soilless medium, covering them with ¼ inch of the medium and then bottom-watering. The moistened pots go onto my heat pad at 75 degrees, and I'll have seedlings in about 7 days. They're moved to a sunny spot, and when true leaves unfold I transplant seedlings to individual cell-packs. They're bottom-watered with water-soluble fertilizer at half strength, and given a day out of full sunlight before going back into full sun. For this fall sowing I always try two or three new varieties, to see how they hold up against my recent favorite, White Sails.

Celery Near the end of this month, I side-dress the slow-growing celery plants with 1 cup of 10-10-10 fertilizer per 10 feet of row. The plants are big enough now that I feel safe in twisting off a few of the larger outer stalks for summer munching. The main harvest will begin in September.

Corn The corn that went into the garden in May will come ready for harvest in mid-July, having survived attacks by crows, raccoons, and insect pests like the corn borer — if I'm lucky and clever. I've read about, and tried, lots of different methods for holding this hungry army of animal invaders at bay. Some gardeners I know recommend putting a paper bag over every ear of corn to protect them from birds. This sounds fine, and the pictures of stalks with two or three bagged ears look convincing. But it's a huge amount of work to bag *every* ear on a corn crop. And there are few more frustrating things than walking out into the garden on the morning after a windy night to find all those carefully placed bags blown throughout the neighborhood. Birds just haven't been that much of a problem in the Victory Garden. If they were, I'd be inclined to defend against them with scarecrows or a prowling platoon of hungry housecats. Raccoons are another matter. They are determined and ingenious. I'm winning the raccoon war, but just barely. The protection begins with a good stout fence about 4 feet high. Then to the top of the fence, running around the entire perimeter of the garden, I mount a single strand of uninsulated aluminum wire. The wire is connected to a device that generates an electrical pulse every second, shocking animals that touch it. Another raccoon deterrent seems to be rock music. A "Victory Garden" contest winner in Knob Hill, Pennsylvania, put a radio under a plastic pail right in the corn patch, tuned it to the local rock station — and never suffered a loss. I've also experimented with humane traps, and have caught quite a few raccoons. But, having caught them, I'm left with the disposal problem: either take them for a long ride in the country, or put them in a weighted bag and toss them in a nearby pond. I'm never mean enough for the pond toss, so it's

Adult candy. . .on the cob!

always a matter of chauffeuring two or three bewildered raccoons to new homes.

Of all the pests that can ravage corn, though, the European corn borer is among the most troublesome. In days past, gardeners sprayed with strong chemicals, but I'd rather lose the crop than eat it after it's been treated with chemicals that could do worse things to my insides than to the bugs themselves. I'm also willing to accept less than perfect ears. I usually go out with a pocketknife, expecting some damage from corn borers and corn earworms. Spraying with *Bacillus thuringiensis* will take care of corn earworms, the 1½-inch-long moth larvae that attack not only corn but beans, peppers, and tomatoes as well.

There are probably as many suggestions for telling when the corn crop is ripe as there are pests that attack it. I still like to watch the silk on the ears. When the silk is all light brown, and the ear feels full from one end to the other, the corn is probably ready. The silk should still be silky, and not at all shriveled. I will also peel back the corn leaves wrapping the ear and puncture a kernel. If the fluid in the kernel is milky rather than clear, I know the corn is ready. I try not to use the peel-and-puncture method too much, though, because if the corn is not ready, it's left hanging on the stalk partly exposed, making a sweet-smelling target for birds and bugs.

Cucumbers   There's always a bountiful July harvest of cucumbers in the Victory Garden, and it's a good thing — I'm especially fond of cucumbers. I rub the soft spines off the long European types and munch them right in the garden, in fact. Even though I harvest young and often, the cucumber vines invariably peter out before the end of summer, so a second generation of cukes goes in this month. The soil's warm enough now that I can direct-seed without any problem, and I prepare the beds just as I did for my earlier sowing (see May), working in compost and slow-release fertilizer before applying black plastic, then sowing the seeds, and finally setting up the A-frame support.

Cucumbers are seldom ravaged by insects, but can be destroyed in short order by an unstoppable bacterial wilt spread by the cucumber beetle. The agricultural fabric that protected a number of spring crops will keep these insects at bay, too, when draped over the cucumber vines. Dusting with rotenone will also help. Some varieties, like Sweet Slice and Sweet Success, have varying degrees of disease tolerance (though not total resistance) bred in.

Kale   One of the inspirations for planting kale is the vision of it standing tall well into December, the heavy green leaves holding firm even under several inches of snow. That said, finding real estate for 6 plants in the busy midsummer garden is never easy. And since kale is a brassica, it should not be planted

Hilling-up corn and weeding are both accomplished in this one step. ▶

A mild, burpless cucumber grows straight and long on the Victory Garden A-frame trellis. ▼

where relatives have recently grown. To do so invites clubroot and that, like bad debts and psoriasis, is very hard to get rid of once it's established. I prepare the kale bed by adding 1 cup of 10-10-10 fertilizer for every 10 feet of row, then raking the bed smooth. The transplants, now deep green and 4 inches tall, are set in the same depth they grew in the cell-packs. Spacing is 18 inches in the row, with 24 inches between rows. I water them in with half-strength water-soluble fertilizer and then pretty much forget this hardy crop. Kale can look after itself right through the season. A later side-dressing (5 pounds of 10-10-10 for every

Kale and cabbage are set in in July for fresh eating from September into November.

This one last feeding and hilling will stretch these leeks to trophy proportions.

100 square feet of bed) and a lookout for aphids (they can be washed off with a hard hose spray) when the weather cools should be all the attention kale needs.

Leeks   The leeks that were planted in May, looking for all the world like anemic grass blades, have grown into robust sentinels in the July garden. Now's the time to give them a final feeding and hilling. The trench has been filled and brought level with grade, and I side-dress with 1 cup of 10-10-10 fertilizer for every 10 feet of row. When that's done, I draw soil from the bed 2 inches up along the leeks' stems. The object is to get the leek to stretch up and out from the thick stem that develops below.

Parsnips   My spring-sown parsnips sometimes suffer from the out-of-sight, out-of-mind syndrome. They are tucked off in a remote corner of the garden, fretted over until they finally come up, and thinned to a single plant per hole. But then they're forgotten. Really, though, after the care that went into preparing each specially designed planting pocket, there is little to be done. A side-dressing boost in July will encourage them to reach to the bottom of the cone I made for them and to thicken up nicely for cool-season eating. Each parsnip gets a half-handful of

5-10-5 fertilizer in a ring around the plant. I scratch the feed in and give the bed a thorough weeding, and yes, forget the parsnips . . . for now.

Peas   I look forward to July for sowing many of the crops that do best maturing into cool fall weather. Peas, however, are an exception. I can't tell you how many fall pea harvests have been disappointing in the Victory Garden. The problem is that if fall comes too cool too fast, the peas' growth is checked before they have time to flower and fruit well. I wish I had a pat answer for this dilemma, but I haven't met anyone yet who can successfully command the weather gods. At least *starting* the peas this time of year is easy. Germination is so reliable now that I seed the peas directly in the soil without a worry. I dig their trench 2 inches deep and 8 inches wide, after having worked in 5 pounds of 5-10-5 fertilizer for every 100 square feet of bed to replenish the nutrients depleted by the very active spring and summer growth. I treat the seeds with legume inoculant and then plant them as I did earlier, broadcasting casually for a spacing of about 1 inch. I draw an inch of soil over them, then keep the bed moist until the seeds sprout. This is also the time to erect the trellises for tall-growing varieties like Sugar Snap. Bush types receive a more natural trellis: branches left over from spring prunings. I just push these into the ground beside the emerging pea plants, which grab the branches and climb right on up.

My row of parsnips, safely off in one corner of the garden, are doing beautifully in their individually tailored planting pockets.

Peppers   Though Americans are accustomed to eating their peppers green, Europeans think that this borders on the uncivilized. They like their peppers red. In fact, almost all peppers will turn red if left on the vine long enough, though from the astronomical cost of sweet red peppers in the grocery stores you'd think they were rare and exotic varieties. They aren't. Growers charge more for them because consumers want the bright colors. When we grow our own peppers, we can take them any way we choose, of course, and in July my first peppers will be large enough to pick. While I leave a good many more on the vine to sweeten and turn red, it is a good idea to pick peppers as they become table-sized, encouraging the plants to produce many more.

When harvesting, I cut the fruit from their vines, leaving ½ inch of stem on the pepper, and I take care not to loosen the main plants themselves in the soil. I also side-dress each plant with half a handful of 5-10-5 fertilizer per plant, scratched in around the base, to encourage a second set of fruit.

Potatoes   My Red Norlands that always come first will already have had a few tubers lifted from under them, and this month will see the vines dying off. When the plants show decline, I'll lift one hill at a time for the table, using my spading

One of my garden
favorites — and a special
taste treat!

fork gently to turn up the tubers. My mid- and late-season varieties should continue to grow through the month, if I keep the
Colorado potato beetle at bay. The fabric covering the potatoes
is not quite wide enough to afford total protection, because the
vines are so robust that they lift it right off the ground, allowing
beetles to slip beneath. However, it does reduce their damage
considerably, and gives the plants a few more weeks of
unchecked growth. It also means less time spent waging hand-
to-hand combat against adult beetles and orange egg cases alike.

July's zucchini is bold, beautiful, and the perfect size for harvesting.

Summer Squash The bright yellow blossoms of summer squash, so soon followed by young fruit, really hold center stage in the July garden, but a single-minded pest can quickly lay waste to the whole patch if I'm not careful. The squash vine borer is active in July, at least in these parts. Females lay eggs at the base of my squash plants. These hatch larvae that feed on the interior flesh of the vines. A deposit resembling sawdust, collecting at the base of the vine or at the point of entry, is the first sign of infestation. Dusting the base of the plant with rotenone can help, if done early in the worms' life cycle. Once the leaves begin to go limp, though, more drastic measures are called for, because this is a sign that the insect has nearly killed the plant. I use my pocketknife to slit open the stem and cut out any borers that are feeding on the squash. This is major surgery, and to help with recovery, I hill up over any area that has been opened, then water well. Squash will root along the stem, and if I've acted early enough, this should save the plant.

Here's another measure, passed on to me by a viewer, that works well and that requires no chemicals. I cut foot-square pieces of aluminum foil, make slits from one border to the center, and slip these mats, shiny side up, around the base of the squash vines. Glare and reflection may disorient egg-laying adults, or the eggs may simply get cooked by solar radiation. Whatever, I suffer no borer damage with these metallic mats in place.

In mid-July I sow another crop of summer squash, using the same techniques described earlier, and after the middle of this month the vine borer is, in my region anyway, much less of a problem.

Tomatoes July has barely begun when Early Girl, Sweet 100, and, a bit later, Gardener's Delight are basket ready. Celebrity, Champion, Better Bush, Jet Star, and Superfantastic come midmonth, and the Beefsteaks (those one-slice-makes-a-sandwich tomatoes) close out July.

Tomatoes in cages are easy to look after, and now that they're supporting plants that look me squarely in the eye (I'm 6 feet tall), my cages really come into their own. This month, I'll side-dress the plants after the first harvest, scratching in half a handful of 5-10-5 fertilizer around the base of each plant, taking care not to let the granules touch the stem itself. The disease-resistant hybrids I grow are flourishing this time of year, undeterred by wilts or mosaics that were once so troublesome to tomato growers. And my Victory Garden regimen of regular watering (1 full inch per week) and carefully maintained pH (6.5 throughout the garden, save the acid-loving potatoes) prevents blossom-end rot and some of the other physical blemishing (catfacing, for example) that can plague this crop.

You'll need a napkin ready for these juicy tomatoes.

VICTORY GARDEN BERRIES

Some of gardening's sweetest rewards come from the berry patches. Fresh-picked strawberries, raspberries, and blueberries slipped from the bushes at peak perfection are tasty delights, indeed. The berry patch is really the garden's dessert shoppe, and all three — blueberries, raspberries, and strawberries —are of easy culture.

Blueberries   I plant blueberries in the spring where they will receive at least 6 hours of direct sunlight. They are perennial shrubs, so siting is important because they will occupy their spot for years. Six bushes will provide well for a family once they've come fully into their own, which takes several years. I plant three different varieties that come ripe at different times during the season. Blueberries are listed as early, midseason, and late in catalog descriptions. Choosing these three varieties will extend the berry harvest a full month. Each group should be represented in the garden. Blueberries are available from garden centers and through the mail, with the latter likely to provide the best choice, especially if you deal with a berry specialist. Blueray (early), Bluecrop (midseason), and Herbert (for late season) are

High bush blueberries ready for the Thomson taste test. ◀

good choices. Having more than one variety also improves pollination and increases yield.

Blueberries prefer an acid soil with a pH of 5.0, rich in organics and well drained. I add several inches of peat moss mixed in thoroughly to each planting hole; 5 inches of sawdust mulch covers the patch, and both help lower the soil pH. The plants are set 6 feet apart in 2-foot squares cut out of lawn, at the same depth they were growing in the nursery. I water them in with water-soluble fertilizer for a strong start. Pruning at this early stage is limited to cutting back any broken or crossing branches and damaged roots.

It will take a couple of years for these bushes to bear a significant amount of fruit. I fertilize every year in June with

half a handful of 10-10-10 fertilizer for every 12 inches of height, and keep the sawdust mulch 5 inches thick around each plant.

The only pruning necessary for the first 2 or 3 years is to remove crossing branches, spindly, twiggy growth, and head back exuberant shoots. I maintain a couple of inches between branches and encourage the thicker, stronger branches to develop. The best berries are on 2- to 3-year-old wood. These will continue producing for several years, then peter out.

When the plants are fully established, I remove about 20 percent of the oldest wood every year, and old, declining branches are removed at ground level.

A row of blueberries mulched with sawdust. I prune back thin, spindly top growth (above), and remove any crossing branches (below).

As soon as the berries start to color up, I cover the bushes with tobacco netting.

Mind the birds when berries become ripe. I protect my patch with tobacco netting strung over lengths of bent plastic tubing, but I always leave a bush or two exposed, in line with my philosophy of sharing a bit of the garden's gifts with the birds (see the feature on "Gardening to Attract Birds"). One last tip: Color is not the best indication of truly ripe blueberries. I wait 2 to 3 weeks after they've turned a ripe, rich blue, and then let the occasional tasting tell me when they're just right. Tough job, but someone has to do it. And an especially nice fall treat is the bright color of the blueberry leaves, which makes them a good choice as a landscape plant.

Raspberries Raspberries are true homegrown treasures. They're so fragile that they want to be vine-ripened, and really should be enjoyed immediately. There are red, black, and gold raspberries, and they can fruit from early through late summer. Those that fruit in late summer are called, illogically, fall bearers. They're *all* delicious!

They're also eager bearers that can be invasive, so they inhabit a separate corner of the Victory Garden. Like blueberries, they need full sun for at least 6 hours and a rich, free-draining soil. The pH level should be around 6.0. I have two rows of raspberries, each of which is 2 feet wide and 15 feet long, with 4 feet between rows.

Raspberry plants can be bought in the spring from garden centers or from mail-order houses, and I make sure to buy stock that's certified to be disease free. The best time to plant any of the three varieties is early spring. I prepare the soil by working in 3 inches of well-rotted manure or compost before setting the canes out.

The canes are planted 2 feet apart in the row, at the same depth that they grew in the nursery. I make sure to water the canes in well and then set up their training system.

I've adopted my training system from a cane fruit specialist I met at the Royal Horticultural Society's Trial Gardens in Wisley, England. For both June- and fall-bearing varieties, I use this system, which keeps the bushes looking neat and provides easy access to pickers. First, I sink 8-foot cedar posts 30 inches deep into the ground at each corner of the raspberry patch. Then, at 30-, 45-, and 60-inch intervals above ground level I string guy wires of vinyl-wrapped, multistrand cable around the 4 posts, securing the wires with galvanized staples. These wires contain and guide the canes as they grow.

Now, about pruning. Raspberries bear in different ways, and this bears on how they're pruned. Summer-fruiting raspberries fruit on wood that grew the previous season. Fall bearers (really late-summer bearers, as I mentioned earlier)

It doesn't get much better!

bear on the current season's growth. In the first year for fall bearers, no pruning is necessary. After the first year, though, fall bearers are cut right back to the ground, leaving just an inch of stubble. They'll put on vigorous vegetative growth the next season, flower, and fruit — after which they'll be cut right back down to stubble again — and every season thereafter. Summer-fruiting raspberries produce canes one year that flower and fruit the following year. In that same fruiting year, they make new vegetative growth for the following season's crop. All the canes that have fruited are removed from summer bearers each fall. These spent canes will be brown and woody-looking. For either type of pruning, stout shears and sturdy gloves are a must.

In June I apply a side-dressing of 10-10-10 fertilizer to the area around each raspberry plant, using 1 pound for every 10 feet of row, then lay down a

Prune back old canes of summer-fruiting raspberries.

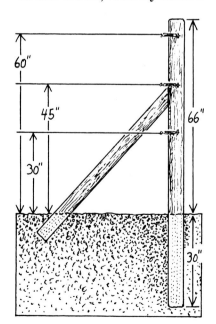

4-inch mulch of sawdust. I water the patch consistently throughout the season, delivering the Victory Garden standard of 1 inch of water per week.

June-bearing raspberries will be ready for the taking in — what else? — June. The fall-bearing varieties will come ready in late July, August, and September. It's important to pick raspberries as soon as they ripen. When they're ready to go, you'll find that they slide easily from the little white core that remains on the stem. I use small containers to pick these little jewels, so that those on the bottom are not crushed as I go along. I don't wash the delicate berries, either — that seems to dull their fine flavor and can hasten rot, even when they are refrigerated.

A fall application of well-rotted manure or compost will improve next season's crop.

Strawberries The glossy photographs and glowing catalog descriptions of strawberries never prepare me for the plants that the mail brings in early spring. A tangle of roots, some still clotted with dead leaves, maybe a hint of green here and there — sorry-looking specimens indeed. The plants come in bundles of 25 or 50, all held together with a single rubber band. Remember, I tell myself, all great strawberry beds started this way.

There are two kinds of strawberries. Everbearing varieties yield lightly through the summer, then produce their main harvest in mid to late summer. June-bearing varieties yield primarily in late spring and June. Though their bearing time is shorter, the overall yield from June bearers is greater. Different varieties are suited to different climatic conditions throughout the country (as well as being imbued with degrees of resistance to different diseases). Your local county extension agent or garden cen-

ter fruit specialist is the best source of advice on which varieties will do best in your particular area.

It's true that strawberries are perennial plants, but one set of plants can't be counted on to produce forever. After a couple of seasons, production from original plants (also called "mother" plants) will decrease, while susceptibility to various diseases will increase. For this reason, strawberries are grown in a way that ensures continual production of new plants. I've tried lots of systems, and have settled on two as being highly desirable. I'll get to them in a moment. First, soil preparation. Spring is the best time to plant strawberries, and a traditional bit of wisdom holds that it's permissible to do so when deciduous trees are beginning to leaf out. When planting time

Sweet strawberry success.

arrives, I soak the straggly plants in a bucket of water to awaken their root systems. While they're doing that, I prepare the soil. My standard Victory Garden pH of 6.5 is fine for strawberries. I work into their beds several inches of compost or well-rotted manure and then go about planting. With either of the systems I'll describe in a moment, spacing between rows is 24 inches.

The first system is the more economical of the two, with slightly lower yields and smaller individual berries. It's called the *spaced matted row* system. In this growing scheme, mother plants are spaced 24 inches apart. They're set in just at the point where roots and stem meet. This is called the crown, and it must

be at soil level. If it's too high, the plant will dry out; if too deep, the growing point will suffocate and stop growing. After the original plant is in place, it will produce runners, and these will root and create daughter plants. Three of these daughter plants are allowed to develop, each about 10 inches from the mother, arranged so that the 4 form a square, with the plants at each corner. In the first year of planting, the mother plant will produce lightly or not at all. Next season, the mother plant will produce heavily, with the new daughter plants also producing well. After this second season, the original plant and 2 daughters are taken out, leaving one new mother to produce 3 new daughters. This system balances the plants' constant spawning of new plants with berry production. The goal is to maintain both, and this system does that. You obviously have to pay some attention to

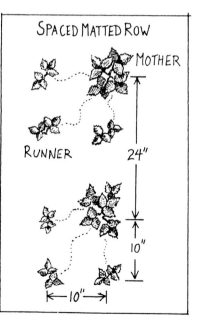

the plants, pruning and directing them after the initial planting, but the reward is a berry patch that will keep on producing for years.

My other system is more extravagant and less work, and uses the black plastic of which I've grown so fond. Before planting, I soak the new plants in water and prepare the raised bed just as I did for the previous type of planting. Before setting the strawberry plants in, though, I work 5 pounds of 14-14-14 slow-release fertilizer into the soil for every 100 square feet of bed, along with several inches of rotted manure or compost. Then, after raking the bed into shape, I stretch the black plastic over it and bury the edges all around. I cut 4-inch squares from the plastic every 12 inches and set the plants in just to the point where roots meet stems, as described above. And that's it. The shoots sent out will quickly wither on the plastic. That means only the main plants grow, and they do *grow*. This system truly produces superplants. The black plastic eliminates competing weeds, conserves moisture, provides more heat for early fruiting. Berries stay clean on the plastic, and, because each plant puts all its energy into producing berries, the latter are huge and supersweet. Depending on the variety I plant, I may have a light harvest the first season and then a super harvest the next year, or just one grand harvest during the second growing season. This system requires that I plant new strawberry plants each season, but the reward in size and quality of berries — as well as the reduced work with the

My preferred strawberry system: plants spaced 1 foot apart on black plastic. This gives me premium berries with almost no weeding and no runners to space out.

black plastic — has led me to favor it, and it's the system I use most in the Victory Garden.

With either system, the Victory Garden regimen of 1 inch of water per week is fine. After harvest, with the first system, I fertilize the plants with 5 pounds of 10-10-10 fertilizer for every 100 square feet of bed space. And I mulch the plants in the matted row system with about 3 inches of salt marsh hay, to keep the berries clean and off the ground once they begin to form. Finally, with either system I pinch off the blossoms that form during the first year. This produces the strongest plants possible.

The berries in both systems will be delectable to birds, so I protect the beds with fine-mesh black plastic netting supported on #12 wire hoops or bent PVC tubing.

Strawberries are ready for harvest about a month after

the plants have bloomed. I harvest only berries that are completely red, and I never pull the berries themselves. Instead, I pinch off the stem behind it with my fingernails and thumb.

Varieties I like are Fairfax, an old standby, Earliglow, Sparkle, and Ozark Beauty. As I mentioned earlier, the varieties best suited for your area may well vary, so consult your local county extension agent or garden center fruit specialist.

So that I get more berries than the birds, I cover the bed with nylon netting.

The August garden shows
broccoli getting ready to
head, onions drying off,
corn needing to be picked
for dinner, and Inca marigolds adding a bit of color
on a gray day.

AUGUST

AUGUST

August's harvest is rich, with all the heat-loving crops coming into full productivity. Melon and pumpkin vines seem about to consume the garden. Eggplants glisten after the morning watering. The Gypsy peppers continue to amaze me with the number of fruit set. Later on, the lima beans are ready to pick, and I'll probably not be able to survive all the zucchini. It's a heady time indeed, but experience has taught me to keep my wits about me now. The days will be getting cooler and shorter, and these mainstay crops from the tropics won't be around, at least in New England, much longer. Thus, despite the bounty, I need to be ready for next month's much cooler weather. That means finding space to set out cauliflower, Chinese cabbage, radishes, lettuce, and spinach. With an early August start, all these lovers of cool weather should produce beautifully through September.

August is also the month when I'm saddled with a particularly enjoyable chore: visiting many of the exceptional gardens entered in my annual "Victory Garden" contest. Every year I'm gratified — and educated — by excellent backyard gardeners all over the country. These vegetable-gardening enthusiasts have developed many ingenious techniques of their own to deal with vagaries of terrain and climate. I'm always impressed by the length to which serious gardeners will go to harvest superb vegetables, and I've noted that two things are common to virtually every one: maximum use of garden space, and careful, regular attention to soil preparation. Those are the keys to successful, productive vegetable gardening, and where they're practiced, the crops flourish.

August, despite the overflowing harvest baskets, is not without problems. Hot weather brings with it the need for vigilant watering. If the weather is really scorching, I pay particular attention to the weeds, which can compete with vegetables for soil moisture, and to my mulches, which I'll deepen just a bit to lessen evaporative loss.

Start Indoors
Chinese cabbage
Lettuce

Transplant
Lettuce

Plant in Garden
Beans
Cauliflower
Chinese cabbage
Lettuce
Radishes
Spinach
Turnips

Fertilize
Chinese cabbage
Eggplant
Okra

Harvest
Beans
Eggplant
Melons
Okra

Mulch
Spinach
Turnips

An unusually warm summer rewards me with a good crop of pole lima beans, but New England's unpredictable weather has taught me that the best bet is with bush varieties.

Beans My crop of bush lima beans will be ready for picking late in August, while the pole beans planted in June have been producing steadily all month. I like to harvest both types of beans when young, because I've found that older beans are too tough for my taste. I keep an eye on the pods and pick them daily if necessary. I want to send the plants the right message: "Keep producing." Pole beans I harvest while they still snap cleanly and before the bean seeds fully develop. With the limas, I let the pods fill out completely, but harvest well before the pods turn yellow.

During the first week of August, I plant a last crop of beans, using quick-maturing bush beans like Provider and Contender. I seed in a wide trench as I did in May, working in 5-10-5 fertilizer at the same rate to get them growing vigorously. I cover the seeds with ½ inch of soilless medium and keep the bed moist until the seeds sprout. This crop must grow quickly through August so it has time to set a good crop for a late September harvest.

Cauliflower   July's seedlings will be ready, in August, for their move to the open garden. I try to pick a cloudy day for this, to help ease the shock of transplanting. The beds will have been limed to raise the pH to 7.5 to help protect against clubroot, and I'll work in 5 pounds of 5-10-5 fertilizer per 100 square feet of bed. I've taken 2 crops off the bed where cauliflower is being planted, and it's very important to fertilize now so growth is vigorous.

After 5 days in the cold frame, I set the seedlings, which are now 4 to 6 inches tall, into the soil a little deeper than they've been growing in their cell-packs, spaced 18 inches apart. I give them a welcome watering of water-soluble fertilizer, too. Keeping the plants well watered is not easy to do on those sweltering days, and as I deliver early-morning and late-afternoon waterings I often envy my father, who, at eighty-five, is still an avid cauliflower grower. He spends 4 or 5 months each year in Maine, where cauliflower thrives. He's not far from the seacoast town of Camden, and there he can grow cauliflower right through the summer. The days often begin wrapped in a blanket of thick coastal fog, which burns off during the late morning and then rolls back in during late afternoon. Cooled and moistened by this ocean air, the cauliflower flourishes.

Chinese Cabbage   Come the first of August, I'm ready to plant out the fall crop of Chinese cabbage. About 6 choice heads is what I'm after for the late September and early October harvest. This season change from warm August to cool fall suits their growing needs just fine. If I have enough open ground, I'll seed out directly into a bed enriched with 5 pounds of 10-10-10 fertilizer per 100 square feet. Three seeds are planted ½ inch deep at 12-inch intervals, and I'll thin to the strongest seedling in a couple of weeks. If space is tight, I'll sow indoors in 3-inch peat pots and move into the mid-August garden when there's room. He who forgets that Chinese cabbage resents being transplanted will suffer plants that prematurely flower, so setting out young plants in peat pots is the perfect solution to that problem. I peel back the tops of the peat pots when I set them in, so the August sun doesn't wick moisture out. I also water them in with a water-soluble fertilizer — this heavy feeder appreciates all the nutrients it can get.

Cucumbers   The cucumber vines that have given their all are pulled and composted now. In the space left by their departure, I can plant a quick crop like lettuce. But if I have enough of that growing elsewhere, I'll replenish the cucumber beds with 2 inches of compost or manure, lime as needed to adjust pH, and add 2 pounds of 10-10-10 fertilizer for every 100 square feet of bed. Then I'll sow the cover crop. If the harvest has been completed in early August, I'll sow 1 pound of quick-growing buckwheat for every 100 square feet of area. Buckwheat is frost tender, and I'll turn it under before it's killed by frost in September or October. If my cucumber harvest has lasted until late in August, I'll go ahead and sow winter rye seed, which will take the beds through the winter.

Eggplant I like eggplant when they're a bit immature — 2 to 3 inches long — but most I leave to size up fully. These get the time-tested ripeness evaluation. I gently press my thumb into the fruit. If the shiny black eggplant dulls and stays a bit dented, it's ready. (If the flesh springs back and shines, then I'm

The taste, of course . . . but also the beauty of eggplant and Ruby Swiss chard.

too early.) I snip off the fruit and 1 inch of stem. I expect my eggplants to produce right through September, and to keep them growing strongly I side-dress with half a handful of 5-10-5 fertilizer around each plant after first harvest.

Another word about verticillium wilt: It may have claimed a few fruit by this time, though Dusky, my favorite variety, has some tolerance to this disease and usually holds up nicely. I've also found that less-tolerant varieties can survive if they're side-dressed and given weekly feedings with water-soluble fertilizer. It may be that the extra nutrients keep them growing just fast enough to stay one step ahead of the disease.

Lettuce   This month I'll be starting, indoors, my fall crop of lettuce. I sow the seeds in 4-inch pots filled with soilless medium, just as I did back in the spring, and bottom-water the pots to moisten the medium thoroughly. I put them on a heat pad at 75 degrees to produce seedlings in 3 days, and then move them to a sunny spot. When the seedlings' true leaves show, I transplant them to cell-packs filled with soilless medium, bottom-water again, and give them a day out of full sun to re-cover from the trauma of transplanting.

Melons   I doubt if there's a crop I look forward to harvesting more than melons. For Northern gardeners they might be called the ultimate challenge; up here it's difficult to achieve the same sweet flavor and tender flesh that come so much more easily to hot-clime growers. Varietal selection has a lot to do with my Victory Garden success, and I'd still nominate Burpee's Ambrosia as my favorite — the one melon I'd take to a desert island with me. But I also know that too much moisture at the time of ripening affects taste adversely. While there's not much to be done about rainfall, I can be careful with watering. The trick is to give enough, but not too much. My approach, which seems to work well, is to hold watering, once fruit has set and reached full size, until the plants just begin to show signs of wilting.

Soon after that, the long-awaited harvest will arrive. There are two reliable indicators of ripeness in a melon. The first is a heady fragrance that grows stronger as the thermometer climbs. The second is a slipping disk. At the base of the stem that attaches the vine to the fruit, there is a ½-inch disk that will recede and start to pull away from the melon when it is ripe. If the disk slides off the fruit with gentle thumb pressure, I know the melon's ready to go.

When the last melon's been harvested, I pull the black plastic off the bed and, if it's in good shape, roll it up for use next year. I work in 10-10-10 fertilizer (2 pounds for every 100 square feet of bed), add 2 inches of manure or compost, and rake the bed smooth. Finally, I sow my soil-replenishing cover crop of winter rye, using 1 pound of seed for every 100 square feet of ground sowed.

My favorite cantaloupe, Burpee's Ambrosia Hybrid, is nearing full ripeness. When the disc that joins stem to fruit begins to shrivel, get the knife ready.

Okra   The key with okra (even more than with most vegetables) is to harvest early. I cut them at 3 to 5 inches, leaving a bit of stem behind. After taking the first harvest, I side-dress with 5-10-5 fertilizer (1 cup per 10 feet of row) to coax continued fruiting.

Radishes   It's time to sow my fall radishes in the Victory Garden, a crop I always anticipate with more pleasure than that of spring. Fall radishes are consistently superior to those grown in spring — large, juicy, cool-tasting — because they so much prefer maturing in cool weather.

Before planting, I replenish the hardworking soil by scratching in 1 cup of 5-10-5 fertilizer for every 10 feet of row, and turning in 2 inches of compost as well. With the bed raked

The mid- to late-August-sown radishes are well spaced and soon will be free of weeds for unchecked growth. The Victory Garden cold frame is back out to extend the growing season well into fall.

smooth, I use my planting board to make ¼-inch furrows, and sow the radish seeds 1 inch apart, with 6 inches between rows. I cover them with ¼ inch of soilless medium, water well, and wait for the seedlings to appear in about a week. When they're up, I thin out every other plant, leaving a final spacing of 2 inches.

Since these radishes will be growing into cool weather, I can choose from lots of varieties: whites, multicolored, cylindrical (Icicle or Breakfast), and even the white, rose, or black-skinned long-storage radishes. The point is that I needn't stick with the red globe types only.

Spinach   It's been too long between fresh spinach harvests, but now that the weather is cooling, it's time to plant a midmonth sowing for September eating. I first work in 1 cup of 10-10-10 fertilizer for every 10 feet of row, then rake the bed smooth. Then I open the spinach trench, 12 inches wide and 1 inch deep. I scatter the seed the length and width of the trench, spacing the seeds about 1 inch apart. An inch of soil covers the seeds. At this time of year, I like to mulch lightly right over the seed bed with salt marsh hay before watering. This will help keep the bed evenly moist while the seeds germinate. They'll be up and growing before long, and — once again — here's my fail-safe harvest rule: When the leaves touch, pick. There will be several harvests before individual plants stand 6 inches apart, the first one being small but *very* tender greens that make superb salads.

Turnips   I said before that turnips are tasty, and that's true. They're also a rich source of nutrients with most of the vitamins C, A, B, E, and minerals concentrated not in the roots but in the greens. An ounce of turnip greens, for instance, has 5 times the amount of vitamin C that's contained in an equal amount of root. That might explain why turnip greens are so popular in the South.

I'm looking for roots with my August sowing of turnips, though, and have chosen two varieties with good flavor, Purple Top and Golden Perfection. I plant seed ½ inch deep in prepared furrows, allowing 1 inch between seeds. One foot separates the rows. I cover the seeds with ¼ inch of soilless medium, water them in, and then thin to a final spacing of 4 inches in the rows when the seedlings are 3 to 4 inches high. In late August, if the weather is still hot, I'll mulch the bed with 2 inches of salt marsh hay to keep moisture in and to keep the plants cool.

An August sowing of Purple Top turnips will produce beauties like these to be enjoyed this fall.

SECRETS OF THE SILVER TROWEL GARDENERS

Since 1979, the "Victory Garden" television show has sponsored an annual vegetable gardening contest. Each year, viewers send in crop lists, diagrams, and photos of their gardens. A preliminary screening reduces the entries to a manageable number. Then our judges make on-site evaluations. From this select group, the finalists are chosen. I visit these with our television crew to record segments for national broadcast on the PBS television series. And from this *crème de la crème*, viewers vote for their favorite. We've showcased the finest gardens throughout this country, and I've learned many useful lessons from these masterful gardeners.

The one common element linking *all* the great vegetable gardeners I've visited is meticulous attention to soil preparation. My own program, pretty conscientious in its own right, is outlined in "Steps to Victorious Gardening." I've been impressed, over the years, with the great lengths to which other gardeners go to enhance

This beautiful and very productive garden is tended by 1986 contest finalist Nan Norseen. Intensive cropping on raised beds with mulched paths, surrounded by lawn, caught our judges' eye. ◄

soil in some pretty unlikely locations. For instance, I'll never forget Andrew Biggerstaff of Portland, Oregon. He was in his late eighties when I met him, and had been gardening all his life. Now retired, he'd *really* become involved in gardening. He lived on one of the hills overlooking Portland, and as we snaked up the steep, winding roads I wondered where on earth he'd find a flat square foot to cultivate. He lived right on top of the hill, and, with the exception of a small level area to one side of his house, the land was very steep. He built 75 steps on either side of the garden, which measured about 80 by 80 feet. And he had tamed the ferocious slope singlehandedly by creating a number of stone wall–contained terraces. Looking after the garden was no easy task, but Andrew solved it with compost and lots of manure. The latter was dropped off at the top of his driveway, where he loaded it into wheelbarrows and then sent it down a chute to whatever level he happened to be working on. He'd set a barricade across at that level, then go down and shovel the manure onto his beds. He grew superb vegetables in this unlikely setting and, with his raised terraces, could garden comfortably at waist level. From Andrew I learned that nothing will keep a determined gardener from his creative endeavors.

I've often sung the praises of leaves as a great source of organic material, and Bob Hardison of Chapel Hill, North Carolina, used them as well as any gardener I've seen. Every year he collected all the leaves on his property, then prevailed on the city to drop a truckload or two as well. He kept them in a cinderblock pen and added them to his compost piles as they emptied. His vegetables thrived on the leaf-enriched soil in his beds.

North Carolina produced another ingenious finalist, Chuck Brackett. His specialty was manure tea. He'd created wood-enclosed raised beds, carefully engineered and featuring elaborate trellising to support his 8-foot tomato vines and equally rambunctious pole beans. Chuck composted and used rotted manure, but also gave his plants frequent boosts with manure tea, adapting the principles of moonshine stills to brew his rich solutions. His basic ingredients were 55-gallon barrels, water, manure, and something to suspend the manure in the barrel. Rather than tying the manure in a burlap bag (traditional but short-lived, as the burlap soon rots), Chuck took a 5-gallon plastic pail and cut several slits in the sides, 1 inch wide and 5 inches high.

The suburban Ohio garden of Eric Mayer — Eric chose to edge his beds with wood and laid his own brick paths for easy garden access. ◄

The Oxford, North Carolina, garden of finalists Marie McGee and Lewis Bell. ▼

He lined the pail with aluminum wire screen, and filled it with manure. A lid held everything in place. This "secret weapon" was suspended in the barrel and steeped for at least 24 hours. The result was a rich liquid fertilizer that plants took up readily. His was such a realistic-looking operation that revenue agents flying over the countryside looking for stills occasionally landed and came by for a closer inspection. Seemed that it wasn't hard to convince them that *his* brand of mash wasn't for human consumption.

Chuck also constructed custom beds that impressed me. They were raised beds walled with brick, with aluminum wire screening covering the soil. To each bed he'd add organic material, adjust the pH, and then custom-fit the season's insect barriers. Some were short, for lettuce and other greens, while others were as much as 3 feet high to allow for growth of taller plants. The overall system was as effective as it was attractive.

One of the most eye-pleasing gardens I saw anywhere belonged to Ewing Walker in Maine. He lived right on the rugged coast in a beautifully restored old home. His vegetable gardening had to be aesthetically pleasing as well as satisfying for the table, to complement that lovely old house of his. His solution was to make raised beds 3 feet above grade, with grass strips lying between. He framed the beds with 6x6 timbers, painted to match the house. The beds were beautiful to look at, and produced vegetables that the bony, unenhanced coastal soil alone could never have managed. Raising the beds so high helped warm the growing area after the long Maine winter, and made for stoopless gardening as well.

Ewing was doing with grass strips what I'd seen done at a number of other contest gardens: incorporating the vegetable garden into a small backyard landscaping plan. Rather than cut an entire patch from the lawn, contest winner Helen Rood, outside Minneapolis, placed individual wide-row beds between grass strips. This gave her access to the garden even during the soggiest weather, and lent an especially refined look (not unlike the maze gardens of stately English mansions) to her yard.

Contest finalists have overcome lots of challenges in their zeal. During the contest's first year, I visited a doctor in rural New York state. His practice was at home, and he left time in his busy schedule, every day, to spend an hour or so relaxing in the garden. His area harbored quite a deer population, which he eventually frustrated with an 8-foot fence all around the garden. That kept them on the right side of the fence, an important achievement to someone who put up as much produce as Dr. Pike, who had an elaborate system of climatically controlled root cellars with rooms at different temperature and humidity levels that allowed him to keep the harvest well into the new year.

Good gardeners tend to be a resourceful lot. Our winners the first year lived right along

A few years ago this now lovely Camden, New Jersey, garden sported only trash, debris, and weeds. Then two dedicated gardeners transformed it into a Silver Trowel Award winner.

the Massachusetts coast, in a particularly windy location. They buffered that by locating the garden in among trees. They also had a sandy patch of ground to contend with, and for help they turned to the sea, hauling up loads of seaweed. It's a fine organic amendment with ample trace elements. They'd rinse the salt off and let it dry in the sun before using it in compost and for mulching. This partly explained the incredible richness of their greens, spinach, chard, and so forth — but not entirely. Credit also had to go to their special fertilizer — sea bird guano collected from a derelict military facility built during World War II to guard Boston Harbor. Gulls and other shore birds found this concrete tower a

useful sanctuary, and this "livestock" took no looking after.

Finally, there was the couple in Camden, New Jersey, who did more than their part to reclaim a former dump site. Michael Devlin and Valerie Frick turned an eyesore into a garden where food, flowers, and herbs thrived. They were even able to use a discarded engine block, turning it into a planter! This intrepid couple personified one of the characteristics I've encountered again and again in my garden visits — the feeling of immense satisfaction that derives from reclaiming badly used land.

That's one of the pleasures of gardening, but certainly not the only. The list is inexhaustible, in fact, and each time I've looked on as a new gardener has regaled me with tales of his super tomatoes or sugar-sweet corn, I've realized this anew. There's no end to it!

The Victory Garden journal is one of my most important aids. Memory dims as the months pass, but the journal never fades. Here, I'm noting how this season's new varieties of kale and summer squash performed: vigor, yield, insect and disease resistance, maturing time, and so on.

SEPTEMBER

SEPTEMBER

Weather can be my undoing in September. Tropical storms with damaging winds often work their way up the coast. And if a harvest moon comes near the end of the month, especially on clear and windless nights, it could bring a killing frost with it. I'm prepared to go out and cover frost-tender crops like tomatoes, peppers, and eggplant for a night or two because I know that this brief cold spell will generally be followed by a period of good growing weather.

In September, the coming on of cool-season crops offers some welcome additions to the table. Planting does slow considerably except in the dusted-off cold frames, which I keep filled with lettuce seedlings. Beds that open up are quickly seeded with soil-improving winter rye, and compost that's been breaking down in summer's heat is ready to be spread over the raised beds.

There are lots of notes logged in my Victory Garden journal this month. My memory from year to year is not nearly as reliable as notes recorded through the season. I find them particularly helpful with new varieties and techniques. I note yield under favorable and not-so-favorable growing conditions; disease resistance; eating quality; vigor and productivity; timing — was I too early or too late? Here's a sample remark:

Experiment with mail-order potato eyes disappointing — yield low — vines looked stunted. Stick to whole, small tubers.

I planted a short row of potato eyes, which have recently been appearing in mail-order catalogs. They weigh almost nothing to ship and are easy to handle, so I tried a row. In this particular season, they were disappointing, taking up as much space as seed potatoes but producing only a fraction of the crop. No improvement there, so I'll go back to whole, small tubers until something new comes along.

Here's another:

Parsnips — mistake to plant a crop before parsnip — delayed parsnip seeding not doing as well.

I tried to get an early spring crop on the bed where parsnip was to go. That worked all right but held the bed too long. By the time I seeded parsnip, it was late and resulted in acceptable but not trophy-sized parsnips.

The grammar may not be flawless, but the information I record on the spot, when everything is fresh before me, will prove invaluable next season and beyond. What's the old saying about those who don't understand history being doomed to repeat it? Not so in the Victory Garden.

Plant in Garden
Lettuce
Spinach

Fertilize
Broccoli
Spinach

Harvest
Beans
Broccoli
Cabbage
Carrots
Cauliflower
Celery
Chinese cabbage
Leeks
Lettuce
Peas
Radishes
Summer squash
Turnips
Winter squash

PLANT	VARIETY	SOURCE	DATE SEEDED	CONTAINER	DATE GERM.	GERM.	1ST TRANS.	2ND TRANS.	COLDFRAME/ OUTSIDE	GARDEN	1ST FLOWER OR HARVEST	COMMENTS
Tomato	Patio	Stokes	3/17	4"	3/23	Good	3/30	4/29	into 3	5/9 in wall water		Still no ripe fruit by 7/19
"	Better Boy VFN	Stokes	3/17	4"	3/22	Good	3/30	4/29		water	7/16	
"	Celebrity	Harris	3/17	4"	3/22	Good	3/30	4/29		5/9 wall water	7/12	Cracking of first fruit. Good fruit set.
"	Supersonic	Harris	3/17	4"	3/24	Good	4/3	4/29		5/9 "		First fruit at orange-pink stage 7/19 Vine small
"	Whopper VFNT	Park	3/17	4"	3/22	Good	3/30	4/29		5/9 "		Good fruit set
"	Better Bush	Park	3/17	4"	3/23	Good	3/30	4/29		5/9 "		Weaker set than Campbell 1327, Revolution
"	Revolution	Twilley	3/17	4"	3/23	Good	3/30	4/29		5/9 "	7/16	Very heavy set, but many fruit malformed
"	President	Park	3/17	4"	3/23	Good	3/30	4/29		5/9 "		
"	Floramerica	Burpee	3/17	4"	3/22	Good	3/30	4/29		5/9 "	7/16	
"	Quick Pick	Park	3/17	4"	3/22	Good	3/30	4/29		5/9 "	7/7	Earliest of regular size tomatoes again. Fruit smaller this year

A sample journal page. Four months from now, when I'm ready to plan next year's garden, the information will prove invaluable.

These Kentucky Wonder pole beans are only one of a dozen or more varieties I grow every year. I'll be harvesting beans all through the month.

Beans My midsummer-sown beans are producing abundantly in September. In fact, with the repeated sowings of short rows, I've had fresh beans for the table continuously since mid-June.

When I was a kid, we grew two types of beans in our garden — bush beans and pole beans, one variety of each. Now I might grow 15 varieties a year, still modest compared to a gardener close by who grows over 200 varieties annually. He's determined to help preserve the rich gene pool among this most valuable crop, so his collection contains varieties long since out of the commercial trade. His efforts are important because some of these varieties are exceptionally flavorful, some are highly disease resistant, some very productive. In fact, one of my favorite beans is an heirloom type, White French Crystal. They are not easy to come by, so I save a crop for seeding next year by allowing a few vines to ripen their bean pods fully. They are shelled when the pod has shriveled but before they split and spill the beans. I store them in a cool dry spot (a covered jar makes a good container) over the winter and then have good bean seeds ready for next year's planting.

When the bean beds finally are finished, I cut the vines off just above ground level, leaving their nitrogen-fixing roots in the soil. I scratch the soil lightly with my cultivator, adding 2 pounds of 10-10-10 for every 100 square feet of bed, then seed winter rye right over the wide bean row, and water in.

Broccoli I harvest broccoli right through September and into October. It will tolerate a bit of frost, so I water with water-soluble fertilizer this month to encourage continued side-shooting. I also keep an eye out for aphids, which tend to be troublesome on fall brassicas. A strong spray of water keeps infestations in check by washing the bugs right off the plants.

When the broccoli harvest plays out, I pull the roots and discard them, to avoid leaving clubroot organisms in the soil. Then

I give the beds my standard fall soil improvement. I work in 2 inches of compost or manure, lime as needed, and 2 pounds of 10-10-10 fertilizer per 100 square feet of bed. This is raked smooth, and then I sow 1 pound of winter rye seed for every 100 square feet of bed. Finally, I water in well and keep the beds moist until full germination occurs.

Cabbage   I think we have to thank the English for expanding our horizons with cabbage, especially the fall types. My winter reading has included some wonderful books by British estate gardeners, and their notes and preferences on cabbage varieties really point out the care they take with varietal selection for almost every month. This doesn't translate so well over here with our harsher climate, but it has made me more attentive to the fine art of selecting cabbage varieties.

My Victory Garden intensive culture is shown at its best here: Growing beautifully in the single 4-foot bed are Savoy cabbage, kale, Swiss chard, oak leaf lettuce, and Brussels sprouts.

I find my September bed filled with ball-head green and red types and the beautiful Savoy Ace, a Japanese breeding success, with its commendable size, nicely savoyed leaves, and creamy yellow heart. These cool fall months are really perfect for cabbage because growth is good but not so exuberant that everything comes at once. The cabbage holds well in the ground and can be harvested as convenient.

It's usually late September or early October before all my fall cabbage is out of the ground. When it's finally finished, I prepare the beds for next year by adding 2 inches of compost or manure, lime as needed, and 2 pounds of 10-10-10 fertilizer for every 100 square feet of bed. I sow 1 pound of winter rye seed for each 100 square feet of area, water in well, and keep the seed bed moist until germination occurs.

Carrots I'll be harvesting carrots throughout the fall, taking them as I need them from the Victory Garden's beds, rather than making a once-over harvest. This is really my favorite carrot season, too. The carrots that I pull and munch now are even sweeter than those grown from spring into summer, because carrots prefer maturing into cool weather.

The carrots catch your eye here, but my Victory Garden soil is the real star. Stone free and enriched with compost and manure, it provides the loose, friable composition carrots must have to develop without splitting and forking.

The September garden in full swing. Many gardeners quit when summer ends, but there's plenty of fall action in the Victory Garden. Beans, squash, lettuce, and leeks are ready for harvesting; the fall crop of radishes has just been planted.

Cauliflower   By late September my fall crop of cauliflower is ready for harvest. The caulis get individual scrutiny as they size up this month. Under cool, early fall conditions, the heads should stay in good shape in the ground until the table calls, but I don't assume anything, and check regularly for curd separation or yellowing. If I see either of those, I harvest quickly.

When the harvest is finished, it's time to give the cauliflower beds their fall soil preparation. I work in 2 inches of compost or manure, lime to raise the pH to the 6.5 level (no brassicas will be growing here next year, as I follow my brassica crop rotation plan, so I don't want the higher pH of 7.5 that I use in brassica beds), and 2 pounds of 10-10-10 fertilizer for every 100 square feet of bed. With the beds raked smooth, I sow 1 pound of winter rye seed for every 100 square feet of area, water well, and keep moist until germination occurs.

Celery   In September — at last — I can expect to harvest the celery plants that I started from seed way back in February. I'll harvest whole plants, cutting them off just at ground level. The

I harvest cauliflower when the head is tight and white, before any yellowing or separation occurs. Blanching produces that beautiful creamy color.

green, crunchy stalks are a welcome taste treat now that fall is arriving.

Celery has been in the ground for a long time, and has taken a lot out of the soil, which will welcome my fall rejuvenating. I work in 2 inches of compost or manure, lime as needed to adjust the pH, and 2 pounds of 10-10-10 fertilizer for every 100 square feet of bed. That's all turned in well and raked smooth, and then I sow 1 pound of winter rye seed for every 100 square feet of area. I water the seed in well and keep the beds moist until germination is complete.

Chinese Cabbage It's time to harvest my fall planting of Chinese cabbage, but first a word about slugs. The moist ground beneath the succulent Chinese cabbage heads is prime slug habitat, and slugs like the taste of this delicious brassica as much as the rest of us. The generous spacing that I give each plant will cut down on the slug population a bit, and careful cultivation also helps send them on their slimy way. But slugs can be even more troublesome in fall than spring. There are a whole host of home remedies. Some folks put beer in saucers to attract the slugs, which then expire from drowning or wretched excess or both. Long-frustrated gardeners also take fiendish delight in sprinkling salt on slugs' tender bodies. Ingenious devices called slug hotels, available at garden supply houses, allow the creatures to check in but not out. I've also tried spreading wood ashes or gritty substances like diatomaceous earth around the bases of plants, but rain seems to wash these abrasives away all too easily.

As long as the weather stays cool, I'll continue harvesting 5-pound heads of Chinese cabbage into October. When the last has been pulled, I'll begin my fall soil-enrichment program. See "Steps to Victorious Gardening" for my soil-enriching instructions.

Leeks   Leeks can be harvested at any time during their growth, but I like to leave them alone until early September, when they'll be fully mature. By then, there should be 10 to 12 inches of blanched, glistening white, mild-flavored stalk under the soil, with the leek leaves spread out like beautiful fans on top. I use a spading fork to harvest them, pushing it into the ground several inches from the plants and making sure to bury the tines deeper than the plants are growing. Then I nudge them up and out with a back-and-forth motion.

My row of leeks will provide for the table right through till Christmas if I lay down a thick mulch of salt marsh hay in November to prevent freezing. If my appetite can't keep up with the supply, I'll try to winter-over a few, taking them in the spring before they go back into active growth.

Lettuce   In September I plant my lettuce seedlings in the cold frame, first forking into the soil 1 pound of 10-10-10 fertilizer for the 4x4-foot bed. I set the lettuce into the soil the same depth they were growing in their cell-packs, water in well with half-strength water-soluble fertilizer, and close the cold frame lid. Once in a while September will bring an unusually warm, sunny day, and I keep an eye on the cold frame temperature. If it starts to climb over 75 degrees, I vent the heat to keep the seedlings safe.

Peas   If September's weather has been kind to my fall peas (warm for good growth without a checking frost), I'll have a good year. But even in a bad year, a crop failure is the beginning of next season's soil-improvement program. If I don't get a crop, I turn the vines right into the soil. Then I work in 2 pounds of 10-10-10 fertilizer for every 100 square feet of bed, 2 inches of compost or manure, lime as needed, and rake the bed smooth. I sow 1 pound of winter rye seed for every 100 square feet of bed space, and that's that until next spring.

I've used my spading fork to lever up this beautiful leek. They can be taken any time during their growth, but won't be fully mature until September. That gorgeous root system is made possible by the Victory Garden's specially conditioned soil: carefully adjusted pH of 6.5, annual addition of compost or manure, and systematic fertilization throughout the season. ▶

My cold frame provides early lettuce in spring and late lettuce in the fall. These Little Gem seedlings, planted as my summer squash harvest winds down, will come ready in October. That gives me fresh salad greens nine months out of twelve!

If there's a good year, and therefore a harvest, I take peas as long as possible to encourage the plants to keep producing. When they've finally given up, I cut the spent vines off at ground level and compost them. They're a bit tough by now and will break down better in the compost bin. The roots I leave in the soil, loosening it with my three-pronged cultivator before working in 10-10-10 fertilizer and manure or compost. The winter rye goes down last of all, to provide a good, thick stand that will hold the soil in place over winter and add a substantial amount of organic matter come spring, when it's turned under.

Radishes I'm in no great hurry to harvest my fall radishes. They're actually improved by cool weather, growing slow and sweet this time of year. I don't leave them *too* long in the ground, though, because they tend to turn woody and tough when old.

Root maggots have not been a problem with the fall radishes, so I don't even bother with protective fabric. And once the harvest is complete, I make the bed ready for winter by working in 2 inches of manure or compost, lime as needed, and 2 pounds of

10-10-10 fertilizer for every 100 square feet of bed. Last, I sow 1 pound of winter rye seed for every 100 square feet of area and water well.

Spinach The fall crop will be maturing now, and to keep it growing vigorously, I give the bed a drink of water-soluble fertilizer early in the month. I *am* fond of this fall crop, which has no leaf miner worries, never bolts (the hot weather is past), and even tastes better, thanks to the right temperature cycle of warm-to-cool weather.

At the end of the month, I'll find an open bed and open another trench, 12 inches wide, 1 inch deep, and about 15 feet long. Here I'll direct-seed a crop of spinach that will grow a little before going dormant for the winter. This crop will come ready for harvest in March and April, and may be the best of all, having grown completely untroubled by pests of any kind. One thing is certain: It's a most welcome sight — and taste — come early spring!

Summer Squash This crop is very frost sensitive, so I keep my ear on the weather reports in September. If the squash are hit with a frost, they will rot on the vine. When frost is predicted, then, I harvest all the fruit, or, failing that, at least try to cover the vines with a sheet of clear plastic, which will give a couple degrees of frost protection and a longer harvest.

When that harvest is finally finished, I pull up the plants, take them to the compost bin, and put away the black plastic for use next season. Then I give the squash beds my standard fall soil improvement. I spread enough lime to bring the pH into the 6.5 range (after getting back results from my soil test), then add 2 inches of compost or manure. I also work in 2 pounds of 10-10-10 fertilizer for every 100 square feet of bed area. With the soil raked smooth again, I sow 1 pound of winter rye seed for every 100 square feet of area and water in well.

Turnips With turnips coming on this month, I'll have all the fixings for a traditional New England boiled dinner, one of my favorites. These quick-growing, tasty turnips that come in September are much better for having matured into cool weather. I'll harvest them at 1½ to 2 inches across, when they're at their tender best. They will keep the table well supplied while their big, even tastier cousins — rutabagas — size up to provide great eating in October and on to Thanksgiving.

Winter Squash If you've been looking for squash entries between here and the June planting, you've been frustrated — there aren't any. That's because so many of the traditional garden "chores" — extra fertilizing, weeding, cultivating, chemical warfare — are eliminated by my streamlined Victory Garden cultural practices. Starting the squash indoors virtually elimi-

Fall spinach, well fed with water-soluble fertilizer in early September. This crop will provide greens for the Thanksgiving feast. I'll seed another, at month's end, for wintering-over.

nates seedling failure, so replanting is a thing of the past. The slow-release fertilizer feeds the hungry plants all through their growing cycle. (If any deficiencies occur, I nip in with quick-fix feeds of water-soluble fertilizer — but they rarely occur.) Insects are held at bay by the plastic, which also conserves water and completely eliminates the need for weeding and cultivating. Thus here it is September — harvest time — almost before I know it.

Frost now becomes a factor in the lives of my winter squash. I think everyone knows that summer squash vines are highly sensitive to frost, but not everyone knows that winter squash vines are also sensitive. Both can be done in by a hard, early frost, although winter squash are somewhat tougher, and will stand a few degrees of frost without harm.

The September garden is literally a treasure trove of colorful winter squash. Tasty Blue Hubbards are coming ready now. So is Waltham Butternut, and the Jersey Golden Acorn. Color is the best indicator of readiness for all of these. Waltham Butternut turns a uniform tan, and loses its green cast. Hubbard becomes gray-blue all over, and Jersey Golden Acorn turns shiny yellow. I cut all with 2 inches of stem attached, then cure them off the vines in the sun for a few days before putting them in cool storage (50 to 60 degrees) for the winter. I handle them gently, because bruises invite rot, and I don't crowd them or stack them on top of each other. It's important to leave space among the fruits.

The winter squash beds have performed long and hard for months now, and it's time to treat them to my regular Victory Garden season-end rejuvenation. I work in 2 inches of compost or manure, lime as needed to adjust the pH to 6.5, and add 2 pounds of 10-10-10 fertilizer for every 100 square feet of garden area. With all that blended in, I rake the beds smooth, sow 1 pound of winter rye seed for every 100 square feet of space, and water well.

A Blue Hubbard winter squash, still green. When it's gray and uniformly smooth, I'll harvest by cutting it off with 2 inches of stem. Though they look tough and gnarly, *all* winter squash should be handled gently, as even small bruises promote rot. ◄

Resembling tiny pumpkins, these Gold Nugget squash are firm, deep orange, and ready for harvest. The mulch of salt marsh hay keeps fruit off the damp ground, retarding rot. ►

MAKING CIDER

The countryside close to where I grew up was dotted with farms, and several of our neighbors pressed their own cider every fall. I well remember autumn trips to one of those farms. My father and I would drive down when the orchards were groaning with Macs and Cortlands. We could smell the tang of the cider press half a mile down the road when the wind was right. At the farm, we'd find mounds of scoured, gleaming apples waiting for the press inside the small mill. Dad always brought along a load of gallon jugs, and the farmer filled them with golden cider fresh from the press. When all the jugs were full, he'd hold a wooden dipper under the stream and give me a taste. I've never forgotten it. The cider was dark and thick, a perfect blend of tang and sweetness, cool enough to quench thirst and rich enough to fill me right up.

There aren't as many cider mills around as there used to be, nor are there as many presses in American homes. That's a shame, because cider is as American as apple pie, and maybe more so. Though the apple was unknown in North America, seeds were brought over by colonists from England in the 1600s. Our most famous apple planter was John

Key cidermaking ingredients: clean, sound apples, a sturdy cider press, spotless containers, and a thirsty gardener. ◄

To make pomace (the pulp from which juice is expressed), I first feed apples into the hand-cranked grinder. You can also make the pomace with a blender or food processor.

Chapman, immortalized in legend as Johnny Appleseed for his planting beyond the Alleghenies in the early 1800s. But apple planting got off to a much earlier start. Historical records show that the first true New Englander, Peregrine White (who was born on the *Mayflower* as she lay at anchor on May 20, 1620), sowed apple seeds in Massachusetts when he grew up. Apple raising and cidermaking reached a peak in this country in the mid-nineteenth century, when almost 80 percent of the population made farming their daily work. We've changed a lot since then, of course, and many of us have lost our ties with the old farming ways. But just

as many are anxious to regain some of that connection with the land, which is one reason for gardening's dramatic increase in popularity.

You don't have to grow an orchard, or live next door to a cider mill, to enjoy the matchless taste of fresh, sweet cider. A very reasonable investment of time and money will produce excellent home-pressed cider. I've made cider at home often, and I enjoy not only the superb taste but also the feeling of self-sufficiency I get from making my own cider. There are few home creations that taste better, and I don't know of many that are easier, either.

I buy cider apples from a local orchard. It is *very* important to use only ripe, sound apples. A "sound" apple has no bruises, worm damage, disease, or rot. The skin is smooth and intact. I buy apples by the bushel, knowing from experience that I'll get about 2 gallons of cider from each bushel. I've also picked my own in the fall, which is a nice way to save a few dollars and have a fun family outing at the same time.

At home, I wash each apple very thoroughly, making sure to clean out the area around the stem, where chemical sprays tend to accumulate and form a residue. Cleanliness, by the way, should be raised almost to the level of fanaticism in cidermaking. Cider is very nearly as volatile as milk, rich with organisms and bacteria, and I sterilize every single cidermaking implement. That means all the scoops and ladles, the cider press itself, our pomace cloth, cheesecloth, containers, lids — *everything*. I use boiling water for the cleaning; soaps and detergents don't do the job. They won't disinfect adequately, for one thing, and they can leave a residue that taints the cider.

Cidermakers agree that it's best not to use one variety of apple, but to blend two or three kinds for the finest flavor. Just *which* varieties to blend has been debated since pre-Christian times, when cider was already a popular drink in Europe. I've found that a reasonable compromise is to blend three varieties, two sweet and one tart — Delicious, Cortland, and MacIntosh. Some friends of mine in Vermont have been pressing cider as a family business for a hundred years, and they're *still* experimenting with different blends, so I never feel bad about trying a new combination. And I never hesitate to ask the advice of local orchardists, who are sure to have their own favorite combinations.

There's no magic to pressing cider at home. It requires only a bit of patience and elbow grease. It's changed little, in fact, in hundreds of years. I use a small manual press, bought from a mail-order

I'm adding washed apples to the press's attached grinder. Pomace collects in the wooden vat, which I've sterilized with boiling water.

The three stages of cidermaking, all in one view. At the top, a half-ground apple. In the middle, pomace collecting in the hardwood vat. And down below, pure cider already flowing into the sterile container. Cider is clear when first expressed, but contact with air quickly turns it a characteristic tawny brown.

house, several of which advertise in magazines like *Yankee, Country Journal, Organic Gardening*, and *Harrowsmith*. Cidermaking supplies can also be found in the Yellow Pages, but look under the "Winemaking Equipment and Supplies" heading.

The use of a food processor to make pomace (the pulp that's squeezed for juice) saves a tremendous amount of time and labor, but it's not the only way — particularly for traditionalists. I have friends who make pomace by slicing the apples very finely with a wooden slaw cutter. And I've read about a hardy homesteading couple who pound their apples into pomace in a big tub with one end of a 5-foot log!

My home press holds about 2 gallons of pomace when it's full. I use a wooden scoop to ladle in pomace and to press it down from time to time as I go. Juice will begin to flow at this point, so I keep a sterilized container under the press's spout to catch this early runoff.

When the press is full of pomace, I set the round wooden platen in place. The only thing left is to engage the metal screw and start turning. *Slowly*. Here's where patience comes in. Cider starts to flow as soon as the handle is turned, and it's tempting to keep right on going. Be warned that cider

And that's it. The cider I've pressed is ready to drink as soon as it starts to flow into the jug. In fact, I doubt if there's a better time to drink it, when it's so fresh that it tingles all the way down. There are ways, though, to keep the cider, and I've used each of them at one time or another. Unless cider is refrigerated, fermentation will begin at once. The expressed liquid is rich with microscopic yeast organisms present in the apples' skin, and, given only the right temperatures, these industrious little microbes will immediately begin turning the sugar into alcohol — and eventually into very fine vinegar. I keep cider as long as 2 weeks in the refrigerator. I've also tried freezing cider to keep it longer, and this works perfectly well — for months, in fact. The only caution is to leave space in the plastic jugs (I don't use glass for freezing — too much danger of cracking) for expansion.

The final product, ready for the taste test.

should not be hurried. Pressing out 2 gallons of pomace should be an all-day affair. That doesn't mean I stand around staring at the press. I give the platen a few more turns to start, and then repeat the process every half hour, giving one or two full revolutions each turning. I'll make ten visits to the press during the day. And if I'm really anxious to engage in the ultimate Yankee frugality to get the last drops of es-

Pressing the pomace is an all-day process. I tighten the press's platen one or two turns at a time, then leave it alone for an hour. The reward for my patience is fresh, pure cider that can be enjoyed fresh or kept in the freezer for months.

sence from my pomace, I'll let the press sit overnight, making the final turns the next morning.

A frost-spared early October garden, still fully productive. One of my garden aims is to extend the growing season as late as possible into the fall, which means being ready to cover frost-tender crops like beans when cold is forecast.

OCTOBER

OCTOBER

In October, the Victory Garden philosophy of intensive culture really comes into its own. I'm still harvesting brassicas, leeks, rutabagas, and lettuce out of the cold frame. The threat of a killing frost sends me out with baskets and boxes to capture the last of the peppers and the remaining tomatoes. The vegetables, in other words, are still coming on strong. Broccoli, Brussels sprouts, cabbage, and kale will give a great harvest right through the month. I learned years ago from my father that Brussels sprouts are helped to mature at this time of year by pinching off the top 6 inches of stem and by pulling off the lower leaves. This stops any additional top growth and sends all the energy into the rapidly developing sprouts. Leeks, Swiss chard, and spinach don't even need this minimal attention. They're all thriving in the cool weather.

Still to come this month is the harvest of pumpkins, and many herbs will be bunched for drying. Braided onions hang in the potting shed. Potatoes and squash are stored for winter.

The Victory Garden will soon have more vacant room, as the last of the crops are taken. I'll continue to amend the soil with compost, manure, lime, and fertilizer. In October, I take soil samples to test for pH and nutrient content. Fall is the best time to correct the pH, as both lime and sulfur take time to act. That pH, as I've said elsewhere, is the key to unlocking nutrients in the soil. If the pH is not close to neutral (between 6.0 and 7.0), many soil nutrients just aren't available to the plants. I never guess at pH, but rely on my county extension service test results. I'm not usually given to unequivocal statements about gardening, but here's one: This attention to pH is one of the most important things I can do for the garden.

Another October certainty is that deciduous trees will lose their leaves. I take my own leaves, and all those that neighbors will bestow, and put them in one of the compost bins, where they'll break down over the winter, turning into next season's most friable soil amendment.

Finally, I take a few special minutes to lean on my spading fork or rake and savor this very special time, the last days of the last month of my growing season. The garden and I have been working together since February, and in a way it's a bit sad, like saying good-bye to an old friend. That sadness never lasts long, though, because I'm so proud of all that we've produced together over the months — the taste of those early tomatoes is still strong on my tongue — and because I know that the gardening year never truly ends. Cycles complete themselves, rhythms change, pace alters, but the garden is always alive and thriving, appreciating my contribution to its growth and awaiting the approach of spring's flourish.

Plant in Garden
Winter rye

Mulch
Asparagus
Kale

Harvest
Brussels sprouts
Kale
Lettuce
Parsnips
Pumpkins
Rutabagas
Tomatoes

Asparagus It's time to give the asparagus beds their wintering-over top dressing of manure. I spread 2 to 3 inches of well-rotted manure over the entire bed this month. Nutrients from the manure will work their way into the soil all winter long, steadily and gradually. And the manure, as always, enhances the soil composition wherever it goes.

Brussels Sprouts In early October, I pinch off the growing tips of the Brussels sprouts plants to drive energy into the developing sprouts. I also prune out the yellowing lower leaves. When the sprouts reach golf-ball size and are tight leaved, like mini-cabbages, I start harvesting from the bottom up. I take the

Pinching off the top and snapping off the lower leaves hastens the maturing of Brussels sprouts from the bottom up.

sprouts by breaking them off with a twist of the fingers. It's trendy now in some of the more fashionable food boutiques to uproot a whole stalk of Brussels sprouts and present them to the table just that way. It's an impressive offering, and I save one such stalk for the Thanksgiving feast at home.

Kale   Kale is one tough plant, able to survive inclement weather, drought, and rough treatment. It even improves with cold weather and frost, so I'm in no hurry to harvest all the kale too soon. I'll leave a few plants, in fact, to overwinter completely, bedding them down under 6 inches of salt marsh hay in late November for use next February. When I do harvest kale, I snip individual leaves from the plants, taking them from the outside without disturbing the central growing point. Leaving that point alone prolongs the harvest considerably.

Lettuce   This may be the most satisfying lettuce harvest of all. I have gone to the October cold frame and found the plastic cover entirely frosted over, only to lift it up and discover, inside, perfectly healthy lettuce plants waiting to be picked. There's little to equal the taste of fresh Red Sails, Buttercrunch, and other savory types at this time of year.

When the harvest is completely finished, I go through the same fall soil preparation for the lettuce bed that all my other Victory Garden soil receives. A soil test tells me how much lime I need to add to adjust the pH back to the desired 6.5 range. In addition, I work in 2 inches of well-rotted manure or compost for soil structure. The bed receives a pound of 10-10-10 fertilizer, and then I broadcast the fall cover crop of winter rye, sowing the seeds thickly. They're watered in, and that puts the bed to bed for the winter.

Parsnips I sample the first parsnips after a good hard October freeze. This crop not only survives cold weather, it is much improved for being left in the ground over winter. The cold helps convert starch to sugar, producing much sweeter parsnips. Most of the crop will be harvested by late fall before hard frost

A few fall-dug parsnips, well shaped and long thanks to the customized planting holes I prepared in April.

locks them in the ground, but I like to sample an early parsnip or two this month. There's no special trick to the harvest. I dig the roots with a spading fork, working both sides of the parsnip row, plunging the fork in well back of the plants and gently levering the soil up by pushing the handle down. At this time I think back to those oversized ice-cream-cone holes that I made with the steel bar. If the parsnips are as big as the holes, I'll be a happy gardener.

Pumpkins   It's easy to know when pumpkins are ready for harvest. They turn that bright, uniform orange we all associate with Halloween jack-o'-lanterns. The vine will die off, and that's also a sure sign that the pumpkins are ready. I harvest them by cutting through the vine with my pocketknife, leaving 2 inches of vine on the pumpkin. I also handle the pumpkins carefully, making sure I don't pull the stem away from the pumpkin while I'm harvesting, because the open wound that results will be more likely to rot.

When the harvest is finished (and I do try to get all the pumpkins before the first hard frost hits, because they'll turn black and rot if punished by a deep freeze), I roll up the black plastic for use next year. Then I put the pumpkin beds through my usual Victory Garden fall soil amendment program. After testing for pH requirements, I add the necessary amount of lime, and work in 2 inches of well-rotted manure or compost and 2 pounds of 10-10-10 fertilizer for every 100 square feet of bed space. After raking the soil smooth, I sow 1 pound of winter rye seed for every 100 square feet of bed, water in, and wait for spring.

Rutabagas   Like parsnips, rutabagas' flavor is much improved by a good, hard frost. I wait until we've received one of those and then harvest a rutabaga or two. The globular rutabagas sit there, half in and half out of the soil, just waiting to be lifted free by their tops. Nothing to it. The harvest will actually last over several weeks as the seedlings tend to grow at different rates, giving plants that come to maturity at different times, rather than all at once.

By the end of October, I still have plenty of rutabagas waiting to be harvested. Since very hard freezing of the ground will not occur until December, it is perfectly suitable to leave them in the ground right up to Thanksgiving.

Tomatoes   There are still tomatoes in the early October garden. Many are green, and it's tempting to let them fully ripen on the vine. I can get them through the light frosts of September by wrapping their cages in polyethylene, but an October frost is usually much harder. If one is forecast, I go ahead and harvest all the remaining tomatoes: green, semigreen, and red. Those with blemishes go to the discard pile. The rest are stored.

These Jersey Golden Acorn squash will fill the day's harvest basket of season's end tomatoes and peppers, broccoli, and a lovely Chinese cabbage.

A classic New England assortment of winter squash and pumpkins.

Any tomato with the slightest blush of pink will eventually ripen off the vine, but conditions must be just right. They must be cool and dry, and it helps to put a piece of apple in the storage container (I use a Styrofoam cooler). The ethylene gas given off by the decaying apple aids the tomatoes' ripening. Each one is wrapped in newspaper before going into the cooler. While these — even when fully ripened — will never match the beauties I pulled fresh from the vine in August, they'll certainly do next month. And green tomatoes have *their* uses, too, as any lover of green tomato relish can attest.

My last bit of tomato housekeeping is to pull the tomato cages, clear them of any leftover foliage or vines, and store them for next season. Empty vines go to the compost bin. Then I prepare the beds for winter by working in 2 inches of compost or manure, 2 pounds of 10-10-10 fertilizer for every 100 square feet of bed, and enough lime to bring the pH to 6.5. I work all this into the soil, rake it smooth, sow 1 pound of winter rye seed for every 100 square feet of area, and water well.

Winter Rye   I'm sowing my winter cover crop of rye on the Victory Garden raised beds this month as they come open. The practice is the same for all the beds. When the harvest is complete, I work 2 inches of manure or compost into the soil, add 2 pounds of 10-10-10 fertilizer for every 100 square feet of bed area, and lime as needed to adjust the pH to 6.5. That's all worked in well, raked smooth, and then I broadcast 1 pound of winter rye seed for every 100 square feet of area being sown. It's watered in and the beds are kept moist until germination occurs. The rye will grow over the winter, holding the beds' shape and, come spring, contributing its organic matter to soil structure when I turn it under before planting.

A good thick stand of winter rye with mums, Mission lettuce, and Inca marigolds. Next year's successful garden begins with fall soil improvement.

WREATHMAKING

When I talk about preserving the harvest, many people think I'm talking about canning or freezing food. Here's another way to preserve the yield of garden and fields. I'm talking about wreathmaking, a craft that was practiced among American colonists and that can still beautify our homes as it did theirs.

To make wreaths, you'll need a few things from the hardware store. Of primary importance is wire for attaching materials to the frame. A bunch of 2 dozen floral wires costs about 59 cents; a whole spool is only about $3. Number 24 wire is a good all-purpose choice. Wire cutters make the job of snipping off pieces much easier, though an old pair of sturdy scissors will do. Needlenosed pliers save my fingers when twisting wire, and serve as tweezers when positioning the materials. Wreath frames are essential. Wire frames are either flat or box-wire types. There are also Styrofoam or floral foam frames. A 12-inch wire frame costs about 79 cents and a 12-inch foam frame about $2.50. You will need something to fix materials to the frame, and I think the very best way is with a light hot-glue gun. Fifteen dollars buys a good gun, which will glue almost

The American native bittersweet winds easily around and makes a simple, rustic addition to the Victory Garden tool shed. ◄

Gathering American bittersweet.

anything. I've added an on/off switch 5 inches down the cord from the glue gun's handle, to extend the life of the tool. Glue sticks sometimes come with the gun, and extras cost about 20 cents each. Finally, you will need a special corner where mess can be ignored until you get around to recycling all your materials.

The list of wreath ingredients is almost endless, and starts, of course, in the garden. From the flower garden, everything from peonies to hydrangea, from roses to dusty miller, and clematis, delphinium, and foxglove seed pods. From the vegetable garden, rhubarb flowers, celery leaves, ornamental kale, carrot tops, okra pods, leek and chive seed heads, and whole, tiny red peppers. The herb garden is another gold mine, providing

flowers from marjoram, mint, tarragon, chives, and lavender as well as the seed heads and seed pods from lovage, dill, coriander, chervil, and sage. Sage, bay, parsley, and savory leaves work fine, too. In fact, just about any herb you grow can be an eager candidate for a wreath.

I have seen tendrils of wisteria, branches of birch, bittersweet, weeping willow, forsythia, and pussy willows all used. They are so flexible that they can be coiled or woven into natural wreath frames, to be used as they are, or decorated further. It's even possible to use many roots as frames, securing the ends with a quick twist of wire or weaving them into each other for a purely natural connection. Look also for berries, seed pods of locust and tulip trees, clematis, delphinium, larkspur, and foxglove seed pods, cones from pine, hemlock, spruce, and evergreens like juniper.

It is also possible to range farther afield, collecting goldenrod, clover, red sumac, tansy, heather, teasel, Queen Anne's lace, and an endless number of weed flowers and wonderful grasses and pods. It's not necessary to know all their names to appreciate their lovely forms and textures. Finally, don't forget to bring bayberry back from the shore, and remember that cemeteries and arboretums are wonderful collecting grounds for the polite guest.

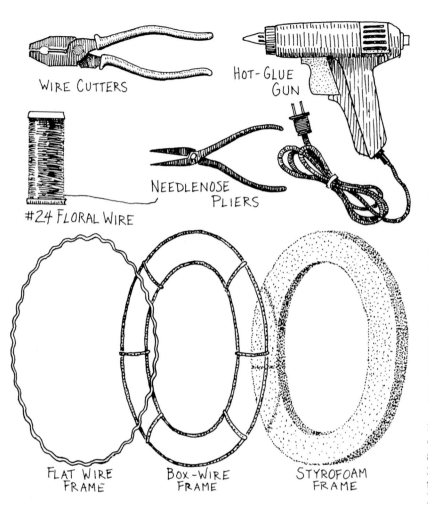

WIRE CUTTERS

HOT-GLUE GUN

#24 FLORAL WIRE

NEEDLENOSE PLIERS

FLAT WIRE FRAME

BOX-WIRE FRAME

STYROFOAM FRAME

Gathering can go on from early spring to late autumn. Try to pick on dry days, in early morning, just after dew has evaporated. Most flowers are best harvested at the peak of bloom, and trial and error is the only way to develop a sense of timing here. It's better to harvest earlier than later, in some cases cutting just as the buds begin to unfurl their color. Those just showing and others at peak bloom are the real eye-catchers in a well-done wreath. But it's nice to work in variety and interest by including flowers at all stages.

After picking, I strip all the leaves from the stem except one or two near the flower itself. Leaves retain moisture and retard the drying process. Stripping outdoors, right after picking, allows me to leave the mess outside.

There are lots of ways to preserve this harvest, but I stick with two simple methods. One is highly traditional, the other ultramodern. The traditional method, practiced by our

forebears, is air-drying. It's easy, cheap, and produces materials in good quantity. It also works on almost anything that grows. To begin, loosely bunch together about 6 of the same type stems and wrap them with a rubber band 2 inches from their ends. Tie again with string and leave a loop for hanging. Choose a drying spot that is dry, dark, and has good air circulation. I hang bunches from the edge of a top pantry shelf. Be sure that the bunches hang freely, and aren't crowded. Drying this way will take 10 days to 2 weeks, after which you can leave the bunches hanging until you want to use them, or store them in cartons away from dust. If you'd like to see them on display, set them upright in baskets throughout the house, avoiding the moist bathroom and direct sun.

The ultramodern drying method is to use a microwave oven. Although it limits the size of materials, it does a perfect job of drying, locking in the exact natural colors. Leaves that yellow in air-drying remain a brilliant green. Experiment by placing a leaf or two on half a paper napkin and covering with the other half. Top this with an inverted ovenproof custard cup to keep the leaves from curling. Set the oven on high and leave it on for 2 minutes. As with foods, let the materials relax out of the oven for 5 minutes while the internal heat continues to dry them. If they're stiff and dry to the touch, they're finished. If almost dry, let them sit out overnight. If still damp, return for another minute in the oven. Experiment with ferns, English ivy, and forsythia. Since

I'm using twine to hold my wreath of American bitter-sweet in good form.

the microwave perfectly captures the colors of a fall leaf and a pansy, why not a rose?

With a wealth of dried materials on hand, you're ready to start making wreaths. A word of advice: If you're not adept with a glue gun, practice first. Plug it in, load with glue according to the instructions, and wait 2 or 3 minutes, so that when you press the trigger, melted glue (it's really plastic) dribbles out. Practice on an old basket or mushroom box. Frame around the rim of either with a sampling from your collection, starting with larger pieces, like pine cones. Hold the gun point right above a spot on the cone, pull the trigger, and hope. You should play around until you can regularly produce a neat, single spot of glue the size of a pea. When the little spot is in place, release the trigger and make a

clean getaway by twisting the nozzle up and away. Quickly connect your cone or other material to the naked rim. Stick with this trial-and-error practice, and you'll be surprised at how quickly you become expert. The trick is to produce the right size drop for the material, just large enough to hold it in place, but no larger.

Now let's go step-by-step through the building of an herb wreath, one of my favorite kinds. First, assemble the materials: a 12-inch saw-toothed wire frame, enough artemesia (or other material) to cover the frame's surface, herbs of your choice, and the basic tools and supplies listed earlier.

Cover the entire surface of the frame with artemesia, or a substitute, anchoring it with a piece of the wire looped over and around the boughs. Don't worry too much about neatness and visible wire. This is your base, and will be covered.

For the next layer, wire on bunches of tarragon, lemon balm, savory, mint — whatever herbs you have harvested. Use the needlenosed pliers to twist the wire tightly around these bunches. Vary the textures, colors, and shades. If a bit of wire shows, tuck in a sprig of lavender or thyme or rosemary. If you are using a glue gun, camouflage any bothersome spots by gluing on a chive or marjoram flower, or dill or fennel heads.

As with any recipe, don't hesitate to substitute, and, above all, don't avoid making because you lack the suggested ingredients. If you don't have artemesia, try lamb's ears, oregano, catnip, or basil. Try it freshly picked, and let it dry on the frame. Vary appearance by using a box-wire frame, which will allow you to attach a much larger selection of materials.

If you want to break off your herbs for cooking, attach them mostly with wire. If the wreath will be purely decorative, you can rely more on a glue gun. Add to the design by wiring or gluing on nutmeg, nuts, or cinnamon sticks. Glue on rich green microwave-dried bay or sage leaves. Stretch the theme and trim with tansy, yarrow, goldenrod, berries, or tiny hemlock cones.

Finally, cut off any wire ends. Decide where you want the top of your wreath to be, and wrap a wire hook around the back of the ring for hanging. There you have it! Your own creation, beautiful, aromatic, and useful. Yet another way to use the things that grow all around us.

I gather all the leaves I can in fall because they are such good soil-improvers. I mulch them, compost them, and sometimes spread them right on the garden and till them in before sowing over with winter rye.

ENDINGS

ENDINGS

The gardener's year is circular; November and December are the months that close the circle. Though I'm already looking forward to the next season's activities, I appreciate this quiet period. It's a time to relax, reflect — and take special delight in the harvest that the Victory Garden provides right through Thanksgiving. It's one of my gardening goals to grace the table with fresh vegetables come the end of November. I want this special meal to include freshly dug leeks, kale, parsnips, Brussels sprouts, as well as stored potatoes, onions, rutabagas, and winter squash. Careful mulching is essential if I'm to enjoy this late-season bounty. I mulch around the leeks, parsnips, and Brussels sprouts after they've had several frosts, but before the ground freezes. When that happens, I use leaves or salt marsh hay, laying the mulch quite thick — 6 to 12 inches. Both mulches work well. Leaves are almost always readily available, and they're a fine soil conditioner. Come spring, I'll dig them right into the soil. Any extra leaves will fill one of the compost bins over winter. I also lay down a 6-inch mulch of leaves or hay on the strawberries now. And both raspberries and asparagus are mulched with 2 to 3 inches of manure.

A few more projects close up the garden for winter. To leave it tidy, ready for next year, I bring in all the equipment I've used over the season. I gather tomato cages and stack them together in the garage. Trellises come down and receive any necessary repairs before they go into storage. After the last lettuce harvest, I take the cold frames apart and store them. I bring watering cans and hoses inside, and blow out underground hose lines with a compressor. (A bike pump with a special fitting will work just as well.) After I fill the compost bins almost to the top, I add a final 2 inches of soil, water well, and then cover with black plastic. This will keep the pile active into early winter. Pots are sorted and cleaned, and any broken ones are discarded.

I'm orderly with my tools. Anything that can be hung *is* hung on pegboard. Before they go to their assigned spots, all tools are cleaned. I wire-brush working ends and metal surfaces, then file all the edged tools. All metal surfaces are wiped down with motor oil, to prevent rusting. I clean wooden handles and give them a fresh coat of linseed oil. The occasional painted handle receives a fresh, bright coat. Pruners, hose-end attachments, string lines, and other small items are "filed" together in an old bureau. Finally, I make a list of items that will need to be replaced come next growing season.

One tradition of long standing at my house is having a live Christmas tree. Several of the landscaping evergreens around my home spent time indoors as living Christmas trees, and

I like to give all my hand tools a good cleaning before putting them away for winter. This includes scraping off soil, oiling metal ends, sharpening edges, and rubbing over wooden handles with linseed oil. ▶

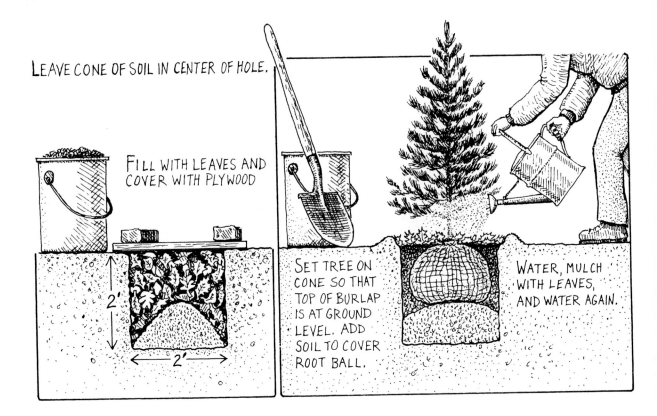

LEAVE CONE OF SOIL IN CENTER OF HOLE.

FILL WITH LEAVES AND COVER WITH PLYWOOD

2'

2'

SET TREE ON CONE SO THAT TOP OF BURLAP IS AT GROUND LEVEL. ADD SOIL TO COVER ROOT BALL.

WATER, MULCH WITH LEAVES, AND WATER AGAIN.

there are few things more satisfying than watching a 3-foot spruce mature over the years.

Before I go shopping for our tree, I prepare the hole in which it will eventually be planted. Because the tree will one day grow into a fully mature forest tree as much as 30 feet tall, it needs ample separation from house, outbuildings, and other trees. I'm also careful not to set it too close to the garden, where shade would rob sun and spreading roots would steal moisture and nutrients from my vegetables. The tree's planting hole is dug 2 feet deep and 2 feet in diameter. I keep the soil from this hole in a large bucket, and store it in the garage or cellar, where it won't freeze. Then I fill the hole with leaves and cover it with a piece of plywood.

Next comes shopping for the tree. Spruce and pine are the most popular Christmas choices. When shopping for a live one, I look for good, dark green color and secure needles. A vigorous shake should not dislodge needles from a healthy tree. Another test is to bend a single needle between thumb and forefinger. If the needle is supple and bends easily, springing back to its original shape, the tree's healthy. If the needle is brittle and snaps, I look for another tree.

During the Christmas season, the tree stays indoors only 3 to 5 days. Exposing it to a longer period of dry warmth is a main cause of winterkill. I keep the root ball moist in a waterproof container (the very large plastic tubs available from nurseries and garden centers work well for this) with about 2 inches of water. I also moisten the burlap-covered root ball daily, and provide humidity for the tree by spritzing it thoroughly every day. After its brief stint indoors, the tree goes outside for planting. I remove all the leaves from the protected hole, and place some of the stored soil in the hole, creating a cone. The root ball goes on top of that cone, and the burlap is left on the root ball. It will rot away and the roots will grow right through it. It's important to plant the tree at the same depth that it was growing in the field, and this means that the top of the burlap should just be covered with soil. After the root ball is in place, I fill the hole with my remaining soil. Then — and this is very important — I water the tree in well. Next I spread leaves all around the base of the tree to help retain warmth and moisture, and then I give the tree another good soaking. Many live Christmas trees die during the winter from drying out, because rain is infrequent and snow is not a usable water source. Whenever there's a thaw in January or February, I go outside to water the tree. And I spray the needles with an antidesiccant, which lets them breathe but slows the rate of water loss.

In December the seed catalogs begin to arrive, and I spend many an hour by the well-stoked fire, turning pages and fantasizing about next year's harvests. I like catalogs that are easy to read, illustrated in color, and full of helpful cultural information. Some companies, for reasons I've never understood, insist on printing their information in microscopic type. My eyes glance off such user-unfriendly catalogs, and they don't get much of my business. I do pay attention, though, to the catalogs from various specialty houses, which offer Oriental vegetables, heirloom varieties, and the like. These complement nicely my assortment of catalogs from the major houses and provide a look at varieties that mainstream houses can't afford to stock.

Finally, December is gift-giving month, and I enjoy this chance to share the garden's glory with friends and relatives. I give relishes, braided twists of onions, potpourri, gardeners' aids (like the planting boards I make in the Victory Garden workshop; see the feature titled "Victory Garden Structures" for instructions), and wreaths (which I've described in a separate feature, "Wreathmaking"). Subscriptions to gardening magazines also go into the stockings of friends, as do copies of the "Victory Garden" video.

GARDENING TO ATTRACT BIRDS

I've mentioned elsewhere my early morning visits to the Victory Garden, when I watch birds helping themselves to a hearty breakfast of insects from the various crops. The birds are beautiful, of course, but their visits serve a very real purpose, reducing plant damage from insect pests and lessening my own de-bugging work. Birds are a welcome addition to the Victory Garden and its environs, and I know that I am not alone in my fondness for them. Something like 70 million people now attract birds with feeders, spending an estimated $500 million annually on birdseed. There's good reason for such enthusiasm. Birds are faithful, and will pay regular visits to any backyard that offers them food — from feeders or more natural sources. Their color and flash add beauty to any home environment. And of all wildlife, birds are the least likely to cause problems for the gardener and homeowner.

Many people start out creating a backyard wildlife habitat with bird feeders, and there's not a thing wrong with that. When I was a boy, we had several feeders around our house,

I like the natural look of this house feeder, hung at a convenient height for re-filling. ◄

Chickadees being offered a two-course meal — suet in the cage and seed in the cylindrical feeder.

and a large nesting box as well. I remember the pleasure of seeing bright flocks of evening grosbeaks come to the feeding tray in winter, and of watching new chickadee families learn the ropes during the summertime. I liked especially the little red hummingbird feeder, and found the tiny, brilliantly colored ruby-throated hummingbirds endlessly fascinating.

One of the nicest things about bird feeders and birdbaths (birds need water, too!) is that they provide almost immediate results. While other aspects of creating a backyard

wildlife habitat may take months or even years to pay dividends, feeders and baths will collect birds in a few days. There are really six basic kinds of feeders, each with certain things to recommend it. The best all-around type, and the one to have if you're having only one, is the cylindrical plastic feeder. Available from hardware stores and garden supply houses, these are best supported on a pole away from large trees and the eaves of your house, from both of which squirrels may leap. Fill the tubular feeder with sunflower seeds of the black oil or striped kind, and nothing else. Sunflower seeds are more popular with more kinds of birds than any other seed, and they provide more fat and energy than do other varieties, an important consideration during cold winter months. Tubular feeders will attract not only seed-eaters, but birds that normally eat insects as well, when the insect population dwindles in winter: nuthatches, chickadees, titmice, and woodpeckers.

The feeding table is really nothing more than a flat plywood tray with a roof, supported 1 to 3 feet from the ground. Bigger birds that like to walk around in their food will come to the tray, as will

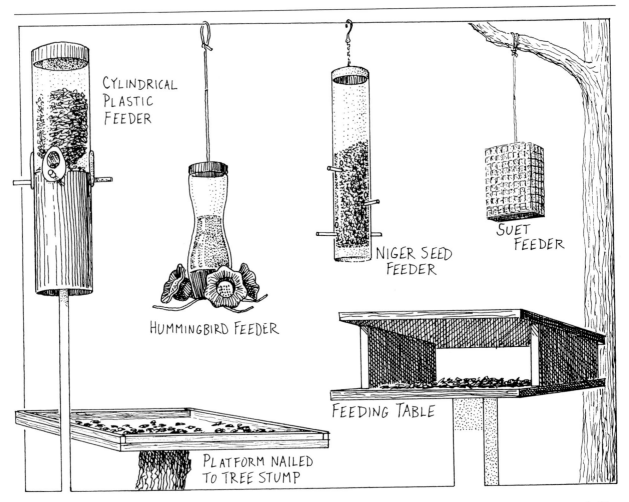

CYLINDRICAL PLASTIC FEEDER

HUMMINGBIRD FEEDER

NIGER SEED FEEDER

SUET FEEDER

FEEDING TABLE

PLATFORM NAILED TO TREE STUMP

gregarious types that like to dine with four or five buddies. You'll see cardinals, mourning doves, blackbirds, finches, and evening grosbeaks pecking happily in your feeding table.

Suet feeders are a third type, and are especially important in winter. Suet is a certain kind of fat (the hard fat around the kidneys and loins of cattle and sheep), which you can find at butcher shops or meat counters. A winter suet feeder invites birds you might not see otherwise — a variety of woodpeckers and nuthatches, Carolina wrens, yellow-rumped warblers, and, in the coldest winters, red-shouldered hawks or

American kestrels. A suet feeder is nothing more than a wire mesh cage hung from the trunk or branch of a tree 6 to 8 feet off the ground.

Hummingbird feeders are usually red plastic or glass containers that hold sugar solutions. They're red because hummingbirds have been found to associate that color with high concentrations of nectar in flowers. A hummingbird feeder should be easy to clean, and cleaned often — every other day — with hot water or a mild

detergent. Use a sugar solution that is 1 part table sugar to 4 parts water.

Niger seed feeders, sometimes called thistle seed feeders, are tubular plastic feeders with very small holes for the very small seed. Niger seed will attract some species, like pine siskins and red polls, that might not gather around other feeders.

Finally, a small platform nailed to a tree stump makes an ideal fruit feeding table for birds. Mockingbirds, bluebirds, catbirds, thrashers, thrushes, and robins all eat a lot of fruit in the winter. Raisins and currants are best, but orange halves will bring orioles, too.

Birds need water as well as food, and many homeowners make the mistake of thinking that wildlife naturally finds ponds and streams to drink from and bathe in. In urban and suburban areas, such natural sources may be few and far between, so providing a backyard water source is a sure way to attract wild birds. A birdbath need not be complicated at all. Any shallow container will do: from a ½-inch deep, 6-inch wide saucer to more traditional pedestal-mounted birdbaths standing 3 feet high. The birdbath should be light enough to tilt easily for cleaning, and not too deep. Birds don't like water deeper than ½ inch. They bathe and drink from the same water, so the bath should be cleaned daily and refilled with clean tap water — no additives!

Bird feeders and baths are an easy, inexpensive way to begin attracting wild birds to your yard, but they do not provide the natural habitat wildlife needs. To really make the best environment for wildlife, you need to think in terms of living plants. Landscaping and gardening with wildlife in mind will create an environment that provides four essential elements: food, water, cover, and a place to raise young. Consider this fact: With the very best feeders, you may attract up to fifteen kinds of birds. With landscaping and gardening, you can expect visits from more than *eighty*.

The first step in creating a habitat for birds and other wildlife is to develop a land

A downy woodpecker enjoying a winter's meal at the suet feeder.

scape plan. Make rough sketches, identifying what's on your property already. Don't just put down the trees and shrubs. Show everything, as illustrated in the accompanying sample plan. Include large deciduous trees, all shrubs and flowering plants, and fruits, as well as heat pumps, swing sets, driveways, outbuildings, and other structures. Early fall is a good time to begin making your inventory. Walk around out there and see what's been growing well and what's been struggling. Look at areas of bright sun and shade, at areas where your land borders that of neighbors, and — of course — at your garden. Through all the surveying, try to be thinking like an animal. Ask yourself which plants provide good food, protective cover, and shelter for raising young. If you're not too sure which varieties *are* best, you

may want to talk to an expert. When we created the new Lexington Victory Garden outside Boston, we worked with some of the best experts in the business, people like Craig Tufts of the National Wildlife Federation. You may not have access to such expertise, but don't disregard your county extension service agent, who's likely to be a wealth of free information. If you'd like to do some reading on your own, I'll pass on three sources that I've found very helpful. A fine starting point is the National Wildlife Federation's "Gardening With Wildlife" kit, available from the National Wildlife Federation, Dept. BN, 1412 16th Street NW, Washington, D.C. 20036. *The Bird Feeder Book* by Donald and Lillian Stokes, published by Little, Brown, provides information on common birds. Ortho Publishing's *How to Attract Birds* is a reasonably priced guide to a very wide range of birds and their preferences. And for the really serious enthusiast, there is *The Audubon Society Guide to Attracting Birds*, by Stephen W. Kress, published by Scribners.

Once you've familiarized yourself with the kinds of birds that frequent your area, and with the general lay of your own land, it's time to make a detailed landscape plan, to scale, on graph paper. As you do this, bear in mind that you're working to create a backyard environment that will provide the four essentials for wildlife survival mentioned earlier. The ideal plant for attracting and maintaining wildlife will be evergreen, with extremely dense growth, thorny and heavily branched, and will provide fruit or berries all year round. Unfortunately, that ideal plant doesn't exist. What we try to do in the Victory Garden, and what you can do at home, is to use our tactic of succession planting to provide a group of plants that all work together to meet the needs of birds.

Food is our first consideration. No one plant will provide fruit or berries all year, so in spring we depend on grape holly and shadbush (also known as amelanchier), which bloom and bear fruit by May and produce through July. I also like to share a little of my berry crops with the birds. Any berries grown for human consumption will delight the feathered friends: blueberries, strawberries, blackberries, gooseberries, currants, or raspberries, for example. I protect most of my berry crops with netting, but I always leave a few plants open for the birds. Dwarf fruit trees — plums, cherries, or peaches — are another source of food for the birds in spring and summer.

Much more critical than those two seasons, though, are fall and winter. The best solution is to provide the birds with massed bunches of plants that make good cover *and* food sources. Berry-bearing shrubs are an especially good bet. Berry bushes will attract birds likely to be different from the seed-eating birds at your feeder, and the bushes that produce berries in fall will hold

Pyracantha **is a choice ornamental, offering berries that birds love.**

Viburnum dentatum.

fruit into late winter, when birds may be finding wild food in short supply. Firethorns, or *Pyracantha*, and flowering dogwood are excellent berry bushes, as are the mountain ashes, winterberry hollies and junipers such as the Eastern red cedar.

I also like the native viburnums, which are especially heavy fruit-setters. Arrowwood viburnum, American cranberrybush, and black haw viburnum will all form a dense shrub mass, and will bear fruit from September through January or February.

Privets are exellent choices for hedging, because they provide fine bird cover with their thickly intertwined branches, *and* if you've left some unpruned to flower they'll hold fruit — blue or blue-black berries — late in winter. Likewise, tree holly holds fruit until April or May. For a wide variety of shapes and forms, I favor the cotoneaster group, which gives a range of food-bearing plants from growth that crawls on the ground to plants 8 to 10 feet tall. A few are evergreen, with berries from early fall through late winter, and very adaptable to many different soil conditions. Junipers are also excellent, providing thick cover and, in the female varieties, an ample food supply. The junipers do need strong sun, but they can be downright spiny, making some of the best cover planting around. I'd hate to be a housecat trying to chase chickadees into a big Hetzi juniper!

As you can see, by planning and planting with the birds in mind, I can offer them food sources throughout the year. The grape holly and Amelanchier start things off in early spring, after which the birds feast on their ample supply of natural foods, augmented tastily by a few of our Victory Garden berries. Come fall, the viburnums, berry-bearing species, and cotoneasters sustain the birds, and berries and fruit produced by those plants keep them going through the winter, as well.

For hummingbirds, I plant as many red, tubular-shaped flowers as I can. Scarlet salvia, (an excellent bedding plant), cypress vine, scarlet petunias, and scarlet gladioli are excellent hummingbird-attracting annuals. Good hummingbird perennials include bee balm, Texas sage (an annual in the North), wild columbine, and trumpet honeysuckle.

Birds like seeds as much as they like berries and insects, of course, and your supermarket is far from the only source of seed. I've discovered over the years that growing my own birdseed is more fun than hauling home bags of supermarket stuff. Sunflowers are perhaps the best of all, but marigolds, cosmos, and zinnias add color to the garden, are heavy seed-producers, and, in the case of the marigolds, help protect the garden from certain pests. These flowers produce seeds that the birds love. Four-

Annual salvia is a real hummingbird pleaser.

Pokeweed (*Phytolacca*).

o'clocks and petunias attract birds in droves, as do the bright yellow flowers of the St.-John's-worts. The best way to insure a hearty seed supply is to resist the gardener's habit of pinching off fading flowers to keep the plants in full bloom. Let the flowers wither, and the seeds will swell in their pods. This will produce lots of bird-seed, plus seed for next year's planting of flowers.

Though shrubs and bushes, along with flowering plants, are the most important sources of food and cover for birds, trees can also be helpful. Many people think only of large deciduous trees when landscaping their yards, but in fact a greater number of smaller trees may be a better option for the average-sized yard to which the homeowner wants to attract birds. Semidwarf or dwarf fruit trees, crab apples, hawthorns, flowering dogwoods, and Cornellian cherry are all good choices. They produce fruit and lots of spring color, along with pleasing fall foliage. I also think the sassafras is a superb choice. Though not widely available, it produces perhaps the most spectacular fall foliage of any tree. The female trees produce fruit, and the leaves are quite aromatic, producing the pungent, surprising scent of gumbo filé, an essential ingredient in Cajun cuisine.

APPENDIX: AGRICULTURAL EXTENSION SERVICES

Alabama

Agricultural Extension Service
Bulletin Room
Alabama Cooperative Extension Service
Auburn University
Auburn, AL 36849
(205) 826-5323

Alaska

Agricultural Extension Service
University of Alaska
2651 Providence Avenue
Anchorage, AK 99504
(907) 277-1488

Arizona

Agricultural Extension Service
University of Arizona
Tucson, AZ 85721
(602) 626-2438

Arkansas

Agricultural Extension Service
Cooperative Extension Service
University of Arkansas, USDA
1201 McAlmont, Box 391
Little Rock, AR 72203
(501) 376-6301

California

Agricultural Extension Service
University of California
Davis, CA 95616
(916) 752-0412

Agricultural Extension Service
San Joaquin Valley Agricultural Research Extension
Center
9240 South Riverbend Avenue
Palier, CA 93648
(209) 646-2794

Agricultural Extension Service
Department of Botany and
Plant Sciences
University of California
Riverside, CA 92521
(714) 787-3432

Colorado

Agricultural Extension Service
Department of Horticulture
Colorado State University
Fort Collins, CO 80523
(303) 491-7018

Connecticut

Agricultural Extension Service
University of Connecticut
Storrs, CT 06268
(203) 486-3435

Delaware

Agricultural Extension Service
University of Delaware
Newark, DE 19711
(302) 738-2531

Agricultural Extension Service
University Substation Division
R.D. 2, Box 48
Georgetown, DE 19947
(302) 856-5250

District of Columbia

Agricultural Extension Service
1351 Nicholson Street, N.W.
Washington, DC 20011
(202) 282-7403

Florida

Agricultural Extension Service
Agricultural Research Center
3205 S.W. 70th Avenue
Fort Lauderdale, FL 33314
(305) 475-8990

Agricultural Extension Service
University of Florida
Gainesville, FL 32611
(904) 392-2134

Georgia

Agricultural Extension Service
University of Georgia
Athens, GA 30602
(404) 542-8861

Hawaii

Agricultural Extension Service
University of Hawaii
3190 Maile Way
Honolulu, HI 96822
(808) 948-7256

Idaho

Agricultural Extension Service
University of Idaho
Box 300
Boise, ID 83701
(208) 334-3209

Illinois

Agricultural Extension Service
Extension Specialist, Floriculture
205 Ornamental Horticulture
Building
University of Illinois
Urbana, IL 61801
(217) 333-2123

Agricultural Extension Service
Extension Vegetable Specialist
208 Vegetable Crops Building
University of Illinois
Urbana, IL 61801
(217) 333-1969

Agricultural Extension Service
Extension Specialist, Pomology
104 Horticulture Field Lab
University of Illinois
Urbana, IL 61801
(217) 333-1522

Indiana

Agricultural Extension Service
Department of Horticulture
Purdue University
West Lafayette, IN 47907
(317) 749-2261

Iowa

Agricultural Extension Service
2 Northcrest Drive
Council Bluffs, IA 51507
(712) 328-0077

Kansas

Agricultural Extension Service
Department of Horticulture
Kansas State University
Manhattan, KS 66506
(913) 532-6170

Kentucky

Agricultural Extension Service
Agricultural Science Center
North, Room N-318
University of Kentucky
Lexington, KY 40546
(606) 257-2874

Louisiana

Agricultural Extension Service
Louisiana State University
Baton Rouge, LA 70803
(504) 388-4141

Maine

Agricultural Extension Service
University of Maine
Orono, ME 04473
(207) 581-2771

Agricultural Extension Service
Highmoor Experimental Farm
Monmouth, ME 04259
(207) 933-2100

Maryland

Agricultural Extension Service
University of Maryland
College Park, MD 20742
(301) 454-3143

Agricultural Extension Service
Vegetable Research Farm,
Route 5
Salisbury, MD 21801
(301) 742-8788

Massachusetts

Agricultural Extension Service
Bowditch Hall
University of Massachusetts
Amherst, MA 01003
(413) 545-2250

Agricultural Extension Service
33 King Street
Northampton, MA 01060
(413) 584-2556

Michigan

Agricultural Extension Service
Department of Horticulture
Michigan State University
East Lansing, MI 48824
(517) 355-5178

Minnesota

Agricultural Extension Service
University of Minnesota
St. Paul, MN 55108
(612) 376-7574

Mississippi

Agricultural Extension Service
Box 5426
Mississippi State, MS 39762
(601) 325-3935

Missouri

Agricultural Extension Service
University of Missouri
Columbia, MO 65201
(314) 882-7511

Montana

Agricultural Extension Service
Plant and Soil Sciences Department
Montana State University
Bozeman, MT 59715
(406) 994-4601

Nebraska

Agricultural Extension Service
377 Plant Science Building
University of Nebraska
Lincoln, NE 68503
(402) 472-2454

Nevada

Agricultural Extension Service
University of Nevada
Reno, NV 89507
(702) 784-6981

New Hampshire

Agricultural Extension Service
Plant Science Department
University of New Hampshire
Durham, NH 03824
(603) 862-1200

New Jersey

Agricultural Extension Service
Blake Hall
Box 231
Rutgers, The State University
New Brunswick, NJ 08903
(201) 932-9393

New Mexico

Agricultural Extension Service
New Mexico State University
Las Cruces, NM 88003
(505) 646-1521

New York

Agricultural Extension Service
Cornell University
Ithaca, NY 14853

North Carolina

Agricultural Extension Service
Department of Horticultural
Science
North Carolina State University
Raleigh, NC 27607
(919) 737-3131

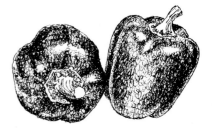

North Dakota

Agricultural Extension Service
North Dakota State University
Fargo, ND 58102
(701) 237-8163

Ohio

Agricultural Extension Service
Ohio Agricultural Research
Development Center
Wooster, OH 44691
(216) 264-1021

Oklahoma

Agricultural Extension Service
Oklahoma State University
Stillwater, OK 74078

Oregon

Agricultural Extension Service
Oregon State University
Corvallis, OR 97331
(503) 754-3464

Pennsylvania

Agricultural Extension Service
102 Tyson Building
University Park, PA 16802
(814) 863-2194

Puerto Rico

Agricultural Extension Service
Departmento de Horticultura
Recinto Universitario de
Mayaguez
Mayaguez, PR 00708
(809) 832-4040, ext. 3004

Rhode Island

Agricultural Extension Service
University of Rhode Island
Kingston, RI 02881
(401) 792-2791

South Carolina

Agricultural Extension Service
Department of Horticulture
161 P&AS Building
Clemson University
Clemson, SC 29631
(803) 656-3011

South Dakota

Agricultural Extension Service
Horticulture and Forestry
Department
South Dakota State University
Brookings, SD 57007
(605) 688-5136

Tennessee

Agricultural Extension Service
University of Tennessee
Box 1071
Knoxville, TN 37901
(615) 974-7324

Texas

Agricultural Extension Service
Texas A&M University
College Station, TX 77843
(713) 845-7341

Utah

Agricultural Extension Service
Utah State University
Logan, UT 84322
(801) 750-2258

Vermont

Agricultural Extension Service
Hills Building
University of Vermont
Burlington, VT 05401
(802) 656-2630

Virgin Islands

Agricultural Extension Service
Box L
Kingshill, St. Croix, VI 00850
(809) 778-0246

Virginia

Agricultural Extension Service
Virginia Polytechnic Institute
Blacksburg, VA 24061
(703) 961-6723

Washington

Agricultural Extension Service
Washington State University
Pullman, WA 99164
(509) 335-2511

West Virginia

Agricultural Extension Service
West Virginia University
Morgantown, WV 26506
(304) 293-4801, 4802

Wisconsin

Agricultural Extension Service
University of Wisconsin
Madison, WI 53706
(608) 262-0768

Wyoming

Agricultural Extension Service
Plant Science Division
University of Wyoming
Box 3354, University Station
Laramie, WY 82071
(307) 766-2243

INDEX

Page numbers in *italics* refer to illustrations

Abbot, Peter, 120
acidity. *See* pH level
action hoe. *See* hoe
aeration, 22
A-frame trellis. *See* trellis
agricultural fabric. *See* polyester fabric, spun bonded
alkalinity. *See* pH level
All-America Selection, described, 24–25, 48
alyssum, 127
Andring, Ron, 74–75
anthracnose, 193, 200
aphids, 42, 45, 95, 130, 169–170, 189, 209, 239
apple mint, 161
apples. *See* cider/cidermaking
asparagus: backfilling, 167; creating bed, 89–91; crowns, 89; diseases, 194; fertilizing, 90, 91, 167, 259; harvesting, 131; mulching, 36, 131, 167, 274; planting, 91; varieties, 89; weeding, 91, 131
asparagus beetles, 45
Attack (*Bacillus thuringiensis*), 43
aubergine. *See* eggplant

Bacillus thuringiensis (Bt), 43, 45, 190, 192, 204, 206
backhilling. *See* hilling-up/backhilling
bacteria, as cause of disease, 193–195, 206
bacteria wilt, 195, 206
basil, 159–160, *199*
beans, bush, 91–92; diseases, 92, 193, 195, 200, 206; fertilizing, 132, 167, 225; harvesting, 92, *196–197*, 198, 199–200, 225, 239, *242–243;* intercropping with, 178, 180; planting outdoors, 131–132, 167, 225, *242–243;* starting indoors, 92–93; succession planting, 167, 200; varieties, 93, 199, 225, 239; *see also* beans, pole; legumes

beans, pole: diseases, 92, 193, 195, 200, 206; fertilizing, 132; harvesting, *196–197*, 198, 199–200, 225, 239, *242–243;* planting outdoors, 131–132, 167; for, 92, 132–133; varieties, 93; *see also* beans, bush; legumes
beets, *202–203;* fertilizing and soil preparation, 93, 200; harvesting, 167, 200; planting outdoors, 92, 167–168, 200; screening, 133–134; thinning, 93, 133, 200; varieties, 93–94; weeding, 42, *133*
Bell, Lewis, *234*
berries. *See* specific berries
Biggerstaff, Andrew, 233
birds, 198; attracting, *278*, 279–283; protecting berries from, 218, 221, 282; protecting corn from, 205, 206
bittersweet, American, *268*, *269*, *271*
blackleg, 117
black plastic mulch, 5, *8–9*, 19, *40–41*, *176–177;* application of, *23*, 34–35; heat and water retention of, 34, *35*, 88, *110*, 141, 154, *183;* insect and weed control, 33–34, 43, 130, 141, 166, *183;* season-end removal, 249, 262
blanching: cauliflower, 172–173; celery, 52, 174–175; leeks, 144; scallions, 112

blight, 117
blood meal, 18
blueberries, 66, *216*, 217–218
bolting, 88
bonemeal, 18
boron, 16, 18
bottom-heating. *See* grow mats
bottom-watering, 26–29; *see also* watering
boxwood, 159
Brackett, Chuck, 110, 233
Brackett, Marion, 110
brassicas, *37;* in container gardening, 127; cool-weather preference of, 68, 70, 205; discarding roots of, 170, 173, 178, 239; raising pH level for, 94–95, 194, 200–201, 226; crop rotation, 48, 50, 94, 99, 106, 136, 168–169, 194, 244; weeding, 42
broccoli, 30, *32*, *33*, *36*, 127, *147*, *222–223*, *263;* crop rotation with, 48, 99, 106; fertilizing, *107;* harvesting, 67, 168, *169*, 239–240; pests and diseases, 94–95, 99, 106, 192, 194, 239; planting outdoors, 68, 94–95, 167, 200–201; soil preparation for, 94–95, 200–201; starting indoors, *64–65*, 68, 167; varieties, 68; *see also* brassicas
browallia, 127
Brussels sprouts, 127, *134*, *240*, 258; crop rotation with, 48, 168–169; harvesting, 259–260; mulching, 274; pests and diseases, 169–170, 192, 194; planting outdoors, 169, *170;* starting indoors, 134; varieties, 134, 169; *see also* brassicas
buckwheat, 14, 226–227; *see also* winter rye
bush beans. *See* beans, bush

cabbage, 68, *147*, *171*, 240; crop rotation with, 48, 99, 106; harvesting, 170, 241; pests and diseases, 94, 95, 106, 192, 194, 204; planting outdoors, 70, 95–96, 170, 200, 204, *208;* starting indoors, *64–65,* 70, 172; varieties, 48, 68, *69,* 70, 172; *see also* brassicas; Chinese cabbage
cabbage looper, 43, 96, 190
cabbage moth, 95, 96, 190
cabbageworm, 45, 190, 204
calcium, 16, 18
cantaloupe, *228; see also* melons
Cape Cod weeder, *42*
carrots, *40–41;* fertilizing, 136; harvesting, 204, 241; pests and diseases, 98; planting outdoors, 96–97, 204; soil preparation for, 97, 204; thinning, 134; varieties, 24, 97, 98; weeding, 96
cart, garden, 85
caterpillars, 43, 45
cauliflower *8–9*, *127;* blanching, 172–173; crop rotation with, 48, 99, 106; fertilizing, 70, 226; harvesting, 173, 241; heat sensitivity of, 70, 205; pests and diseases, 70, 106, 136, 172, 192, 194; planting outdoors, 99, 136, 226; starting indoors, 70, 205; varieties, 70, 205; *see also* brassicas
celery: blanching, 52, 174–175; diseases, 195; fertilizing, 71, 174, 205; harvesting, 244–245; planting outdoors, 174; starting indoors, 52; transplanting, 71; varieties, 52
cell-packs, 27, 29, 31
Chan, Peter, 144
Chapman, John (Johnny Appleseed), 253
cheesecloth, *40–41,* 97, *98*
Chelsea Flower Show (England), 115

chemical fertilizers, 14, 15, 16; amount, 19, 20, 34; and black plastic mulch, 34; cautions, 20; liquid/water-soluble, 19–20, 29, 33; at midseason, 198; numerical designations of, 18–19; and raised beds, 22; side-dressing with, 19, 198; slow-release, 19; *see also specific vegetables*
cherry tomatoes, 120, 121; *see also* tomatoes
chevril, 160
Chinese cabbage, *32*, *263;* crop rotation with, 48, 99, 106; fertilizing, 99, *100*, 136; harvesting, 175, 178, 245–246; heat sensitivity of, 70, 175; planting outdoors, 226; pests and diseases, 136, 178, 194, 245–246; transplanting, 71–72, 99; weeding, 136, *137; see also* brassicas
chives, 159, 160
Christmas tree, living, 274–277
chlorine, 18
chlorophyll, 18
cider/cidermaking, *252,* 253–255
clay soil, 12, 15
clubroot, 16, 51, 117, 194; discarding brassica roots to avoid, 170, 173, 178; preparing soil to minimize, 94–95, 200–201, 226; rotating crops to avoid, 48, 50, 94, 136, 168–169
cocoa bean hull mulch, 163
cold frame, 31–32, *58,* 274; construction of, 60–61; to extend season, 36, *40–41,* *229;* lettuce in, 26, 45, *73,* 74, 107–108, *248*

Colorado potato beetle, 43, 130, 150–151, *188*, 190, 211
composition of soil, 12–16; *see also* soil preparation
compost, 14, 15, 16, 18, 258, 274; as mulch, 34; three-bin system, 20; two-bin system, 20–22; *see also* compost bin
compost bin, 21, 66; construction of, 59
compression sprayer, 85
container gardening, *124*, 125–127
copper, 18
corn, *222–223;* fertilizing, *19*, 137, *139;* harvesting, 99, 198, 205–206; hilling up, 138, *207;* location in garden, 48, 99, 137; pests, 45, 192, 205–206; planting in garden, 136–138, 141; pollination, 136–137; starting indoors, 101; supersweet genotypes, 4–5, 100–101; varieties, 24, 101–102, 141
corn borer, 205, 206
corn earworm, 45, 192, 206
cotyledons (seed leaves), 29
county extension service, 7, 16, 195, 258, 284–289
Cranshaw melons, 109; *see also* melons
Crockett, James Underwood, 4, 5, 12
crookneck squash. *See* summer squash
crop rotation, 48, 50, 94, 99, 106, 136, 168–169, 194, 244
crowbar, *112*, 113
crows, 205
cucumber beetles, 45, 144, 191, 206
cucumbers, *8–9*, 102–103, *127;* fertilizing, 141, 226; harvesting, 206; mulching, 34; pests and diseases, 191, 193, 195; planting outdoors, 141, 206; starting indoors, 103; support for, 63, 88, *102*, 103, *140*, 141, 206; varieties, 103, 206
cultivator, three-prong, *42*, 85, 163
cultivating hoe. *See* hoe
cutworm, 191–192; collars, 95, 183, 191–192

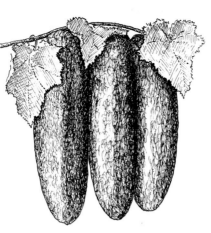

sage, *161*
salt marsh hay mulch, 34, 36, *133, 250*
sandy soil, 12
sawdust: to improve soil composition, 14; as mulch, 34, *217*
scab, 117
scallions, 112, 181; *see also* onions
schedule. *See* garden schedule
scuffle hoe. *See* hoe
Seabrook, Peter, 115
season extenders, 5, *40–41, 256–257;* raised beds, 22; cold frame, 36; Wall O' Water, 5, 36–37, 154, 156
seed catalogs, 24, 48, *49,* 277
seed leaves (cotyledons), 29
seedlings: buying, 30–31; fertilizing, 19–20, *27,* 66; hardening off, 31–32, 34; planting outdoors, 31–33; separating, 29; thinning, 39, 42; transplanting, *27,* 29–30, *178;* watering, 66; *see also specific vegetables*
seeds: germination, 26, 28–29, 96–97; pelleted, 96, 97, 134; planting outdoors, 31; sorting, 66; starting indoors, 25–30; storing, 66; *see also specific vegetables*
shade, 10, *11*
shallots, 80–81, *184,* 185
shock, in transplanting, 31
side-dressing, 19; *see also specific vegetables*
Simmons, Adelma Grenier, 163
site selection, 10–11
size of garden, 11
slope of garden, 10–11
slow-release fertilizer, 19

slugs, 136, 155, 245–246
small-space culture, 5, 125–127
snow peas, 79, 182; *see also* peas
sod, 15–16
soil acidity. *See* pH level
soil alkalinity. *See* pH level
soilless growing medium, 26, *27,* 29, 31, *187*
soil preparation, 11–20, 233, 235; composition, 12–16; for container gardening, 125; in fall, 14–15, 16, 239, 240, 244, 245, 246, 248–249, 250, 258, 261, 262; fertility, 17–20, 59; pH level, 16–17, 258; for raised beds, 19, 23–24; in spring, 15, 16–17; *see also specific vegetables*
solnine, 149
spade, 15–16, *82,* 84
spading fork, 16, *82,* 83
spearmint, 161
Speedling flats, 53
spinach: fertilizing, 19, 81, 230, 249; harvesting, 81, 152, *153,* 230; heat susceptibility, 81; pests, 119; planting outdoors, 66, 81, 230, 249; thinning, 119; varieties, 81
spittle bugs, 162
sprayer: compression, 85; hose-end, *38,* 125
sprinkler: oscillating, 37, *38,* 39; impact, *39*
spun bonded polyester fiber. *See* polyester fiber, spun bonded
squash. *See* summer squash; winter squash
squash vine borer, 43, 191, 215
sterile growing medium. *See* soilless growing medium
storage: herbs, 258; seeds, 66; tools, 274, *275;* vegetables, 152, *184,* 235, 258
strawberries, 66, *127,* 219–221, 274
succession planting, 5, 22, 48, 51
Sugar Snap peas, 4–5, 79–80, *148; see also* peas
sulfur, 17, 18
summer squash, 8–9, 127, *199, 236–237;* fertilizing, 18, 19, 154;

harvesting, 84, 185, 187, *242–243,* 249; pests and diseases, 43, 191, 193, 195, 215; planting outdoors, 154; starting indoors, 119, 215; varieties, 119
sunlight, 10–11
supersweet corn. *See* corn
Swede turnips. *See* rutabagas
sweet basil, 159–160, *199*
Swiss chard, 119, *227, 240;* fertilizing, 19, 120, 187; harvesting, *186,* 187; planting outdoors, 120; starting indoors, 120, *121;* varieties, 120

Tanaguchi, Glenn, 199
tarragon, 163
thermometer, soil, 85
thinning plants, 39, 42; *see also specific vegetables*
Thompson, Delbert, 52, 174
Thuricide (*Bacillus thuringiensis*), 43
thyme, 163
tiller, 84
tobacco mosaic, 117, 122
tomato cages, 155–156, 266, 274; construction of, 62; plastic-wrapped, 30, *40–41, 142–143,* 262
tomato horn worm, 192
tomatoes, *35,* 36, *55,* 120–122, 127, *143, 214, 263;* fertilizing, 18, 54, 56, 57, 154, 215; harvesting, 6, 54, 57, 198, 215, 262, 266; pests and diseases, 122, 192, 194, 195, 206; planting outdoors, 33, 56, 154; starting indoors, 26, 30, 54, 122; super-early, 26, 30, 54; support for, 56–57, 62, 154–156, 215; varieties, 54, 120, 122, 215

tools, *42*, 51, *82*, 83–85, 274, *275;*
see also watering, equipment
topsoil, 22; see also soil composition
top-watering, 26; see also watering
trace elements, 16, 18
transplanting seedlings, *27*, 29–30, 31–33; fertilizing, 19–20; see also *specific vegetables*
trees and shrubs, *46–47;* to attract birds, 279–283; in garden plan, 10, 275; living Christmas, 274–277
trellis, *8–9*, 66, 88, *176–177*, 274; A-frame, construction of, 63; for beans, 91; for cucumbers, *102, 140*, 141; for peas, 78–79, 88, *148*
trimmer, gas-powered string, 85
trowel, 31, *82*, 84
true leaves, *27*, 29, 30
Tufts, Craig, 281
turnips, *123*, *231;* harvesting, 249; pests, 192; planting outdoors, 122–123, 230; varieties, 230

varieties, 4–5, 24; pest and disease resistance, 24, 130; selection, 48; see also *specific vegetables*
verticillium wilt, 104, 122, 178, 194, 195, 228
"Victory Garden, The" (TV series), 4, 6, 99; contest/contestants, 6, 11, 52, 67–68, 74–75, 108, 110, 120, 205, 224, 233–235
vine borer, squash, 43, 191, 215
viruses, 193, 194, 195

Walker, Ewing, 234
Wall O' Water, 5, 36–37, 154, 156
water-soluble fertilizer. See chemical fertilizers
watering, 20, 37–39, 163, 224; for container gardening, 125; drip/trickle system, 38; equipment, 37–39, 84–85; excessive, 30; in making compost, 22; newly planted seeds, 26, *27*, 28, 29; in raised beds, 22; and black plastic mulch, 34, 88, 141, 154
watering can, *31*, *38*, 39, 85
watermelon. See melons
Waterson, John, 103
wax beans, 93. See also beans, bush
weeds/weeding, 42, *128–129*, *137*, 166, *207;* mulching to minimize, 33–34, 166
WGBH-TV, 4, 12
wheelbarrow, 85
White, Peregrine, 253
white fly, 45
wilts: fusarium, 122, 194; potato, 117; verticillium, 104, 122, 178, 194, 195, 228
winter squash, 249–250, *263–265*, 274; fertilizing, 18, 19, 157, 187; harvesting, 84, *242–243*, 250, *251;* pests and diseases, 43, 191, 193, 195; planting outdoors, 157, 187; starting indoors, 157; support for, 156; varieties, *25*, 157, 250

winter rye: planting at season end, 227, 228, 239, 244, 245, 246, 248, 249, 250, 266, 267; and soil composition, 14, 15, 17, 19, 20; turning under, *56*, 57, 66, 88
wireworms, 98
Wisley garden (England), 72
wood ashes, 18, 181, 246
woodchucks, 130, 184
wreaths/wreathmaking, 159, 269–271

Young, Bob, 157

zinc, 18
zinnias, 127
zucchini, 119, *126*, 154, *212–213;* see also summer squash